RETHINKING
MEDIA EDUCATION

CRITICAL PEDAGOGY
AND IDENTITY POLITICS

THE HAMPTON PRESS COMMUNICATION SERIES

Women, Culture and Mass Communication
Karen Ross and Marjan de Bruin, *Series Editors*

Rethinking Media Education: Critical Pedagogy in Action
Anita Nowak, Sue Abel, & Karen Ross (eds.)

Gender and Newsroom Cultures: Identities at Work
Marjan de Bruin & Karen Ross (eds.)

Forthcoming

Women/Advertising/Representation: Extending Beyond
Familiar Paradigms
Sue Abel, Anita Nowak, & Marjan de Bruin (eds.)

Commercializing Women: Images of Asian Women in the Media
Katherine T. Frith & Kavita Karan (eds.)

RETHINKING
MEDIA EDUCATION

CRITICAL PEDAGOGY
AND IDENTITY POLITICS

edited by

Anita Nowak
McGill University

Sue Abel
Victoria University

Karen Ross
Coventry University

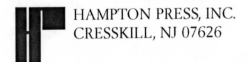
HAMPTON PRESS, INC.
CRESSKILL, NJ 07626

Printed in the United States of America

Library of Congress Cataloging-in-Publication Data

Nowak, Anita
  Rethinking media education : critical pedagogy and identity politics /
  edited by Anita Nowak, Sue Abel and Karen Ross.
    p. cm.
  ISBN 1-57273-726-3 (hardbound) -- ISBN 1-57273-727-1 (paperbound)
  1. Mass media--Study and teaching. 2. Mass media and youth 3. Critical
thinking. 4. Critical pedagogy. I. Abel, Sue. II. Ross, Karen, 1957-III. Title.

  P91.3.N69 2007
  302.23071--dc22
                          2007007005

Hampton Press, Inc.
23 Broadway
Cresskill, NJ 07626

CONTENTS

ACKNOWLEDGEMENTS

As a first-time co-editor of an academic text, I am superbly proud (and more than a little elated) by what I believe is a compelling collection of essays about media education in particular, and critical pedagogy more broadly. I would therefore like to thank each of our 18 contributors for their brilliant insights and superbly well written chapters, the passion they exhibited for the topic and their dedication to this project. I would also like to convey how much they have helped shape my thinking as a doctoral candidate. Bravo and thank you! To my terrific co-editors, all I wish to say is how rewarding and enjoyable it has been working with you both. I couldn't imagine a more constructive joint project spanning three continents. Sue, I thank you in particular for your patience, support and untiring personal touch. And Karen, I thank you for always believing in me. It has also not gone unnoticed that two seasoned academics such as you both are, steered away from treating me as a junior. It is a gift I deeply appreciate and hope to emulate as I grow professionally. Lastly, I wish to thank my Master's thesis supervisor, Dr. Gan Su-lin, to whom I dedicate my contributions to this book. She entrusted me with unconditional academic freedom, and in return, I was dedicated to rigorous scholarship. My success as a young scholar and decision to pursue a life in academia is irrevocably thanks to her. She was the best mentor and thesis supervisor a young scholar could hope for. Xie xie ni, Su-lin.

Anita Nowak

I started my teaching career as a secondary school teacher driven by a desire to save the world, and saw teaching Media Studies as a vital part of this. In my early teaching years I thought that my main role was to demonstrate to my students how the media distorted the "truth," and (in the well-word phrase) "inoculate" them against media effects. The work of writers such as David Buckingham, and the responses of my students, made me realize that media education is not as simple as this. I currently teach at Massey University in Auckland, New Zealand, where I try to take a much broader approach. I have nothing but admiration for the teachers who describe their philosophies and experiences here. I see my frustrations echoed in many of these chapters, and am inspired by the concern shown for both pedagogy and students. I thank them all for firing up my enthusiasm again.

Sue Abel

I would like to thank my co-editors, Sue Abel and Anita Nowak, for their inputs to a novel three-way collegial relationship in the production of this edited collection and for providing complementary scholarly perspectives in an area of research and practice which has such salience in a media landscape scarred by highly contested words and images.

Karen Ross

INTRODUCTION

This book arose as a result of another anthology *Women/Advertising/Representation* (Hampton Press, forthcoming) co-edited by Sue Abel, Anita Nowak and Marjan de Bruin. We had anticipated that the final section of *W/A/R* (as we dotingly refer to it) would contain two chapters looking at issues of media education, specifically with respect to the representation of women in advertising. However, we received so many excellent abstracts for this section that we decided to devote another book in its entirety to the outcome effectiveness of media education, and widen the scope to consider issues such as the teaching of critical thinking, especially in relation to identity formation in youth. Our aim was also to include essays from a wide range of countries. As such, this volume includes chapters written by scholars and media pratitioners in Hong Kong, New Zealand, Australia, Great Britain, Canada, and the United States. We acknowledge and regret that there are large areas of the world not represented here and therefore suggest the need for such a book at some future date.

In our call for abstracts, and eventual book proposal to our publisher, we announced our intention of bringing together a collection of essays that would critically discuss and analyze the efficacy of media education around the world, paying particular attention to if and how it improves the critical thinking skills of its students. The central questions we asked our contributors were: Is media education effective in helping young people negotiate better with the mass media. If so, how? And if not, why not?

Thus, from the onset our aim was to push past arguments that simply support the need for media education, or a call for action. We wanted to know if and how media education is actually achieving its said goals. Many books on the market describe the importance of media education, and many include suggestions for pedagogy, but none currently available evaluate its outcome effectiveness. Implicit in this anthology, therefore, is a belief that without a critical understanding of the extent to which media education achieves its aims—or fails to do so—its potential cannot truly be fulfilled. Significantly, then, our 18 authors (who include media education experts, practitioners, and communication scholars) offer a rich account of media education initiatives and critical analyses from their personal experience of media education in practice. Obstacles, challenges, and disappointments are discussed, as are success stories, lessons learned, and suggestions about how to bring media education closer to achieving its emancipatory goals.

This book will be of interest, then, to anyone concerned with the intellectual development of young people, as well as the process and importance of teaching critical thinking. In particular, it will be useful for practicing teachers and teacher trainees, and those concerned about the role of the mass media and new communication technologies in the lives of youth. This volume will also be valuable to undergraduate students across a wide range of disciplines such as media studies, cultural studies, sociology, mass communications, liberal arts, and feminist and gender studies.

In the opening chapter, *Reviving a Culture-debating Public Through Media Education*, Wendy Wyatt and Kumi Silva provide a compelling theoretical framework in which to situate the potential of media education. By focusing on the work of German philosopher Jürgen Habermas and his theoretical perspectives about the public sphere, communicative action, and the ideal communication community, they argue that media education programs can foster a distinctive, pragmatic type of inquiry, one that neither encourages students to assume a kind of blind faith in media messages, nor develops a skepticism that views media as representative of all that is wrong with today's culture. The chapter also serves as a useful theoretical lens through which to consider all the other media education programs discussed in this anthology.

In Chapter 2, *Closer Than You Think: Bridging the Gap Between Media Effects and Cultural Studies in Media Education Theory and Practice*, Erica Scharrer compares the cultural studies-based approach to media education to the intervention-based approach. Not only does she find many commonalities, but she argues that elements of both philosophical camps can actually be successfully integrated in media education and operate together to enable students to explore issues of identity. She also describes and evaluates an ongoing case study project she is working on with her undergraduate students around the issue of media violence.

Ruth Zanker, author of Chapter 3, *The Media and Me: An Experiment in Reflective Writing in an Applied Media Degree*, argues that critical pedagogy, such as media education, is a radical activity, intimately involved in developing students' moral awareness and political agency. Anchored by a cultural studies perspective, this chapter centers around her analysis of how students responded to an exercise of three "media auto-biographies"completed in the first year of their degree. She concludes that the media offer a range of subject positions and identifications from childhood on that are "played with" during the process of "growing up" in order to negotiate cultural identities and a sense of citizenship.

Sara Bragg is the author of Chapter 4, entitled, *What Kevin Knows: Students' Challenges to Critical Pedagogical Thinking*. In it, she explains that although media education has proved capable of providing pleasure and inspiring considerable commitment in both teacher and young people, it is often questionable whether it achieves its aim of producing "resistant" or "critical" students. Through a biographical note and close reading of a discussion of sexual imagery in horror films by a class of young British Media Studies students, her chapter analyzes "critical" media education's assumptions about students and its failure to engage with the complex power dynamics of the classroom. She also argues that attending carefully to students' responses can reveal their existing strategies for managing their media and classroom environments. Finally, she concludes that educators should build on these to develop postmodern pedagogies of everyday life, which connect to youth audiences' experiences of and pleasures in the media, and promote socially just educational practices.

In Chapter 5, *Cruelty, Compassion, Common Sense and Critical Media Literacy*, Bill Yousman assesses the outcome effectiveness of media education by analyzing how students negotiated different meanings about class position and mobility from an advertisement for the Levi Corporation juxtaposed against a music video by the rap artist Everlast. Students were grouped according to whether or not they had previous exposure to critical media literacy, and based on an analysis of transcripts taken from focus group discussions, he reveals whether or not "media literate" respondents were better equipped to critically analyze the conflicting messages implied in the texts. He concludes with a discussion of the implications of his results for the practice and application of media education.

Chapter 6, *Global Teens: Marketing, Politics and Media Education* is by Barry Duncan. In it, he makes the case that societal changes such as globalization, the corporate take-over of public space and the rise of branding require that educators consider a new agenda for media education. He contends that "digital teens," who readily exploit new and converging media technologies, need to be exposed to discussions about the full spectrum of discourses (i.e., commercial, utopian, and dystopian) present in their lives and consider the impact thereof. He goes on to argue that the role of protest and resistance has evolved, with more sophisticated analyses of global corporate and government hegemony. The challenge for media educators as far as he is concerned, therefore, is to become more involved in that process without being seen as a dogmatic ideologue. From culture jamming (i.e., *Adbusters*) to localized critiques, educators can and are making major breakthroughs and providing a pedagogy of hope—that which involves global citizenship and the reclaiming of public spaces and identities. His chapter also offers class exercises to cultivate such dynamics and outcomes.

In Chapter 7, *Springing Up a Revolution: Media Education Strategies for Tweens*, Salina Abji critically analyzes research published by *MediaWatch Canada* on the effects of increased media attention on "tweens," girls aged 11 to 14 years. Her findings are situated within the context of contemporary feminist discourse on gender and the media, and are analyzed using a feminist poststructuralist approach, which calls for a more nuanced analysis of media effects, as well as a re-evaluation of the efficacy of contemporary strategies to empower girls through media literacy education. As such, feminist poststructuralist understandings of embodied subjectivity, discourse and power are utilized in this chapter to address two major questions: What is the process by which girls choose, use, and reject advertising messages; and How can feminist activists and media educators continue to develop new strategies for resistance and resiliency—strategies that incorporate, rather than alienate, the opinions and experiences of girls? Her chapter, therefore, challenges contemporary feminist theorists and activists to develop new theoretical paradigms for understanding and challenging sexism in media advertising.

Media Education and Negotiating Body Image, written by Michelle Wolf and Kelly Briley is Chapter 8. For seven years leading up to the study discussed in this volume, Wolf posed a series of discussion questions about mass media and body image to heterosexual, gay, lesbian, and transsexual men and women between the ages of 17 and 75. The primary goal of these questions was to stimulate in-depth discussions of media-cultural-personal ideals, media representation and exclusion, feelings about body image, and sources of body image feelings. The video *Body Image: The Quest for Perfection*, based on Wolf's research and produced by Briley, explores these questions in-depth during a 3-day retreat. This chapter compares the pedagogical strategies and outcomes of posing these questions to several groups of heterosexual women, aged 18 to 35, who were gathered in different settings and in groups of various sizes.

Chapter 9, *Media, Teens and Identity: Critical Reading and Composing in a Video Production and Media Education Classroom*, by Monica Pombo and David Bruce, provides a dual-voice narrative account of a 4-month field research project at an American high school. Students from an introductory video production class were asked to create a self-reflection video to explore their identities. In them, students were also asked to demonstrate their understanding of a media education concept that had been discussed in class. An analysis of the videos produced revealed that students were adept at exploring mass media representations of themselves as youth, but tended not to "resist" them. Given this outcome, the authors conclude that creating a safe space for students to explore their identities relative to the ones provided by the mass media is of paramount importance. Consequently, they encourage critical pedagogy teachers to develop and nurture closer relationships with their students. Additionally, both the researcher (Pombo) and teacher (Bruce) involved in this study provide their own self-reflective thoughts about how they as individuals helped shape and influence the research project.

Critically Reading Race in the Media and in the Classroom: A Media Literacy Project, written by Alicia Kemmitt, is the book's 10th chapter. In it, she describes and critically assesses a media literacy workshop she conducted in a diverse American 6th grade classroom. The workshop aimed to help students understand the culturally produced links between images in advertisements and the meanings they connote. To do so, she asked students to identify culturally dominant meanings of images depicted in ads, and then create alternative meanings. She next asked them to transfer this analysis of media texts to an understanding of how racial meanings about themselves and others are also culturally constructed. In addition to describing and evaluating the process and outcome of this workshop, she discusses the potential and limitations of connecting media literacy efforts to broader curriculum goals and educational policies on multiculturalism.

Alice Y. L. Lee and Eileen Mok are the authors of Chapter 11, entitled *Media Education in Post-colonial Hong Kong: Cultivating Critical Young Minds*. Together, they examine the role, effectiveness, and challenges of media education in a postcolonial environment. They begin by contextualizing how prior to 1997 media education had no opportunity to grow under the colonial rule of Hong Kong, and then explain that young people were considered weak in creative and independent thinking relative to western students. Following this discussion, they describe and evaluate two media education programs in Hong Kong that were designed to improve young people's critical thinking skills. They candidly outline the challenges such programs face within a postcolonial education system and offer recommendations for media educators, especially those working in such a context and environment.

In Chapter 12, *Media Education Toward a More Equitable World*, Rashmi Luthra discusses the processes, methods, and learning outcomes of international media education in relation to the events surrounding 9/11 and the ensuing war in Iraq. By focusing specifically on the attacks and the subsequent war on terrorism, she describes how she prompted her class to consider questions of intercultural difference, international news coverage, cultural imperialism, and globalization. According to her, these already charged topics were rendered even more challenging—and fruitful—due to the large Arab American community at the University and in the area. She argues the challenge of media education in this context is to make the issues as concrete to the students as possible, to make effective bridges from existing knowledge and assumptions to new information and new ways of seeing. Furthermore, an experiential component is necessary for the students to come at the conclusions and insights on their own, in a way that will make a lasting difference. As a whole, then, the chapter discusses both the possibilities opened up by specific teaching methods as well as the limitations they present in terms of creating an awareness of existing inequalities and injustices in global communication, and envisioning alternatives toward creating a more equitable and sustainable communication regime.

The concluding chapter of the volume, *The What, Why and How We Know of Media Education*, is written by two eminent media education pratitioners and theorists, Robyn Quin and Barrie McMahon. This final chapter summarizes and comments on the arguments and pedagogical methodologies discussed throughout the book. It then looks at the future of media education, and offers details of a proposal to create an International Literacy Learning Continuum Project.

ABOUT THE EDITORS
AND AUTHORS

Anita T. Nowak is currently pursuing her PhD in Education at McGill University (Canada), where she is studying media education as praxis for social justice. She earned her MA in Communication Studies at Nanyang Technological University (Singapore), a Graduate Diploma in Communications at Concordia University (Canada), and a BCom in Marketing, also at McGill. She is particularly interested in the outcome effectiveness of nontraditional pedagogical initiatives such as media education programs, especially with at-risk youth. She is the co-editor of *Women/Advertising/Representation: Extending Beyond Familiar Paradigms* (Hampton Press, forthcoming).

Sue Abel teaches Media Studies at Victoria University, Wellington, New Zealand. She also taught media education for many years at the secondary school level and was involved in training secondary school teachers to teach media education. She is the author of *Shaping the News: Waitangi Day on Television* (Auckland University Press, 1997), and a range of articles about issues of race, gender, representation, and audience. She is co-editor of *Women/Advertising/Representation: Extending Beyond Familiar Paradigms*.

Karen Ross is Reader in Mass Communication at Coventry University (UK) and was a visiting professor at the School of Politics, Queens University Belfast (2001-2004). She has written extensively on issues of in/equality in communication and culture and her previous books include: *Women and Media* (with Carolyn Byerly, 2004); *Media and Audiences* (with Virginia Nightingale, 2003); *Mapping the Margins: Identity Politics and Media* (2003); *Women, Politics, Media* (2002); *Women, Politics and Change* (2001); *Black Marks: Minority Ethnic Audiences and Media* (2001); *Managing Equal Opportunities in Higher Education* (with Diana Woodward, 2000); and *Black and White Media* (1996). She is currently working on a pan-European project focused on gender and reporting the European Elections 2004, as well as an independent study of the Northern Ireland Women's Coalition.

* * *

Salina Abji holds a Master's degree in Women's Studies from Oxford University. For over a decade, she has been a member and volunteer for MediaWatch Canada, a nonprofit feminist organization working to improve the portrayal of women and girls in the media through research, advocacy, and media literacy education. Salina is currently based at the Faculty of Environmental Studies, York University, Toronto, where she manages a resource center for students and graduates.

Wendy Wyatt is on faculty at the University of St. Thomas where she works to combine her undergraduate training and professional experience in journalism with her graduate degrees in media ethics. Wendy is particularly interested in issues of media and society, including the theoretical bases of media literacy, the moral agency of the news media, and the role that the mass media—both news and entertainment—play in our moral identities.

Sara Bragg is co-author of *Young People, Sex and the Media: The Facts of Life?* (Palgrave Macmillan, 2004, with David Buckingham) and *Students as Researchers: Making a Difference* (Pearson's, 2003, with Michael Fielding). She works as a lecturer in media studies at the University of Sussex, UK, and as a consultant at the Centre for the Study of Children, Youth and Media at the Institute of Education, University of London. She has researched and written on young people and violent media such as horror films, on media education, and on young people's participation rights in schools.

Kelly Briley is a media producer and information designer specializing in educational media development. Her recent video, *Body Image: The Quest for Perfection*, is designed to motivate open dialogue on the issue of body image and women. The program has won first place in the National Council on Family Relations Media Awards and was honored at the Western Psychological Association and National Media Education Conferences.

David Bruce is an Assistant Professor at Kent State University in the department of Teaching, Leadership and Curriculum studies. Prior to earning his PhD, David taught high school English and Media Studies for 11 years at Solon High School where his students' media compositions won numerous local, regional, and national awards.

Barry Duncan is an award-winning teacher, author, consultant, and founder and past president of the Ontario-based Association for Media Literacy. Co-author of the best-selling textbook, *Mass Media and Popular Culture* (Harcourt, Canada, 1996), he has presented workshops and keynote addresses to over 10,000 teachers in Canada and the United States and at international conferences in the UK, Brazil, and Spain.

Alicia Kemmitt is a PhD Candidate in Communication at the University of Massachusetts, Amherst. She is currently completing her dissertation based on 19 months of ethnographic fieldwork conducted in San Francisco, California. Her research examines the production of social issue media campaigns that use documentary film as tools for dialogue, community organizing, and social change. She has taught media studies at the University of Massachusetts, Amherst, and the University of San Diego, in addition to teaching media literacy and general instruction in K-12 classrooms in San Diego County and the San Francisco Bay Area. She received her MA in Communication from the University of Massachusetts, Amherst in 2000. Her thesis was entitled: *Viewing the Troubles: Irish-American Audience Interpretations of Political Violence.*

Alice Y. L. Lee is an Assistant Professor at the Department of Journalism of the Hong Kong Baptist University. Her research interests include media education, online news media, knowledge society, and info-media literacy. In the past 10 years she has conducted media education research in Canada and Hong Kong. She has published journal articles on media education in both English and Chinese. She was also a contributing author for several local media education curriculum kits. She is now the vice-chairperson of the Hong Kong Association of Media Education.

Rashmi Luthra is Associate Professor of Communication at the University of Michigan-Dearborn. Her research interests include women's movements and media, gender and international communication, and media and diaspora. She has published in various journals including *Gazette: International Journal of Mass Communication Studies; Knowledge: Creation, Diffusion, Utilization; Feminist Issues; Women's Studies in Communication;* and *Journalism and Mass Communication Educator* and in various anthologies including *Making Waves: An Anthology of Writings By and About Asian American Women; Feminism, Multiculturalism and the Media: Global Diversities; Religion and Popular Culture: Studies on the Interaction of Worldviews;* and *Women Faculty of Color in the White College Classroom.*

Barrie McMahon is an Adjunct Senior Lecturer at Edith Cowan University and the Western Australian Department of Education and Training's Manager of Youth Advantage, a program to ensure all 15- to 19-year olds are in effective education, training, or work. In his Edith Cowan role he is developing an international project to create a Media Literacy Learning Continuum that is suited to the needs of many countries. Barrie has been a consultant in media education for the Department of Education and played a major role in the development of media education in Western Australia. Together with Robyn Quin, he has written several teacher and student media texts, and has delivered keynote addresses at several international media conferences. The most recent texts by Rod Quin, Barrie McMahon and Robyn Quin are *In the Picture, The Big Picture* and *Picture This* (Curriculum Corporation, Melbourne, 1998).

Eileen Mok is multitalented in music, media education, cultural programs, and youth leadership training. She is Manager of the Cultural Pavilion, Breakthrough Youth Village, and has headed MILE and WELL concerto projects of Media Education and Cultural Heritage. Eileen graduated from Macquarie University (MA, International Communication), University of Technology in Sydney, Australia (MA, Arts Management), and Wilfrid Laurier University in Canada (HBA, Music). Before she joined Breakthrough, she worked with the SBS Radio Station in Sydney as news narrator and music program host, and taught music in the Hong Kong Music Office and Academy of Performing Arts.

Monica Teixeira Pombo was born in Campinas, Brazil. In 2003, she received her PhD from the College of Communication at Ohio University. Dr. Pombo is an Assistant Professor at Appalachian State University in North Carolina where she teaches in the Department of Communication.

Robyn Quin is the Professor of Media Studies and Executive Dean of the Faculty of Communications and Creative Industries, Edith Cowan University in Western Australia. She has taught courses on the media and identity, cultural theory, and new communications. Her major research interests include media education and curriculum development and change, gender issues, and audience studies. She has published widely in the field of media education.

Erica Scharrer is an Assistant Professor in the Department of Communication at the University of Massachusetts Amherst. She studies the media, especially television and video games, and their role in the lives of individuals young and old. Each spring she works with her undergraduate students to offer several media literacy sessions in local sixth-grade classrooms. She is second author (first author George Comstock) of the book *Television: What's On, Who's Watching, and What it Means* and her articles have appeared in *Women & Politics, Journal of Broadcasting & Electronic Media,* and *Media Psychology.*

Kumi Silva has a PhD in Communication and Society from the University of Oregon. Her research examines the relationship between gender and the media, as well as issues of nationalism, immigrant identities, and the South Asian diaspora.

Michelle A. Wolf is a Professor of Broadcast and Electronic Communication Arts at San Francisco State University. She has been active in media literacy efforts and issues surrounding electronic media representations of disenfranchised groups since the 1970s. Her primary research interests center on the range and diversity of mediated images of groups without power in the United States (including gay, lesbian, bisexual and transsexual persons, and persons with physical disabilities), the mediated construction of body image, children and television, media uses and gratifications, and media and social cognition. Dr. Wolf is president of TILT (Teaching Intermedia Literacy Tools; www.tiltmedia.org) and co-founder and president of NCDJ (National Center on Disability and Journalism; www.ncdj. org).

Bill Yousman received his MA in Communication from the University of Hartford in 1999 and his PhD from the Department of Communication at the University of Massachusetts Amherst in 2004. His dissertation is a study of representations of incarceration in U.S. film and television, and inmate responses to those images. He has published work in *Communication Research Reports, Communication Quarterly, Communica-tion Theory, The Journal of Popular Film and Television,* and *Race, Class and Gender.* He is an Assistant Professor at Suffolk University in Boston.

Ruth Zanker is a member of the team that grew the New Zealand Broadcasting School into the premier broadcasting education and policy research institution in New Zealand. Her knowledge of educational theory and design as well as her active engagement in current media practice, policy, and research enable her to address key challenges facing media educators. She is a founding member of National Association of Media Educators, a founding chair of the Children's Television Foundation, and was instrumental in setting up the Canterbury Teachers of Media. Her recent research explores the political economy of children's popular culture and young people's use of emerging digital media environments.

1

REVIVING A CULTURE-DEBATING PUBLIC THROUGH MEDIA EDUCATION

Wendy Wyatt

Kumi Silva

In the introduction to her book, *Redeeming Modernity: Contradictions in Media Criticism*, Joli Jensen (1990) writes that her first forays into teaching about media, culture, and society were done from the perspective that media embody the "corruptions of modern life" (p. 9). Jensen notes that after a semester, she and her students had scholarly justification for believing that they—or at least the nebulous *everyone else*—were victims of media manipulation. As they read on, however, Jensen and her students could only find what she calls a feeble and individual antidote to this manipulation—critical wariness.

> All I could offer my students (and myself) were exhortations to be alert to the dangerous influences that surround us, in the hope that this knowledge would mitigate the influences of media in modernity. This is the dispiriting end-point of the dominant media critique—a call for increased critical capacity, so that at least some of us will not fully succumb. (Jensen, 1990, p. 10)

Many share Jensen's frustration with this less-than-ideal remedy. Although the importance of developing skills in critical analysis cannot be overestimated, the remedy of which Jensen speaks seems to rest on a strictly mediacentric view of the problem. Our relationship with media and media culture, however, should not end with critique. Although media education—or *media literacy* as the populist version of the movement is known in the United States—can teach students to be critical analysts, it can also empower them to become active participants in the development of their own moral identifies and the development of the social world in which they live. This chapter seeks to explore a theoretical basis for these possibilities.

THEORIZING MEDIA EDUCATION

Although the practices of media literacy are much debated and discussed, little has been done to establish a theoretical foundation for the engagement of such. It is to this end that we hope to utilize the work of German philosopher Jürgen Habermas. Though Habermas has never written explicitly on media education and his name appears only occasionally in the theoretical discussions of the movement, we believe he has much to offer in regard to what media education can accomplish, particularly in the social/political realm.

Habermas has been called the leading systematic philosopher of our time and one who has been able to "go into discussions in political theory, in sociology, in psychology, in legal theory—in a dozen different disciplines—and become one of the dominant voices in each one" (McCarthy cited in Stephens, 1994, p. 26). It is this breadth that makes Habermas so important to any social/political question of the day, and because the media play such a crucial role in these questions (many critical media scholars argue that the media, in fact, construct our social/political reality), who better than Habermas to address the theoretical potential of critical media education? In fact, we would argue that Habermas' work is so germane to the notion of media education that it can provide a solid theoretical framework on which many of the ideals of the practice can be grounded. Thus, this chapter explores some of Habermas' ideas and considers them in relation to critical media education. We hope this will provide a theoretical lens through which to consider the particular media education programs and initiatives presented in the chapters that follow.

The discussion begins with a brief introduction to critical media education and a summary of some of its most important goals. It then moves to Habermas and his ideas on the public sphere, his theory of communicative action and the particular ways in which media education that focuses on creating an ideal communication community can help students become debaters of culture rather than simply cultural consumers. It then explores some of the limitations of the Habermasian model that we feel can be addressed through engaged, feminist pedagogy. We conclude by arguing that media education modeled on a Habermasian framework can contribute to the social development of students' moral identities as well as empower them to be active and engaged moral citizens.

CRITICAL MEDIA EDUCATION

Media education has been treated as a public policy issue, a critical cultural issue, a set of pedagogical tools, and a topic of scholarly inquiry from physiological, cognitive and anthropological traditions (Christ & Potter, 1998). Although media education advocates have provided many and varied definitions of the movement, they do agree on five core concepts:

- Media are constructed, and construct reality.
- Media have commercial implications.
- Media have ideological and political implications.
- Form and content are related in each medium, each of which has a unique aesthetic, codes, and conventions.
- Receivers negotiate meaning in media (Aufderheide, 1992).

Recent work in media education has developed along two lines of thought: a protectionist perspective and a critical or cultural studies perspective. The former position generally posits that popular culture is a blight on society and the goal of media education is protecting audiences from negative media influences. If children can be taught to deconstruct media texts, the magic mantra goes, then they won't be taken in by the fantasy, seduced by the violence, or manipulated by commercial ploys. Media education, in this scenario, is the pedagogic equivalent of a tetanus shot (Bazalgette, 1997, p. 72). This protectionist position resembles the dead end in which Jensen and her students found themselves at the beginning of this chapter. Through the deconstruction of media texts, students learn to become critical consumers of the media, but the "activism" ends with critique.

The critical/cultural studies approach attempts to move beyond critique. This paradigm is well represented by Justin Lewis and Sut Jhally (1998), who argue that the goal of media education is to help people become sophisticated citizens rather than sophisticated consumers. Media education is not only about the analysis of messages but an awareness of why those messages are there. Therefore, the critical media education movement integrates textual analysis along with questions of production and reception. For critical media education scholars, the movement "is a way of extending democracy to the place where democracy is increasingly scripted and defined" (Lewis & Jhally, 1998, p. 109). This kind of media education is essential if audiences, who encounter thousands of media messages every day, are to be capable of making rational decisions about them—decisions that go beyond simply evaluating the messages as "true or false, realistic or misleading, stereotypical or positive, but rather as authored voices with certain interests or assumptions about the world" (p. 119).

In addition to working toward an understanding of both texts and the production of texts within sets of social and political relations, critical media education can encourage media democratization by providing students with the necessary tools to produce media messages of their own. As Stuart Ewen (1996) notes, media education "must be understood as an education in techniques that can democratize the realm of public expressions and magnify the possibility of meaningful public interactions" (p. 414). In regard to teaching media production, however, it is critical that production does not become equated with literacy. Lewis and Jhally (1998) argue, for example, that students who have become seduced by the form may attempt to imitate commercial media. Here, exploring the potential of a medium, rather than copying it, is the key.

Finally, as students embark on a process of critically analyzing media messages and the motivations behind the messages, as they begin actively engaging with the media, as they develop citizenship skills, and as they even work to produce media texts of their own, something else begins to happen. In the midst of this process, students can start to discover that their own identities do not have to be constructed by a media culture of mass consumerism. Ideally, along with critical media education comes a kind of freedom from these stifling constraints, a freedom that permits students to discover their own unique and authentic identities and allows and encourages them to participate in the public sphere.

THE PUBLIC SPHERE

Nearly forty years ago, Habermas introduced the notion of a bourgeois public sphere, a sphere that developed in the coffeehouses, salons, and literary societies of eighteenth-century Europe (Habermas, 1991). The conditions of the time allowed for a public—albeit one comprised solely of society's elite—to engage in critical debate about public issues. Within this sphere, private persons discussing public issues were willing to let the force of a better argument, rather than the power of status, determine their decisions (Calhoun, 1992).

With the onset of mass-produced technology and ensuing mass consumption, the end of the nineteenth century saw the decline of a public sphere characterized by active civic engagement. Instead, in today's neoliberal society, critical debate has largely given way to the consumption of mass culture. The media make pretenses of representing the public sphere, but this sphere has become so commercialized that it is now little more than a venue for advertising, where the personas of state and corporate actors are not only publicized but are highly acclaimed. Public opinion, which once developed within a sphere comprised of citizens, has now taken on the meaning of an object to be "molded in connection with a staged display of, and manipulative propagation of, publicity in the service of persons and institutions, consumer goods and programs" (Habermas, 1991, p. 236). In other words, in the absence of a genuine public sphere, public opinion has become little more than a representation of the collective choices we make as consumers. For Habermas and other critical scholars, what must be found is a place for democratic discourse, a place for a rejuvenation of critical debate, a place where the public sphere can be reclaimed. Without an active, engaged public sphere that truly involves its citizenry, there is no true democracy.

Saltman (2000) argues that in a genuine democracy schools provide places for deliberation, consideration of bolstering the common good, and democratic decision making; the school is a place where students can learn to transform the social order. This would suggest, therefore, that the classroom is a place in which to begin the reclamation process. Although it is true that even schools are now under attack by corporate actors, they perhaps represent the closest approximation of a site in which a genuine public sphere can be actualized. In a classroom where efforts are made to equalize power differentials and to ensure that all voices get a hearing, students can learn to confront the mass media-generated public sphere and work toward creating a new public sphere—one that extends beyond the limitations but capitalizes on the strengths of the eighteenth-century bourgeois sphere that Habermas described. For Habermas and other proponents of radical democracy, the re-emergence of a public sphere of citizens—one that includes *all* citizens—would mark a crucial first step toward a society that is built on the ideals of a participatory democracy with active civic engagement rather than active consumption.

This vision for a public sphere raises two questions: first, what does this mean for students of media education? And second, how is a public sphere manifested in a classroom setting? When considering these questions, it is important to consider that the notion of citizenship extends beyond the voting booth, and most definitely beyond the cash register. Of late, this second point has become particularly cogent. For example, in the days and weeks following the September 11 terrorist attacks in the United States, patriotism became synonymous with consumption. Americans were told over and over again by advertisers that being a "good citizen" meant supporting the American economy by traveling—particularly by air—and buying retail goods such as cars. Although many of us—particularly those who devote a good deal of time toward understanding and theorizing political and civic engagement—realize that citizenship ought to be expressed in far more profound ways, this may not be true for many students. Thus, as they hear about consumptive patriotism in the media, the classroom provides a space to engage with students about democratic participation and citizenship in its more authentic form.

The classroom can create conditions whereby students have an opportunity to exercise their citizenship, and in doing so, they can begin to build their own public spheres. Several scholars have referred to these small-scale public spheres as subsidiary spheres (see Calhoun, 1992). Not only do they serve the purpose of providing an accessible forum for discourse on cultural issues, but as the spheres grow, they also begin to overlap, and the discourse that occurs within them extends across their boundaries. The idea is that the public spheres created in media education classrooms eventually grow large and plentiful enough to merge together with one another as well as with other subsidiary public spheres created by, for example, social movements. These united spheres are then able to contend with the public sphere of the mass media.

The idea of a classroom-generated public sphere may sound more at home in a social studies, civics or political science class where questions of citizenship and democracy typically arise. But although these courses are certainly good candidates for the task, the media education classroom is particularly relevant because of the extent to which the social and political issues of the day are expressed by and through the media. It is in the media that important debates take place. It is from the media that the newest trends emerge. And it is to the media that we look for the stories of our culture. In other words—as noted earlier—the media construct our reality, the reality in which we are expected to act as citizens. The difficulty with this is that participants in media debates are most often "experts" who represent two opposite sides of an issue. The debates we hear and see in the media are representative of only a few voices, often manufactured from above by businesses with profit motives; this process tends to render the voices of many silent, leaving out important stories of our culture.

To a great extent, then, the media generate an inauthentic public sphere, one that functions superficially, but on closer examination proves to be more hegemonic than democratic. The first step in media education is recognizing this fraudulence and gaining the kind of critical wariness that Jensen spoke of in the beginning of the chapter. The second step involves picking up the conversation where the media leave off, filling in the missing pieces, telling the untold stories, or creating new stories altogether. This is different from simply consuming the information the media provide because this material should spark important conversations about our social and political world. As such, media education students, by embracing a philosophy of the public sphere, can sustain these conversations, doing their best to ensure that all voices are heard. By engaging in such "communicative action" and constructing a true public sphere, students are able to better understand their responsibilities in a democratic system.

COMMUNICATIVE ACTION

As Mitchell Stephens writes of Habermas, behind his contributions to the many disciplines on which he has had an impact, there is one central theme in his work—the theory of communicative action (Stephens, 1994). This theory revolves around the notion that human social life depends on our capacity to have more or less clear communication with each other. Seyla Benhabib notes that although this idea may seem insignificant, it calls into question a widely held belief by thinkers on both the right and the left that "human behavior is a battlefield upon which each of us is merely out for our own strategic interests" (Benhabib cited in Stephens, 1994, p. 26).

In contrast to this strategic action, communicative action aims at achieving mutual understanding through rational debate rather than through any kind of force. It is here that we get the widely used phrase associated with Habermas' theory: the only force in communicative action is the unforced force of the better argument. Debate, or *argumentation* in Habermasian terms, rests on the presupposition that the process has unconstrained, unifying, consensus-bringing force (Habermas, 1984).

But is this kind of communication even remotely possible? Stephens (1994) articulates well the concerns that many have about Habermas' theory:

> A rather antiquated, idealistic message to be spreading, some might think, in a world of abusive talk-show hosts, misogynistic rap groups and earphone-encased teen-agers. Habermas is, to be sure, as concerned about pop culture as the next philosopher. But he continues to believe that somewhere behind the better of our attempts to communicate with each other, there have to be some shared values, shared respect and acknowledged equality. He sees the *participants in conversations*, in other words, as playing on the same teams. (p. 26; our emphasis)

This concept of "participants in conversation" is critical to Habermas' work. It is here that we begin to fully appreciate his commitment to communication as the answer to many of the most important social and political dilemmas of the day, many of which are represented by and constructed through the mass media. It is also here that we see the connection between communicative action and the public sphere. Within the public sphere, engaged and active citizens participate in conversation about important public issues and rely solely on the force of the better argument to help them reach consensus. In other words, participants within a public sphere take part in communicative action where they present claims; these claims are subsequently accepted but also possibly criticized. As argument progresses, participants revise the claims that have been presented and move toward an understanding that can be agreed upon by all.

So, how does a theory that is based on clear communication, one that has a goal of reaching mutual understanding, connect to the idea of media education? It does so in several ways. First, the theory of communicative action helps us recognize that not all claims are, in fact, communicative. Many claims—particularly those made by and in the media—are strategic and have goals based not on mutual understanding but rather on self-interest. When we consider the largely strategic motivations of the media, we must further consider that these strategic motivations penetrate the discourse of the mass media-generated "public sphere." The entire foundation of a democratic public sphere is one of communicative—not strategic—action. Thus, the work that media education students can do to appropriate the discourse of the mass media's public sphere and use it to build a more democratic public sphere must be done through communicative action, where the primary goal is understanding, not persuasion or manipulation.

To think about this more concretely, consider the claims the media make about what it means to be a woman or a girl in Western culture. Here, we are not simply talking about the typical media culprits such as teen or preteen magazines, commercial films, or the vast majority of music videos. Most media, in fact, generally make the same claims and tell the same stories about women, and these stories often center on issues of body image and heterosexual relationships. In many instances these two go together to propose that physical attributes and success in life are directly related to each other. In a media education classroom, students can take this typical story and engage in debate about it. They can explore what the motivations might be for presenting women this way and what the media, in so doing, are hoping to achieve (Adams, Bell, & Griffin, 1997).

Of course, there is no substantive goal to this exploration, no particular place where students should arrive. Where the discourse goes is entirely up to the participants. One possible conclusion that students may draw, however, is that most media stories are told for strategic reasons—to sell a product or to get ratings, for instance. Through their exploration, students may find that within the media, communicative discourse—the kind that is so important to a public sphere—has been replaced by strategy. In order to reappropriate the idea of Woman back from the media, students may then decide to take action, revising the media's stories or rejecting them altogether and starting afresh with their own stories about what it means to be a woman.

To facilitate this process, one activity we have used in a class that directly speaks of women, minorities, and the media is the "rewriting" of a "traditional" fairy tale. Students choose a fairytale with which they have grown up, such as *Snow White and the Seven Dwarfs, Cinderella,* or *Hansel and Gretel,* and rewrite the narrative in ways that reflect the complex and multiple relationships between gender, race, class, and sexuality in contemporary society. The ensuing discussion, as the students present *their* fairytales, allows the instructor to introduce points to facilitate a discussion about the fractures between traditional tales; the use of these narratives in contemporary media—from advertisements to news coverage; and the multiple realities that the students present themselves. Therefore, through engaging in communicative action as articulated by Habermas, students are able to recognize the disparity between the multiplicities of their own lived experience and realities and the generic stories that the media are telling them.

THE UNLIMITED COMMUNICATION COMMUNITY

One additional piece must be added to the theoretical puzzle to complete the picture of how Habermas' theories can contribute to the practice of media education. This is the notion of the unlimited communication community. This ideal speech situation serves as a metaphorical blueprint for the essential qualities that a media education program must have to empower students to become engaged citizens and take an active role in the development of their own authentic identities. The unlimited communication community is a setting in which true communicative action can be realized. In this community, there exists an unconstrained dialogue (Outhwaite, 1994). Here, students and teachers endeavor to ensure that (a) all voices in any way relevant get a hearing, (b) the best arguments available given the present state of knowledge are brought to bear, and (c) once again, only the unforced force of the better argument determines the responses of all participants (Habermas, 1993, p. 163).

The unlimited communication community represents a kind of partnership among all who are present, a place where students can engage in
the discourse that is so critical to Habermas' project and, we would argue,
to the entire notion of media education. The work that participants in
media education undertake is absolutely dependent on an environment
that promotes this kind of discourse, an environment where students can
share their own insights and work toward insights that are shared and
understandings that are mutual. Media education cannot be done monologically; students cannot be given a text to read or a video to watch and
then left to their own devices to decipher it. For Habermas, life is about
being able to engage; the ideal communication community is just that—a
community comprised of many. It is through our engagement with others
that we create not only our own identities but also the identities of the
social and political systems in which we live.

Fostering an unlimited communication community in a classroom is
something to which everyone must contribute—teachers and students
alike. Interesting things happen when participants in a class are presented
with the possibility of unconstrained dialogue; the debate takes a definite
turn. No longer does it matter who is speaking, but rather that everyone
has had a chance to speak. No longer does it matter what information
aligns with "popular" opinion or the status quo, but rather what information provides the best knowledge. And no longer does it matter which
argument is the most eloquent, artful, or flashy, but rather which can be
best justified.

From a moral development perspective, this kind of unconstrained and
noncoercive dialogue is invaluable. Only by hearing the better argument
will students—and teachers—learn to recognize it. Again, learning and
developing comes not monologically but dialogically. One of the biggest
challenges with so much of today's media is that it is monological—it is dissemination and not dialogue. The unlimited communication community of
a media education classroom, therefore, provides this space to engage in
dialogue and debate about the social and political issues that the media disseminate to us for our consumption.

THE RELATIONAL SELF

So far, this chapter has spent time discussing how Habermas' work can
contribute theoretically to the practice of media education, specifically as
the work relates to ways in which culture-consuming students can develop
into culture-debating citizens. Intrinsic to this process is another form of

development that has been mentioned briefly but deserves further discussion: the social development of one's identity.

Much recent work on identity—particularly that in postmodernism—views the self as a by-product of negotiations within relationships; "the self—both in terms of public identification and private surmise—is born of relationship" (McNamee & Gergen, 1999, p. 21). In other words, "our identity grows and develops in relationship to the endless dialogue that we have with others, with culture and with ourselves" (Bybee & Overbeck, 2001). Although Habermas is often criticized by postmodernists, the notion of discursively formed identity fits well with his work. For Habermas, only in a discursive context can identities fully develop; pursuits as fundamental as "Who am I?" must go through the world and are subject to disputations of the community.

It is in this sense of a discursively formed identity that interactions with the media become so meaningful. In a media education forum—ideally one that approximates the ideals of an unlimited communication community—students have an opportunity to engage in communicative discourse about prevailing cultural identities as they relate to the self. These cultural identities are, of course, constructed by and represented through the mass media. The media's portrayal of age, class, ethnicity, and gender—together with the claims that accompany these portrayals—are crucial to confront as students integrate themselves into a social system and form identities of their own (Habermas, 1975).

In a media education program that empowers students to converse, particularly about issues such as media-constructed identities, we see democracy inducing a development effect on the self (Warren, 1995). Media education gives students a chance to be in relation with one another in a communicative (nonstrategic) setting while, at the same time, confronting the ways in which relationships are portrayed in the mass media. Within contexts of media education, groups of engaged and critical students who are working toward creating a more democratic, participatory and inclusive community can confront and negate the status quo community—the one presented by the mass media. Engaging in this kind of communicative discourse helps students move from an egocentric view of the world to a more decentered view. For Habermas, it is this decentered view that represents moral maturity.

Furthermore, in the course of confronting and criticizing prevailing cultural identities, groups whose identities have been misrepresented or altogether lost through the media may be able to re-establish those identities. Media education can serve as a counter-hegemonic tool for groups that are marginalized and oppressed based on class, ethnicity, gender, or sexuality. In this sense, media education takes on a therapeutic dimension as well as one of discursive identity formation.

Muslim women constitute one of the most pressing examples of a misrepresented group in contemporary media. A closer look a the media will reveal that most media tend to refer to a generic amalgam of "Muslim women," who are often presented as traditional and conservative and visually symbolized through the practice of purdah—the cultural practice that requires women to cover their bodies and conceal their shape. Through the narratives surrounding the purdah, stories and images usually focus on Muslim women as disempowered or disenfranchised. This monolithic representation doesn't account for the different ways the religion is interpreted in different locations and cultural contexts. It also doesn't account for the ways in which the purdah is used strategically as a political symbol by women's movements in various regions. Instead, this representation juxtaposes a traditional Muslim woman against an empowered "Western woman." This binary between the East and West is used with little explanation or context by the media and, in turn, is naturalized as an inherent cultural difference.

With critical wariness as a first step, media education students can work together to determine the story about Muslim women that is circulating in the media-generated public sphere as well as the motivation for telling that story. Students can then move from critical wariness to action, using their combined resources to investigate possible alternative stories, which represent the voices of Muslim women. And from there, students can even make efforts to tell these new stories by creating media messages of their own, messages that are founded on the ideal of communicative action and have as their motivation mutual understanding rather than the selling of a stereotype.

MEDIA EDUCATION IN PRACTICE

Habermas' notions of the public sphere, communicative action, and the ideal communication community are not without limitations or criticism. It is, therefore, important to acknowledge these limitations, while concurrently seeking to capitalize on the strengths of the theoretical framework. Habermas has been criticized, particularly by feminist scholars, for his idealistic construction of a public sphere that ignores the discourses and realities of power struggles in contemporary society (Fraser, 1995), but these same critics acknowledge that the limitations do not completely negate the value of his work (Braaten, 1995; Johnson, 1994). In fact, many feminist scholars point out that there may be some sympathy between the ideological thrust of feminism and Habermas' theory of communicative action that promotes the values of community and social justice (Braaten, 1995).

The same debates on the relationships between visibility, power, and discourse between Habermas and feminist scholarship are salient to the classroom setting when trying to employ a model of communicative action. To this end, we feel that employing methods of feminist pedagogy may be useful. One of the primary concerns of an instructor who is an engaged pedagogue is the power dynamic between instructor and student, even within the most democratic classroom setting. Although we recognize that it is indeed difficult to eliminate this power imbalance, we also feel that openly discussing and setting the *extensions* of power in the classroom is an important part of engaging in a theory of communicative action. Here, we see feminist pedagogy as most useful; it provides both physical and ideological mechanisms to diffuse power dynamics while promoting an unlimited communication community. As such, in our classes, we most often—space permitting—encourage students to sit in a circle. We explain on the first day of class that we do this because we feel it facilitates conversation and encourages students to speak up. It also eliminates the physical superiority that the instructor has when she or he *presides* over a classroom at the front of the room. In addition, we carry out several small group activities, placing ourselves in one of the groups. This allows for students who are reluctant to speak up in the larger group to have their voices heard. Once the physical environment of the class is established as inherently democratic, it facilitates the process of communication and subsequent critical thinking through this communication.

But teaching media education using a theory of communicative action is not merely creating an environment in which everyone gets to speak and be heard. It also calls for reaching a point of critical knowledge of the subject under discussion. In many instances, achieving this critical understanding requires a marriage between the classroom and outside events, which is where Habermasian theory is most useful. It is the understanding that critical discourse is not only taught and debated in the classroom, but that it is—and must be—learned and practiced outside the classroom setting as well.

This notion is exemplified by the experiences of one of the authors, who teaches a class under the theme of popular culture and media at a university in the American midwest. In a discussion that looked at the merits of news coverage of the recent war in Iraq, students debated the validity of the news that was being presented. Although most students felt that the news factually constructed the events leading up to the war, some disagreed. Unwilling to expound on personal politics, the instructor encouraged her students to attend a series of lectures on the war at the university. Following the lectures, students were then asked to write a two-page reaction paper that examined the validation or negation of their assumptions and reasons for their conclusions. The discussion following this activity, which included more insightful support for the stands students took, highlights the value of teaching media education in the classroom and then encouraging students to exercise their knowledge in public forums as part of a conscious, civic engagement.

A VISION FOR MEDIA EDUCATION

Market-driven news and entertainment industries are "penetrating culture and inundating people with information at an ever-accelerating pace" (Christ & Potter, 1998, p. 5). With the one-way nature of this media flow, critical engagement has been almost entirely replaced by blind consumption—a condition that disallows the discourse so important for an active and functioning democracy.

Media education can help awaken today's culture-consuming public, particularly the young people for whom mass media are so pertinent. Using Habermas as a theoretical guide and coupling him with tools such as those from feminist pedagogy, media education can help students build active, engaged, and critical relationships with the media. When students become involved in a space that allows for communicative discourse, they also become empowered to critically confront the spaces that do not make such allowances, particularly the space generated by the mass media.

Critical media education is a movement with goals of transformative practice and the realization of a more democratic society. The movement not only teaches students "to learn from media, to resist media manipulation, and to empower themselves vis-à-vis the media, but it is concerned with developing skills that will empower citizens and that will make them more motivated and competent participants in social life" (Kellner, 2001, p. 9).

For Habermas, this kind of participation/engagement/discourse is essential for the development of society, as well as for the social development of individuals' authentic identities. Using Habermas as a theoretical framework helps us recognize how the media have appropriated the public sphere, commercialized it, and stripped away any opportunities for dialogic participation with it and within it. Furthermore, his notions of communicative action and the ideal communication community help us understand how media education can act as a catalyst that creates opportunities for the public to engage—or reengage—in the practice of debating about, rather than merely consuming culture. With this debate comes the opportunity for students to create a public sphere that is truly public and to embark on a process of self-discovery and self-development that aims not at a media-constructed identity but rather at an identity that is relational, unique, and discursively formed.

REFERENCES

Adams, M., Bell, L. A., & Griffin, P. (1997). *Teaching for diversity and social justice*. New York: Routledge.

Aufderheide, P. (1992). *A report on the national leadership conference on media literacy, strategies for media literacy*. Available at: http://interact.uoregon.edu/MediaLit/FA/MLArticleFolder/aspen.html (Retrieved November 10, 2001).

Bazalgette, C. (1997). An agenda for the second phase of media literacy development. In R. Kubey (Ed.), *Media literacy in the information age* (pp. 69-78). New Brunswick, NJ: Transaction Publishers.

Braaten, J. (1995). From communicative rationality to communicative thinking: A basis for feminist theory and practice. In J. Meehan (Ed.), *Feminists read Habermas* (pp. 139-161). New York: Routledge.

Bybee, C., & Overbeck, A. (2001). Homer Simpson explains our postmodern identity crisis, whether we like it or not: Media literacy after "The Simpsons." *Studies in Media and Information Literacy Education, 1*(1). Available at: http://www.utpjournals.com/ simile (Retrieved May 15, 2002).

Calhoun, C. (Ed.). (1992). *Habermas and the public sphere*. Cambridge, MA: The MIT Press.

Christ, W. G., & Potter, J. (1998). Media literacy, media education and the academy. *Journal of Communication, 48*(1), p. 5-15.

Ewen, S. (1996). *PR: A social history of spin*. New York: Basic Books.

Fraser, N. (1995). What's critical about Critical Theory? In S. Benhabib & D. Cornell (Eds.), *Feminism as critique—on the politics of gender* (pp. 31-55). Minneapolis: University of Minnesota Press.

Habermas, J. (1975). *Communication and the evolution of society*. London: Heinemann.

Habermas, J. (1984). *The theory of communicative action*, Volume I. Boston: Beacon Press.

Habermas, J. (1991). *The structural transformation of the public sphere: An inquiry into a category of bourgeois society*. Cambridge, MA: The MIT Press.

Habermas, J. (1993). *Justification and application: Remarks on discourse ethics*. Cambridge, MA: The MIT Press.

Jensen, J. (1990). *Redeeming modernity: Contradictions in media criticism*. Newbury Park, CA: Sage.

Johnson, P. (1994). *Feminism as radical humanism*. Boulder, CO: Westview.

Kellner, D. (2001). *Media literacy and cultural pedagogy*. On-line course materials. Available at: www.gseis.ucla.edu/courses/ed253a/dk/ML&CP.htm (Retrieved November 10, 2001).

Lewis, J., & Jhally, S. (1998). The struggle over media literacy. *Journal of Communication, 48*(1), 109-120.

McNamee, S., & Gergen, K. (1999). *Relational responsibility: Resources for sustainable dialogue*. Thousand Oaks, CA: Sage.

Outhwaite, W. (1994). *Habermas: A critical introduction*. Stanford, CA: Stanford University Press.

Saltman, K. (2000). *Collateral damage: Corporatizing public schools: A threat to democracy.* New York: Rowman and Littlefield.

Stephens, M. (1994, October 23). The theologian of talk: The question is whether justice exists and reason can benefit society. It's postmodern to say no, but Jürgen Habermas, a German philosopher disagrees. *The Los Angeles Times Magazine*, p. 26.

Warren, M. (1995). The self in discursive democracy. In S.K. White (Ed.), *The Cambridge companion to Habermas* (pp. 167-200). New York: Cambridge University Press.

2

CLOSER THAN YOU THINK

*Bridging the Gap Between Media Effects
and Cultural Studies in Media Education
Theory and Practice*

Erica Scharrer

Much media education scholarship falls somewhat neatly into one of two schools of thought: a cultural studies-based perspective and an intervention-oriented, media effects-based approach (Kubey, 1998). The two camps represent somewhat differing philosophies about media and media influence. In this essay, I argue that both views can be successfully integrated into media education curricula. Of course, it is impossible to provide a complete discussion of the relationship between the media effects and cultural studies paradigms in a single chapter (see Ruddock, 2001, for a more nuanced discussion). What follows, then, occasionally verges on a thumbnail sketch of each, but intends to focus on the ways in which media education is conceived and carried out under either heading.

The cultural studies perspective views media education curricula that attempt to "inoculate" against the negative effects of media exposure as ineffective and misguided pursuits, largely for two intertwined reasons (Buckingham, 1998, 2000; Hart, 1997; Tyner, 1998). First, such endeavors inauthenticate the experiences of pleasure many youth derive from their relationships with media. Second, they can be construed as elitist in that the media educator is purporting to know what is best for youth and making judgments of "high" and "low" culture. Those in the intervention-based camp, on the other hand, do see value in speaking to young people about the negative influences that media can have. Some have found that such discussions can mitigate media influence (Brown, 2000; Cantor, 2000). Interventionists believe that children and teenagers are more susceptible to media influence than adults because they have a limited number of real-world experiences to use to counter media messages (Comstock & Scharrer, 1999) and their sense of identity is in flux, which may make them vulnerable to persuasion (Brown, 2000).

In this essay, I attempt to find common ground between these two theoretical approaches by pointing out how each offers valuable and important considerations for those engaging in media education. I discuss briefly my own ongoing project as a case study that seeks to integrate the two schools of thought into a primarily intervention-based curriculum on the topic of media violence. The curriculum is derived from the media effects tradition but is also informed by some of the central concerns of the cultural studies view. Particular attention is paid to assessing media education curricula and their outcomes.

THE ROLE OF CRITICISM

One commonality across the two theoretical stances is the central role of criticism and the facilitation of critical thinking in most, but not all, manifestations of media education. Neither approach would necessarily advocate a purely celebratory tone for media education in which only positive, progressive, or prosocial media achievements and roles were raised. Rather, both camps often deal in the negative, and by definition media education typically centers around a process of "questioning" or "critiquing" the media (Brown, 1998; Hobbs, 2001), which may (but does not have to) generate negative judgments. Indeed, the concept of critical thinking, which consistently occupies a central place in media education, has been defined as analysis that requires "standards for thought" and judgments of whether topics, practices, or texts meet such standards (Paul & Elder, 2001). Thus, media education, regardless of the theoretical perspective, may take a negative tone when the media processes, messages, or effects discussed do not meet such standards. A theoretical difference emerges in the two camps, however, regarding whom or what is seen as negatively influenced, how (and how likely) audiences resist that influence, and whose standards take center stage, student or media literacy teacher.

The intervention approach focuses on microlevel effects on individuals' thoughts, attitudes, opinions, and behaviors, derived from the tradition of media effects scholarship. Although this research has found that media effects on individuals occur fairly commonly and often in measurable patterns, it also indicates that people are influenced differently depending on their individual characteristics, the characteristics of the media message, and situational variables (Bryant & Thompson, 2002). Identity of audience members, then, is considered in the form of their "individual differences," which range from varying demographic descriptors (gender, income, race, age, ethnicity, education, sexual orientation, etc.) to differing personality traits and points of view. These, in turn, are considered in determining their role in media effects (Oliver, 2002). Yet, the emphasis remains on broad patterns that indicate similarities among audience members.

Traditionally, negative media effects—such as effects of gender stereotypes, of violent depictions, or of advertising appeals—have received prominent attention in media effects scholarship, and interventionist media education curricula often take the form of encouraging young people to become aware of, challenge, and perhaps even resist those effects. A common theme in media education endeavors in this area involves the critical examination of the potential for problematic portrayals of gender, race, sexuality, age, and so forth to have a negative influence on audience members' positive identity and self-esteem. For example, Irving and Berel (2001) examined whether viewing a media educational video on advertising and body image would decrease the likelihood that students would become dissatisfied with their bodies after watching thin models presented as an ideal. Although media-effects research has also studied positive roles and effects of media, such as educational television's fostering of school preparedness or news media's role in learning about current events, media education curricula on these topics are rare. A prominent exception is the kids voting curriculum that encourages political participation through news media use (Kiousis, McDevitt, & Wu, 2005; McDevitt & Chaffee, 2000).

The cultural studies approach "tends to see mass media effects as long term, diffuse and difficult to see," rather than as occurring in decipherable patterns (Ruddock, 2001, p. 3). Macro-level effects are a frequent subject of inquiry in media education that falls loosely under the cultural studies heading, such as the role of media as cultural producers or the implications of the globalization of media conglomerates. Such scholarship often raises critical (i.e., negative) issues pertaining to the media particularly when matters of power and ideology are considered, as they are in critical cultural studies. When the emphasis in cultural studies scholarship is on individual audience members, much attention is paid to the complicated and highly individual elements that comprise one's identity and their role in shaping the complex relationships that audiences have with media texts (Fiske, 1987). Potential influences on audiences are viewed with a lens that foregrounds differing readings of media texts (Hall, 1980), which therefore allows for differences in the valence of influence. Media education curricula in this area might, for instance, ask students to conduct in-depth, detailed analyses of the explicit and implicit values about race, ethnicity, class, gender, and so forth that are sent via media texts, as well as the power structures in society that help reproduce those ideologies.

Therefore, we can conclude that although both approaches often raise issues that are critical or negative in nature, they both also allow room for discussion of positive roles of media in individuals' lives as well. According to Masterman (1985), media education should attend to both. He argues that ideally students engaging in media education should neither uphold "a quite unwarranted faith in the integrity of media images and representations" nor espouse "an equally dangerous, undifferentiated skepticism which sees the media as sources of all evil" (1985, p. 14). Encouraging students to recognize both positive and negative roles of media in their lives as well as in society at large is a crucial guideline in media education that can (and should) be present in the curriculum regardless of the philosophical approach. Knee-jerk dismissal of positive roles of and relationships with media is just as critically unsophisticated as knee-jerk dismissal of negative roles and effects.

THE NATURE OF THE TOPIC

Some media education curricula raise multiple issues for critical discussion whereas others focus on one central issue, such as media violence, images of beauty and issues pertaining to body image, ethics in advertising claims, or representations of gender, race, or class. I will argue that regardless of the theoretical tradition from which one operates, the nature of the topic often carries with it an inherent moral or political stance. Although the cultural studies camp rightly cautions against elitist moralizing in media education (substituting values imposed by the media with values imposed by the media educator), I believe that there are inevitable sociopolitical judgments being made when issues about the media are raised in a critical context. A media education curriculum on media violence, for instance, presumably carries with it an inevitable ethical stance of the media educators that is *anti*violence. Similarly, a curriculum about media representations of race, ethnicity, gender, or sexual orientation presumes that there are "better" and "worse" ways of presenting these traits in the media, and that stereotypical representations are not a good thing. Media production exercises are frequently framed as opportunities for students to respond to the narrow ways in which mainstream media represent the qualities that make up the students' identities (e.g., their age, gender, race, etc.) by producing alternatives. Indeed, many media education curricula argue, either directly or indirectly, for change toward more inclusive, progressive representations and socially responsible practices. Thus, there are underlying judgments at work that contain an unavoidable element of morality. I have written about the ethical dimensions of my own media education work in another essay (Scharrer, 2006).

Although I do not think we can (or should) construct a media education curriculum that is devoid of values, we can recognize that our values as media educators are inevitably present in the curriculum, from the subjects we choose to raise to how we choose to raise them. Though the subjectivity of the researcher is more fully acknowledged in the cultural studies compared to the media effects tradition (Ruddock, 2001), the subjectivity of the media educator can, and should, be recognized by both. While acknowledging the role of our own subjectivity, however, we can also be conscious of trying to limit its influence, by encouraging students to employ *their own* ideas about "right" and "wrong" and "good" and "bad" to develop individual critical strategies. Students can question the values that are embedded in media and determine whether they meet their own, potentially highly personalized, standards. Perhaps media educators operating from a "critical" stance might "stack the deck" toward a particular conclusion, but pleasure is acknowledged and students are given a central voice. In other words, the preferred conclusion of the teacher can be more obliquely advanced while still avoiding didacticism.

PROCEDURES AND EXERCISES IN THE CURRICULUM

To avoid elitism and moralizing, there are a number of techniques that can be employed in media education curricula. First, a comprehensive view of the topic that transcends inter- or intradisciplinary boundaries can be adopted in order to avoid an isolation of the effects of the media from other related processes and issues. For instance, not only can media messages be scrutinized from a media effects point of view, but the social, political, and economic forces that shape those messages can be considered as well (Lewis & Jhally, 1998). That way, we are not placing blame on young people for their media practices and preferences, but rather we are analyzing the system that shapes the number of choices and the appeal of such choices that are available to audiences.

Second, attempts should be made to personalize the curriculum and encourage students to consider how their relationships with and responses to media are, at times, similar to that of others, and, at times, unique to their own positions and perspectives. Both theoretical camps allow for such an element. Students' judgments of the positive or negative elements of media depictions, for instance, can be seen as being partially shaped by their own characteristics, whether these are in the form of membership in social demographic groups or in the form of other layers of identity. One concrete way in which this can be accomplished in media education is through media production exercises. Such exercises empower students to view themselves as creators rather than merely consumers of media, encourage rewarding and fun interactions with media, and help students to understand that there are many forces, factors, and decisions made by producers that shape media content (Aufderheide, 1993; Hobbs, 1998). They also allow students to use media as a means of expressing their identities by countering mainstream media portrayals that they feel do not represent them well.

Third, the tone or the delivery of the curriculum should be carefully considered. By using an interactive approach, media educators can advance "deconstruction of how the media impart particular cultural values" as a goal without, in turn, "imposing specific cultural values" in their place (Kubey, 1998, p. 64). An exchange of information or points of view can occur, rather than a unidirectional delivery by the media educators. By pointing out examples of media portrayals and practices that are more or less "guilty" of the criticisms raised, we can limit sweeping moral statements about the "evils" of all media. Finally, by framing our goals as developing *already existing* tools of media analysis, we can recognize that young people already engage in media criticism and not position ourselves as the sole experts (Buckingham, 2000).

DESIRED AND EXPECTED OUTCOMES

Among the differences between the two camps are divergent views concerning desired outcomes associated with media education and, at a more basic level, different views of whether and how "outcomes" can and should be identified and measured. What can we expect participation in media education to achieve? Most interventionists advocate for media education as a preventative measure to protect audiences against undue media influence, whereas cultural studies media educators object to the inherent paternalism of such a goal. Although intervention-based curricula appear to advance the goal of decreased influence of the media on individuals, the notion that guided media criticism leads to diminished media influence has not often been tested (Singer & Singer, 1998). Scholars in the cultural studies camp would presumably argue that such a goal is protectionist and artificially positivistic in suggesting that participation in a media education curriculum would change such complex phenomena as individuals' responses to media messages. Even from my position as a media effects scholar, I am sympathetic to the issues raised in the latter objection. I believe that although such an influence of media education may be achieved in the short term or temporarily, it may not be enduring without constant updating. For example, if we think while we are watching a commercial, "I know what you are trying to make me do," does that mean we won't find the product appealing? Or, if we believe that the media present an unrealistically thin image of women as a beauty ideal, does this preclude us from the occasional lapse in our own self-esteem after we've watched a Victoria's Secret commercial?

There are a number of problems with an expectation of enduring, as well as immediate diminished influence of the media due to media education. First, how long would that resistant state last? I suspect that if such resistance occurs it is most likely to be rather fleeting due to the massive influx of subsequent media interactions that students would experience compared to the limited number of media education interactions. Second, then, there is the important issue of competing messages from the media themselves. Can we expect participation in a media education curriculum, inevitably limited in duration, to successfully compete with the countless media messages that we encounter everyday? It seems like a tall order to expect a relatively contained media education curriculum to counter these messages and lower their influence once and for all. Finally, the media effects tradition suggests that individual (such as pre-existing personality traits and demographic characteristics) and situational (such as moods, social context, etc.) differences make important differences in determining whether and to what degree individuals are affected by media. Similarly, then, differences that individuals bring to the experience (such as prior critical media discussions with parents and media use) and situational differences (such as how the curriculum was administered or current mood states) could mitigate the influence of media education.

Regardless of my cautionary point about difficulty in sustaining outcomes that signify diminished media influence, it should be noted that there is growing evidence that such outcomes can be achieved in the short term from media literacy education. A number of media literacy interventions in the area of media violence, for example, have succeeded in either reducing aggression or in weakening the statistical link between television violence consumption and aggression among elementary school-aged children (Huesmann, Eron, Klein, Brice, & Fischer, 1983; Robinson et al., 2001; Rosenkoetter, Rosenkoetter, Ozretich, & Acock, 2004). Importantly, the latter two of these studies employed rather long curricula, 18 sessions for the Robinson and colleagues' intervention and 31 for that of Rosenkoetter and colleagues, so perhaps duration (or, for that matter, the young age of the participants)played a central role. There is some reason to suspect, therefore, that media education *can* mitigate behavioral influence from the media. However, I believe strongly that even if media education does not achieve this goal, it has not failed to be useful. If participation in media education allows individuals to learn something new or something more about media practices, processes, institutions, or influence, that is an important cognitive outcome. If participation can contribute positively to identity formation, feelings of empowerment, or enhanced self-esteem through the challenging of narrow media representations of people and behavior, then media education has been successful. If participation contributes to new or newly reinforced feelings of disapproval of some media representations and approval of others, this, too, is a laudable accomplishment. If participation inspires students to write a letter to the editor or contact the FCC (Federal Communications Commission) to argue against media consolidation, then this is a major achievement. Therefore, I believe outcomes for media education should include changes in knowledge, skills, and attitudes, in addition to behavior. I suspect the development of critical attitudes, new information, and media analysis skills can lead to diminished media influence in the long term.

In general, all media education scholars, regardless of their theoretical camp, would do well to further consider the outcomes that are to be expected from participation in media education. As the literature stands, this topic is not often fully developed theoretically or methodologically (Christ & Potter, 1998; Scharrer, 2002). In the cultural studies tradition of media education, Masterman (1985), for instance, reports on curriculum statements published by the British Film Institute that, rather than identifying outcomes per se, outline topic areas to raise in media education. These include media agencies, categories, technologies, languages, audiences, and representations (Bazalgette, 1989; Bowker, 1991). Yet, guidelines for assessing the understanding in students that ensues from addressing these topics are largely absent.

ASSESSING OUTCOMES

Once the media educator determines what types of outcomes can be expected from participation in a media education curriculum, the next step is determining how to measure such outcomes. The intervention camp typically uses quantitative methods and the cultural studies camp qualitative methods in research. Yet, in addition to decisions about what methods to incorporate, media educators must also decide what questionnaire items, focus group or interview questions, or other measures should be employed to best arrive at a sound determination of the effectiveness of the media education endeavor.

One quantitative way to measure the effectiveness of media education curricula is to compare the thoughts and opinions of students before to those after participating, using closed-ended items on a questionnaire. The design has the advantage of assessing changes in thoughts, knowledge, feelings, and attitudes that occur in response to participation, and a delayed postmeasure could determine how long such changes last. Use of a control or comparison group eliminates the possibility of an external factor (instead of the media education) explaining such changes. The most important disadvantages of such a design include the large number of students necessary to make such comparisons and possible sensitivity to the design on the part of the students. Interventionists are most likely to use this design due to their history of employing primarily quantitative research methods.

From a qualitative perspective, personal interviews, open-ended surveys or other reflection/writing assignments, or focus groups could be conducted before and after the students have participated in the media education curriculum. Again, pre- and postcomparisons could be made to determine whether students had gained new perspectives, obtained new language, or strengthened their views in response to the curriculum. The advantage of this design is that students could bring in their own potentially diverse interpretations and their varying opinions and experiences with media, rather than being constrained by closed-ended questionnaire options. The primary disadvantage is the length of time and access to students required, as well as the possible lack of generalizability of the results. Cultural studies–based media educators would traditionally use this type of design.

In any research scenario, the quality and usefulness of the information collected also relies heavily on what types of questions are posed. The lack of published accounts of measures that have been used effectively to study the effects and effectiveness of media education in the past makes this tricky terrain for media educators to traverse (Scharrer, 2005). I outline three categories of measures that may be useful for media educators who are engaging in assessment, regardless of what methods they employ.

First, some items may seek to measure whether key concepts or information contained in the curriculum were effectively conveyed. For instance, if the curriculum pointed out ownership conglomeration issues or the political economy of the media, pre- and postcurriculum questions could be asked to determine what participants thought of these issues before and whether they've learned specific ways of discussing them. Such questions could be open-ended and general, such as *What are the conse-quences of having a small number of companies control the media?*, or more pointed, such as *Television programs exist to entertain us; Television programs exist to provide audiences for advertisers,* with options of *strongly agree* to *strongly disagree.* If the curriculum were effective, we would expect more fully developed, specific answers to the first question and greater agree-ment with the second option (audience for advertisers) in responses to the second question after participation.

Second, other items may measure attitudes and opinions about the media before and after participation in media education curricula. These items may ask students to make judgments concerning the diversity and accuracy of media representations or to give specified media practices or depictions high or low marks for social responsibility. Some items may be general in nature (e.g., *What cultural values are frequently delivered through the media? Which ones are de-emphasized or ignored?*), whereas others may be more specific to the topic(s) of the curriculum (e.g., *How is media vio-lence created in such a way to make it appealing to young audiences and why is this an important issue?*). Other items may ask students what they would like to see more or less of in the media (e.g., *The media should show a greater variety of body sizes of women; The media should give more attention to third-party political candidates;* with response options of *strongly agree* to *strongly disagree*). Students can also be asked whether they view themselves or others in a different light after critically analyzing media representations (e.g., *If your only source of information were commercials, what characteristics would you think women and girls have? How about boys and men? From the people you know in your own life, what other characteristics do you think are absent in advertising portrayals of gender?*). Once again, we would expect an increase in agreement with the closed-ended question and a more specific and developed response to the open-ended questions after participation.

Finally, the skills of analysis or the ability to "deconstruct" the media can be measured to determine whether students have learned new (or honed existing) critical thinking skills to apply to the media. Students would view, hear, or read media content and then be asked to analyze it. For example, both before and after participation in the curriculum, stu-dents could be shown a clip from a cartoon featuring violence and could be asked either, most generally, *What's important to note about this clip?* or, more specifically, *How is violence depicted in this clip? What messages about violence might it convey to the audience?* We would expect a more detailed and focused response, utilizing specific language, concepts, or ideas from the curriculum, after students had participated. For closed-ended items, students could be asked about the presence of certain features (e.g., *What types of violence are present in the clip? Check all that apply*, with response options including *justified violence, rewarded violence, violence without consequences*, etc.), or could be asked to count acts of violence in the clip after having a discussion about how to define and identify media violence.

These three types of measurements are certainly not exhaustive but can provide a useful way of thinking about how to assess media education. I would advocate an approach that uses both open-ended and closed-ended measures, in order to obtain the advantages and avoid the pitfalls of both types. I would also caution media educators to keep in mind what Masterman (1985) noted about ideal media education outcomes involving neither the complete acceptance nor the complete rejection of media. Therefore, when we interpret responses of students we should not necessarily construe total rejection of all media as evidence of having learned effectively from media education. Rather, where appropriate, we should look for a measured response that recognizes some examples of responsible depictions and positive roles of media as well as their negative counterparts.

CASE STUDY: MEDIA VIOLENCE

What follows is a brief description of an ongoing project I have been conducting on the topic of media violence that is administered by my undergraduate students at the University of Massachusetts, Amherst. The curriculum attempts to bridge the gap between the interventionist and cultural studies approaches to media education. In this report, I have included the methods and measures I use to assess the effectiveness of the curriculum and a synopsis of the results. The case study demonstrates many, but not all, of the preceding ideas about the integration of both theoretical perspectives. (For a more complete description of the study, see Scharrer, 2005, 2006.)

The authors of the National Television Violence Study (Smith et al., 1998) suggest that not all violent acts in the media are equally likely to negatively affect audience members. They identify specific features in violent portrayals that have been associated in past research with an increased likelihood that the audience will learn aggression after being exposed to them. The study at hand uses four of these features as the primary subject of a media education curriculum administered to sixth-grade students, designed to increase knowledge and critical awareness of portrayals of violence. By discussing with young people that there are some ways of depicting violence in media that may encourage aggression, whereas other depictions are less likely to carry such risks, a balanced analysis that recognizes positive and negative aspects of media is facilitated, rather than an all-encompassing judgment of harm. The curriculum also contained a media production element. The sixth-grade students were briefly trained in the use of a digital video camera. They produced a script and a storyboard, and then shot and acted out their own fictional media scenes, in which they solved conflicts that they had seen in favorite television programs or movies in a nonviolent manner. Participating students described the media production as fun and educational.

My students (who were enrolled in an upper-level undergraduate seminar on television violence) and I created a reading packet designed to introduce the sixth graders to the concept of media education as well as to the issue of television violence. It defined, described, and gave examples of the four selected content features (rewarded violence, justified violence, violence perpetrated by appealing characters, and lack of consequences in violent portrayals—such as harm, pain, or grief). The packet was a guide for the undergraduate students to follow while administering the curriculum and also contained discussion questions and activities. My students and I met weekly to design the packet, choose video clips to analyze with the sixth graders, and design the research strategy that would measure the effectiveness of the curriculum. I observed the curriculum sessions and provided feedback for the discussion leaders.

The curriculum consisted of four one-hour visits to sixth-grade classrooms (later increased to six). Ninety-three sixth graders from four classrooms in three towns participated. A pretest questionnaire was implemented on the first day, before beginning, to measure students' pre-existing knowledge and opinions about the topic. In the remaining time in the sessions, each content feature was introduced, defined, and discussed with special emphasis on why it was associated with the learning of aggression. Then students viewed media clips and were asked to identify whether and how the content feature(s) was portrayed and to analyze the clip in general. In the general analysis, the media education instructors asked the students about what messages about gender and, where relevant, race and ethnicity were being advanced. In the final sessions, the students worked on their creative media productions. The post-test questionnaire was an exact duplicate of the pretest questionnaire, so that changes in knowledge or opinions in response to the curriculum could be determined. The opinions and experiences of the sixth graders were elicited and discussed in each session, and every effort was made to avoid didacticism and to allow the students to develop their own interpretations and ideas based on the analytical tools introduced. I encouraged my students to view the project as a mutually beneficial exchange of expertise with the sixth graders.

For each of the four content features, two to three questionnaire items measured students' perceptions of their presence in television violence and the degree to which they perceived them as leading to the learning of aggression. All questionnaire items were original measures that I wrote and pretested with a small group of sixth-grade students. Most items were closed ended, although three open-ended items were also included. Some were reverse-coded to prevent a response-set bias when completing the questionnaire. The second questionnaire also sought sixth graders' evaluations of the curriculum itself, using additional open-ended items. Truncated versions of the closed-ended questionnaire items, all with response options measured on a five-point scale of agreement, are found in Appendix 1.

The open-ended items asked for students' more detailed and less-prescripted opinions. Students were asked, What makes something you see on television "violent?" How is TV violence different from real-life violence? Why is there violence on television? and What do you think explains it? These questions were posed to students before the curriculum and then again immediately following. Responses to the second question are analyzed here.

To test whether participating in the media education curriculum would significantly increase awareness and critical evaluations of television violence, repeated measures analysis of variance was run (see Appendix 1). The two groups were defined according to the time in which the students completed the questionnaire, premedia education curriculum and post. In all items, a higher number indicates more agreement with the statement or more critical opinions. Results show significant changes for each measure over time, supporting an increase in learning and a shift toward more critical opinions after participation in the curriculum.

Important variations in responses to the open-ended item that asked about differences between real-life and televised violence occurred before compared to after participation, as well. Before, the majority of students (62 of 90) pointed to such relatively simple explanations of difference as "TV is fake and real life is real" and "People on TV aren't really getting hurt." After participating in the curriculum, 23 students continued to mention the former and 12 the latter theme. Sample quotes include, *"It is fake," "It is different because it is not real," "It is just acting,"* and *"The people aren't really getting hurt, but in real life people are," "TV actors don't get hurt."*

However, after the curriculum these responses were joined by a substantial number that were relatively more complex, indicating more sophisticated scrutiny of media violence and the application of specific language learned from the curriculum. The next most common theme, discussed by 19 students, was the lack of consequences in media violence, one of the four content features emphasized in the curriculum. Sample quotes include, *"TV violence doesn't show real-life consequences," "They don't show what happens to the person when they get punched, kicked, shot," "People don't act hurt. They get back up after being thrown to the ground," "TV violence does-*

n't usually show mourning for a lost person," and *"On TV you could fall off a cliff and not get hurt and in real life you would go kersplat."* Twelve students mentioned after the curriculum that TV violence is more frequent or exaggerated than real violence (e.g., *"TV violence is almost always exaggerated," "Often violence you see on TV is more violent than the stuff in real life," "TV violence happens more often."*).

The next most frequent theme in the post-item was another of the content features emphasized in the curriculum—rewards and punishments associated with violence, mentioned by ten of the students. Sample quotes include, *"There is no punishment on TV but there is in real life," "TV violence is different than real-life violence because when a good guy kills the bad guy, everyone cheers!" "On TV sometimes people get rewarded for being violent."* Finally, a third of the four content features emphasized in the curriculum, violence by appealing characters, was mentioned by seven students in the second questionnaire. Sample quotes include, *"Usually the good person wins the fight," "On TV you always know who's the good guy and who's the bad guy." "Good guys use violence and are thanked for it."*

After the curriculum, additional open-ended items invited feedback regarding whether and what the sixth graders felt they had learned from the curriculum. The media production exercise was often cited as the favorite element of the curriculum, and students reported that it was fun to create a scene that shows young people in a positive light, avoiding violent conflicts through peaceful resolutions. In general, many students noted that they learned about themselves and their power to question the media and "not accept it at face value." Indeed, twenty students mentioned that the curriculum helped them to engage in critical thinking about media violence.

CONCLUSIONS

The central thesis of this chapter is that the media effects–based interventionist and the cultural studies–based schools of thought both have much to contribute to the theory and practice of media education as well as to its assessment. By outlining the design and assessment of the case study example of a media education curriculum on the topic of media violence, one can see that the contributions of both points of view can peacefully coexist and can strengthen the effectiveness and alleviate the limitations of the other. At the center of the difference between the two theoretical approaches, I argue, is the identification of outcomes and their assessment, and this chapter provides a few suggestions regarding how to design and implement an assessment strategy.

The major themes of this chapter—the role of criticism, the nature of the topic, procedures and exercises, desired and expected outcomes, and the assessment of outcomes—were critically examined in the case study example to attempt to arrive at an approach that was sensitive to multiple arguments and concerns. Negative critique of violent media messages was a key element, for example, but by using the National Television Violence Study perspective, which recognizes that some features in some media depictions (but not all) make the learning of aggression more likely from exposure, negativity was balanced rather than being universally applied. The nature of the topic, as discussed above, carried with it an inherent moral stance that the media educators were antiviolence. But, attempts were made to limit moralizing by the media educators through inviting students' opinions and perspectives even while the exercises and discussion generated by the curriculum pointed toward critical analysis. Procedures and exercises in the curriculum encouraged an exchange of experiences and included a fun and instructive media production component. Desired and expected outcomes of the rather short curriculum did not include students being less influenced by media, but rather were defined as the learning of concepts and the adoption (or strengthening) of critical thinking. Finally, methods used to measure outcomes associated with participation in the curriculum included both closed-ended and open-ended questionnaire items and quantitative and qualitative analyses.

The case study's results demonstrate that learning and critical thinking did, indeed, occur in response to the media education curriculum. Whether these outcomes will contribute in the long term and in combination with other factors to a diminished, though certainly not completely eliminated, influence of the media remains to be seen. Only longitudinal data using the same participants could determine that. Nonetheless, regardless of the relationship between the short-term knowledge and opinions measured here and future behavior, I contend that the contributions of the curriculum to students' thoughts and views on the subject represent an achievement of media education.

Whether viewed as an intervention between media influences and audiences or as a study of media as the primary producers of culture, media education has much to contribute. Additional research and theory regarding anticipated outcomes and the assessment of those outcomes is of paramount importance to further our understanding of the potentially profound role that media education can provide. The utility of different emphases and approaches for students of different ages should also be examined. For example, perhaps an interventionist emphasis is most appropriate for younger children, while a cultural-studies emphasis on pre-existing critical analysis abilities and a central role for pleasure is best for older children, teens, and adults.

In short, I hope this chapter begins to address what Kubey (1998) sees as a necessary condition for the widespread adoption of media education in the United States, the integration of the cultural studies and interventionist perspectives. Kubey notes "Until there can be better accommodation between the two camps, and it can be seen, perhaps, that some inoculatory goals might be accommodated within a more student-centered approach . . . a broader acceptance of media education may be very difficult to achieve. There needs to be give on both sides" (1998, p. 66).

APPENDIX 1

Repeated measures analysis of variance, showing changes in mean scores over time. Higher mean numbers indicate more agreement with the statement shown, except for the items labeled*, in which higher numbers indicate more disagreement.

Variable	Mean	SD	F	df	sig.
When audience members like TV characters, they are more likely to learn from them.					
Precurriculum	3.58	1.04			
Postcurriculum	4.13	.78	17.99	1, 92	$p < .001$
Audience members are more likely to copy violence done by good guys vs. bad guys.					
Precurriculum	3.49	1.10			
Postcurriculum	4.14	.70	24.53	1, 89	$p < .001$
The actions that TV heroes use to get rid of bad guys are not really violence.*					
Precurriculum	3.97	1.07			
Postcurriculum	4.43	.94	14.83	1, 88	$p < .001$
When characters have a good reason to be violent, the audience is more likely to learn from them.					
Precurriculum	3.17	1.10			
Postcurriculum	3.80	.79	15.29	1, 88	$p < .001$

Many television programs
show violence as a necessary
way to solve problems.

Precurriculum	3.29	1.21			
Postcurriculum	4.01	1.04	16.98	1, 89	$p < .001$

People are more likely to
copy a violent act if the
character gets away with it
vs. if he/she is punished.

Precurriculum	3.58	1.13			
Postcurriculum	4.02	.96	10.48	1, 91	$p < .01$

A lot of violent acts in the
media are celebrated or
rewarded in the plot.

Precurriculum	3.62	.88			
Postcurriculum	3.97	.84	8.77	1, 89	$p < .01$

Getting shot on TV looks
pretty much the same as
getting shot in real life
would look.*

Precurriculum	2.89	1.09			
Postcurriculum	3.67	1.09	20.57	1, 89	$p < .001$

When fighting occurs
between cartoon characters,
it's not really violence
because it's not real.*

Precurriculum	3.48	1.37			
Postcurriculum	4.18	.97	17.21	1, 88	$p < .001$

TV programs should show
people getting punished
for violence more.

Precurriculum	3.73	1.35			
Postcurriculum	4.22	1.00	7.73	1, 91	$p < .01$

TV shows do a good job
of showing the grief that
loved ones of victims feel.*

Precurriculum	2.74	1.13			
Postcurriculum	3.80	1.04	44.46	1, 89	$p < .001$

REFERENCES

Aufderheide, P. (1993). *National leadership conference on media literacy. Conference report.* Washington, DC: Aspen Institute.

Bazalgette, C. (Ed.). (1989). *Primary media education: A curriculum statement.* London: British Film Institute.

Bowker, J. (Ed.). (1991) *Secondary media education: A curriculum statement.* London: British Film Institute.

Brown, J. (2000). Adolescents' sexual media diets. *Journal of Adolescent Health, 27*(2), 35–40.

Brown, J. A. (1998). Media literacy perspectives. *Journal of Communication, 48*(1), 44–57.

Bryant, J., & Thompson, S. (2002). *Fundamentals of media effects.* New York: McGraw Hill.

Buckingham, D. (1998). Media education in the UK: Moving beyond protectionism. *Journal of Communication, 48*(1), 33–43.

Buckingham, D. (2000). *After the death of childhood: Growing up in the age of electronic media.* Cambridge, UK: Polity.

Cantor, J. (2000). Media violence. *Journal of Adolescent Health, 27*(2), 30-34.

Christ, W. G., & Potter, W. J. (1998). Media literacy, media education, and the academy. *Journal of Communication, 48*(1), 5–15.

Comstock, G., & Scharrer, E. (1999). *Television: What's on, who's watching, and what it means.* San Diego: Academic Press.

Fiske, J. (1987). British cultural studies and television. In R. Allen (Ed.), *Channels of discourse, reassembled* (pp. 284-326). Chapel Hill: University of North Carolina Press.

Hall, S. (1980). Encoding/decoding. In S. Hall et al. (Eds.), *Culture media, language* (pp. 128–138). London: Hutchinson.

Hart, A. (1997). Textual pleasures and moral dilemmas: Teaching media literacy in England. In R. Kubey (Ed.), *Media literacy in the information age* (pp. 199–211). New Brunswick, NJ: Transaction.

Hobbs, R. (1998). The seven great debates in the media literacy movement. *Journal of Communication, 48*(1), 16–32.

Hobbs, R. (2001). The great debates circa 2001: The promise and the potential of media literacy. *Community Media Review*, 25–27.

Huesmann, L. R., Eron, L. D., Klein, R., Brice, P., & Fischer, P. (1983). Mitigating the imitation of aggressive behavior by changing children's attitudes about media violence. *Journal or Personality and Social Psychology, 44*, 899-910.

Irving, L. M., & Berel, S. R. (2001). Comparison of media-literacy programs to strengthen college women's resistance to media images. *Psychology of Women Quarterly, 25*(2), 103–117.

Kiousis, S., McDevitt, M., & Wu, X. (2005). The genesis of civic awareness: Agenda setting in political socialization. *Journal of Communication, 55*, 756-774.

Kubey, R. (1998) Obstacles to the development of media education in the U.S. *Journal of Communication, 48*(1), 58–69.

Lewis, J., & Jhally, S. (1998). The struggle over media literacy. *Journal of Communication, 48*(1), 109–120.

Masterman, L. (1985). *Teaching the media*. London: Routledge.

McDevitt, M., & Chaffee, S. H. (2000). Closing gaps in political communication and knowledge: Effects of a school intervention. *Communication Research, 27,* 259-292.

Oliver, M. B. (2002). Individual differences in media effects. In J. Bryant & D. Zillmann (Eds.) *Media effects: Advances in theory and research* (2nd ed., pp. 507–524). Mahwah, NJ: Erlbaum.

Paul, R., & Elder, L. (2001). *How to study and learn a discipline using critical thinking concepts and tools.* Dillon Beach, CA: The Foundation for Critical Thinking.

Robinson, T. N., Wilde, M. L., Navacruz, L. C., Haydel, K. F., & Varady, A. (2001). Effects of reducing children's television and video game use on aggressive behavior: A randomized controlled trial. *Archives of Pediatrics and Adolescent Medicine, 155*(1), 17-23.

Rosenkoetter, L. I., Rosenkoetter, S. E., Ozretich, R. A., & Acock, A. C. (2004). Mitigating the harmful effects of violent television. *Journal of Applied Developmental Psychology, 25,* 25-47.

Ruddock, A. (2001).*Understanding audiences: Theory and method.* London: Sage.

Scharrer, E. (2002). Making a case for media literacy in the curriculum: Outcomes and assessment. *Journal of Adolescent & Adult Literacy, 46*(4), 2–6.

Scharrer, E. (2005). Sixth graders take on television: Media literacy and critical attitudes about television violence. *Communication Research Reports, 24,* 325-333.

Scharrer, E. (2006). "I noticed more violence:" The effects of a media literacy program on knowledge and attitudes about media violence. *Journal of Mass Media Ethics, 21*(1), 70-87.

Singer, D. G., & Singer, J. L. (1998). Developing critical viewing skills and media literacy in children. *The Annals of the American Academy of Political and Social Science, 55,* 164–180.

Smith, S., Wilson, B. J., Kunkel, D., Linz, D., Potter, W. J., Colvin, C. M., & Donnerstein, E. (1998). *National television violence study: Executive summary* (Vol. III*).* Santa Barbara: Center for Communication and Social Policy, University of California.

Tyner, K. (1998). *Literacy in a digital world.* Mahwah, NJ: Erlbaum.

3

THE MEDIA AND ME

An Experiment in Reflective Writing in an Applied Media Degree

Ruth Zanker

A turning point in tertiary media pedagogy arrived for me in 1998 when, in the middle of a formal lecture, sixty students sang an entire McDonald's advertisement to me joyfully and in unison. What made this episode even more bizarre was that this ad was no longer on air; it had been broadcast half a decade before, during the early 1990s. This unnerving event occurred half way through a sober lecture that I had designed to introduce them to the paradoxical "push and pull" of local and global cultural appeals in advertising. I had chosen McDonald's because it was a global brand that had tapped into the national imagination of New Zealanders and I had hoped that this example of "glocalization" would enable me to tease out the complex relationship between a global brand (e.g., McDonald's) and local culture (McDonald's deliberate appropriation of kiwi cultural symbols). The quirky advertisement in question was for a line of hamburgers called "kiwi-burgers." It began its television version with the headline "Remember when every hamburger had beetroot?" and then the song followed—a long list of Kiwi icons (including McDonald's) with pictures attached:

> Kiwis love,
> Hot Pools, Rugby Balls, McDonald's, Schnapper schools, World peace,
> Woolly fleece, Ronald, And raising beasts, Chilly bins, Cricket wins, fast
> skis, golf tees, silver ferns, kauri trees,
> kiwi burger, love one please . . .

As I collected myself after the chorus, in order to embark on the serious business of dissecting how and why this global company wished to position itself in heartland New Zealand, a student interjected. She argued that I was "picking to bits" precious childhood memories of birthday parties at McDonald's, summertime "Happy Meals" and Disney collectables. She didn't like me "putting down" McDonald's. Clearly, this student felt that critical analysis intruded on her unself-conscious pleasure in a treasured media memory.

I was rather taken aback and remember feeling that this moment must have significance for my teaching practice in an applied undergraduate broadcasting program, but at that time I was far from clear about what the significance might be. But one thing *was* certain: I had tapped into passionate peer-group attachment to a much loved childhood media icon. As Barcan (2002) describes it:

> Many students reach . . . (tertiary) . . . study unused to critical or analytical thinking and thinking which they may experience as baffling or an unwelcome intrusion into their everyday pleasures. (p. 352)

MEDIATED POPULAR YOUTH CULTURE

Upon later reflection, I realized that this episode should not have surprised me. New Zealanders have long been enthusiastic consumers of imported brands. Despite living at the end of the earth we have cosmopolitan tastes and have, since the beginning of television (and even radio), enjoyed access to popular hits from the United States, Britain, and Australia, leavened with a modest amount of local content. Young people here have always been cultural magpies, quick to pick up new global trends, whether Mouseketeer ears or Pokemon, Elvis Presley or Madonna, Pizza Hut or McDonald's.

Scholars in other nations have observed how films, television, music, internet, video games, comics, magazines, and merchandising cultures teach young people about themselves and their relationship to the world (Kinder, 1991). This tiny episode in a New Zealand classroom simply illustrated, yet again, that the shared cultural capital of young people at the turn of the century is powerfully shaped by the marketing campaigns of global brands and entertainment companies. But some scholars go further. They assert that children's consumer culture during the 1990s became, for better or worse, a "whole system" central to peer group identity and gender identification (Kapur, 1999; Kline, 1995; McChesney, 2002; Steinberg & Kincheloe, 1997). Other theorists suggest that we lighten up and stop worrying like old Marxist pessimists. We should simply celebrate individual popular texts as sites for new subversive forms of community. Jenkins (1992), for example, argues that communities of fans define the textual pleasures of a program like Star Trek in their own terms, and others have suggested how children's programs work in similar ways for children, often providing shared peer-group meanings and pleasures not available to their parents (Seiter, 1993). Meijer (1998) perhaps argues the most radical case for audience agency. She contends that advertising, not programming, "has a potential as a form of public communication and a setting for the actualization of contemporary citizenship . . . a feature of culture, operative as a dimension of individual and collective identities" (p. 235).

THE STUDENT PROFILE

These different theoretical viewpoints provide the means of accessing fresh ways of reading media texts for those engaged in a cultural studies program in a liberal arts degree. The aspiring young media professionals sitting in front of me in 1998, however, were not enrolled in a liberal arts degree, but rather in a highly applied undergraduate broadcasting program. They were situated not only as fans and audiences, for whom there was unproblematic critical value in the exploration of media texts/audience responses within postmodern culture, but they were also aspiring producers, programmers and marketers who needed to grapple with the shifting workplaces of the cultural industry. These students were aiming at careers in the mainstream media industry.

The Bachelor of Broadcasting Communication is a vocational degree designed to provide graduates with intense craft production experiences that fast-track them into careers within the New Zealand media industry. My course, sandwiched between two levels of immersion craft, was designed to enable them to understand the cultural, economic, and political context that structures local broadcasting and production media, while hopefully inspiring them to consider their public responsibilities within it.

BACKGROUND TO THE DEGREE

A decade or so before, when the degree was envisioned, it was still possible to ask "What do employers expect of graduates of tertiary vocational degrees?" The job of educators was to provide it. During the extreme neoliberal educational climate of the English speaking world in the 1990s, it was even politically fashionable to suggest that:

> . . . the partnership of universities with employers was mainly one of supplier to customer, as if new graduates were to be seen as "products" more or less shaped by universities to the "specification" of the demanding employer. (Coldstream, 1997, p. 4)

But at the turn of the century, major employers, none more so than in the muddle of workplaces tagged "the audio-visual and media industry" (global corporate to cottage industry), confess they are unlikely to provide life-time careers. It is increasingly clear that students need the means to be flexible and adaptable in an uncertain working world. They need skills to learn and develop throughout their lives.

Fortunately, this emphasis on "learning how to learn" is already embedded in the "capability" philosophy of the degree (Stephenson, 1991), through heavy emphasis on independent, real-life learning in traditional craft groups and close connections with industry advisors. But the ability to be capable learners within the fluid and uncertain post-Fordist media landscape provides new challenges. How can one enable students, who enter a degree with dreams of broadcasting jobs, to deal with the speed of obsolescence, while envisioning new opportunities?

This longer historical view made me realize that whatever the traditional problems of introducing young people to critical or analytical thinking in an applied degree were, they were about to become even more challenging. How could one enable "capable" educated graduates who, " . . . at the end of their university course are impressed less by the extent of what they have been taught than by the limitless prospect of learning opening ahead of them" (Coldstream, 1997, p. 4)?

There were two issues to consider. Not only was traditional broadcasting evolving into the broadband digital future, but this was happening as students' shared cultural memories and expectations were narrowing to those shaped by the global sweep of post-1980s neoliberalism.

My students in 1998 (and thereafter) had been the child fans of the commercial "goodies" that swept the globe in the wake of early 1980s FCC deregulation.[1] They had grown up during the explosion in the children's consumer goodies, themselves the result of children's tastes becoming the site of intense market research and development. Vertical and horizontal integration of entertainment, food, and drink industries in the 1990s created new media platforms and saw merchandising and rights opportunities expand in creative and complex ways. I knew from my own research that the tiny New Zealand market had been particularly quick to pick up new fads for Transformers, Cabbage Patch Dolls, Super Stars of Wrestling, My Little Ponies, Smurf and Lion King collectables at fast food outlets, Mighty Morphin Power Rangers, Pokemon and Spice Girls. Marketers bemoaned that the tiny New Zealand market quickly "saturated." Children moved "overnight" to the next "big television promotion" (Zanker, 2002). Teachers complained about the sweep of many short and sharp cycles of play inspired by toy fads marketed through television. Newsrooms picked up on the waves of associated parental panic on slow news days.

So, it can be said that these students in my class had the distinction of being the group of young New Zealanders whose entire cultural memory had been shaped by audiovisual deregulation. They had grown up in a nation (earlier, the first highly regulated welfare state) that was increasingly individualistic and materialistic, marked by widening social divides, often along tense racial lines. Deregulated commercial television meant Gameboy "give aways" and T-shirts for hit CDs on the national afternoon children's show, followed by reruns of *Gilligan's Island* and *The Fonz*. Deregulated radio in the evenings meant "give aways" of Pizza, soft drinks, and the latest Sony album. Had ads, as Meijer hypothesized, become the shared public spaces of young people?

It might seem logical to me, a double-dipping intellectual who had access to and appreciated the best of cultural experiment and popular culture, that anyone about to enter the local culture industry in a small nation would be keen to understand the political forces that might shape future local creative possibilities. But this was far from clear to students who had absorbed the notion that they were free agents and sovereign consumers, able to choose what they liked best from the media market. How could one expect young people brought up in an individualistic environment that argued "freedom of choice" and commercial free speech to find it easy to accept that, in Fiske's words, they lived in a commodified "mediated world" that was "socially constructed?" How could they understand that there was nothing natural or inevitable about their popular culture and that favorite memories were simply the winners of bitter corporate power battles? How could they accept that their fondest media memories had been shaped simply by what transnational and national commercial media found profitable to offer them?

It was not necessarily cultural diversity, nor was it necessarily risk-taking creativity. Most of the students were ignorant of, or couldn't care less about, what public service broadcasting might offer them. If they did happen to find public service radio stations, they would find little to attract them there in the stuffy coziness of middle-aged cultural hegemony and definitions of "quality." In the meantime, other imaginative horizons for the "public sphere" had shrivelled. So, why should they be interested in debating hypothetical models for a range of futures when they had no models for what an alternative to current provision might be?

Yet, despite all this, it was clear that there was creative energy and ambition aplenty in the group. I was drawn to the energy of many students, fans who knew the fine detail of their chosen shows and music and were witty creatives in their own right. In the class there were scratch DJs, film makers with a nice eye for hybrid intertextuality, web site designers, and song writers with an ear for irony. They gained intense pleasure from creating new forms of sophisticated cultural bricolage. These artists were also potential heirs of new cross-currents of postcolonial energy related to a cultural renaissance amongst the Maori tribes (since 1985), and immigration from Pacific and Asian cultures, if there was access to shared public spaces and experimental funding.[2]

All these factors made constructing a course on the role of media in cultural citizenship based on old binary notions of national/global, margin/center and public/private a challenge. How could I engage students in critical and political economic analysis without being viewed as a puritanical kill-joy when they just wanted to get back to their production toys?

TWO SETS OF PEDAGOGICAL ISSUES FOR AN APPLIED COURSE

Lewis (2001) suggests two key student-centered problems inherent in persuading "youth" to view their culture critically. Firstly, there is the pedagogical issue centering on "politics of pleasure—and, in particular, the specific forms of investment that undergraduates bring to popular youth culture," which the McDonald's episode at the beginning of the chapter dramatically illustrates. Secondly, there is the awkwardness of a pedagogy where "the past and present of popular culture tend to separate the teacher from the student, and where our frames of reference will be quite different" (p. 318). Clearly, it was not useful for me to pretend to have a fan's insights into *Buffy*, or Doom, or Maori hip-hop; indeed it would be viewed as highly embarrassing, but I needed to find a way of helping them view their own intertextual culturescapes critically.

It seemed that there were two clear sets of pedagogical issues to consider in the applied degree. At a pragmatic level, a career in broadcasting, as had been understood for fifty years, was evolving into a broadband future. Their dream jobs (news anchor, cameraperson, DJ, editor, programmer) were disappearing. How could I connect their impressive media-consuming credentials to a critical analysis of the galvanic political/economic forces that had been reshaping the media over their lifetime? How could I convince students, demonstrably already enthusiastic fans, of the personal strategic value of becoming critical thinkers in terms of their future creative lives? I wanted to provide them with critical tools that enabled them to analyze the forces radically reshaping the creative industries, in order to empower them to carve out (possibly yet-to-be-defined) niches in the reconfiguring digital mediascape.

At a more idealistic level, it also seemed to be important to illustrate how the cultural industries mediate all other processes of democracy and culture. How could I demonstrate that media workers exercise moral and political power because they regulate "the images, meanings and ideas that frame the agendas that shape everyday life" and thus shape how people make sense of their lives (Giroux, 2000, p. 9)? How could I engage media savvy young students in abstract issues like the commodification of local public spaces, the importance of range and diversity of representation in the media, and the key role of media in shaping future citizenship and cultural identity?

All this was pretty heavy stuff, but I did not want my course to be viewed as an inoculation against being alert to new business ideas and the value of creative "rights." Nor did I want it to be a form of leftist cultural pessimism. Above all, I wanted students to remain politically hopeful and flexible early adaptors to new creative and social possibilities. Most of the rest of this chapter describes an experiment designed to address these challenges and discusses the difficulty faced in creating what might be called a "pedagogy of hope" for students with a deep investment in the current and future media business. On the one hand, it was important to provide them with critical political economic frames that could make sense of industry realities, but on the other hand, they needed to feel able to maintain openness to change in order to speculate about future possibilities.

I am drawn to Henry Jenkins' definition of theory as "speculation . . . a set of propositions larger than the individual example" (quoted in McKee, 2002, p. 311) because it usefully describes the theoretical intent of the exercises designed to help students jump the perceived gaps between their own private media consumption and pleasure, their applied learning in the craft courses, and critical analysis. Reflective exercises stretch across both so-called "applied" and "theory" levels of the degree. In them, the undergraduate students are encouraged to make connections between their personal media histories as "audiences" and "fans," their craft experiences as "producers," and their responsibilities as producers to future audiences and fans. Theory frames are not the focus of the course, but they are used as a means to an end, to enable students to view their familiar terrain of media memory through new eyes.

WEEK ONE, SEMESTER ONE: GROUP MEDIA HISTORIES

On the first day of the semester, the students are allocated to small groups to prepare skits summarizing their most memorable media memories. Small groups provide a safe confessional environment where it is fun to make connections with students from other parts of New Zealand. During this process they discover the dimensions of their shared media memories. A sheet of prompt questions is supplied to cue them to consider both early and more recent memories and to recall the emotion attached to particular memories. Their "research" is presented in five-minute long theater-sport style performances at the end of the week. This has a performative role; it allows the extroverts their "head," often presenting the thoughtful material supplied by quieter members. It is hard to be formal and sing Kermit's "Being Green." Furthermore, there is healthy competition between groups, and this in turn further extends to a "research community" over beers at the nearest pub. Improvised sets (no budget or access to media equipment), whacky costumes, verbal wit, and keen audience participation are key features.

PERFORMANCE PATTERNS

What is striking is the extent of detail presented. Entire theme tunes, scripts from *Playschool* and *Sesame Street*, the Bart Simpson "rap," impersonations of Raphael the Ninja Turtle, McGyver, *The Young and the Restless*, *Oprah*, Michael Jackson's "Bad," "Wilmaaaaaaa!" *Fresh Prince of Bel-Air*, "Smarter than an average cookie," "Captain Planet, he's our hero, gonna take pollution down to zero!" are performed with gusto and each well-executed "riff" is received with acclaim by the audience. This helps build the sense of inclusive shared history among students, many of whom are far from home. What is also striking is how many skits are performed in American accents. As one journalism student later explains in her autobiography "it just seemed normal for action heroes to have one."

Another recurring riff is the glee of shared memories of parental disapproval (Freddy Kruger, playing *Doom*, training bras) and there is a strong theme of gendered peer group culture. Males vigorously enact *Super Stars of Wrestling*, girls "talk" the peer group politics surrounding *My Little Pony* and *Sally Jessy Raphael*. In such a way, theories of active audience and fan culture come alive for later discussion. Shared media experiences and expertise (i.e., "I found another *Star Wars* and comic fanatic") were cited as a key way of making friends in the course. As Bill from television puts it in the following written autobiography:

> Born in 1982, I am a typical product of a very media focused genera-
> tion. Great pleasure can be had from reminiscing over old TV pro-
> grams, advertising, jingles, catch phrases and toys . . . now after endless
> flashback conversations, I realize how universal media experiences can
> be.

THE ARCHIVED AUTOBIOGRAPHY

The first group task was a means of stirring up memories. The individual reflective media autobiography that followed gathered and archived personal recollections. This written exercise is handed in after a week or so of the course, but is not marked. It is simply a means of capturing their memories of the media as audience members and as fans before taking on the role of media producers. They are told that the exercise will be handed back to them at the beginning of semester two for further consideration. For the rest of semester, the students immersed themselves in "hands-on" craft experiences creating a radio station, working in studio television production, and working in a radio newsroom.

What is most striking about the tone of the autobiographies is the clarity of detail and highly colored emotions (ranging from a sense of safety, to happiness, envy, or terror) attached to early media memories. A strong confessional tone saturates the autobiographies and many confess to finding the process of recall surprisingly engrossing. Sam from the radio stream tries to explain how earlier memories are different: "More recent programs won't stick in my head forever because I am past my prime when it comes to important television viewing." Jane from journalism comments that "it's hard to explain, but I can't imagine my life without the people I came to love on *Play-School* and after school television." Nick from radio suggests that early childhood memories of Elvis shared with his dad mean that "when he is an old man with a 'hottie,' the music of Elvis will send tears streaming down his face." Peter from television talks of "warm safe comfortable feelings evoked by the theme tune to *Coronation Street*." Rod from radio describes the ecstasy of being chosen by his older brother to play Raphael from the Ninja Turtles. Many present their first "flashback" experience in detail. For some it is a moment in a narrative (*Jaws, Wizard of Oz, Dr. Who*), or a recurring dream based on forbidden glimpses (the journalist being eaten off the loo in *Jurassic Park* features more than once!). For several, it is war footage from the first Gulf war, here described by Patrick from radio:

> We always watched the news as we ate dinner. The golf (sic) war was my first "I will always remember where I was moments." It feels like the moment when I realized for the first time that my parents couldn't protect me from everything. I had nightmares about Saddam Hussein bombing Christchurch, New Zealand.

For others, it is as recent as the death of Princess Diana in 1997, described by Anna in television as feeling "similar to Harry, the way his aunt and uncle saying that James and Lily Potter died in a car Crash."

Many expressed a sense of television being the primary measure of "history" in their lives. Suzanne, in journalism, puts it clearly:

> I started watching *The Simpsons* when I was 10. I am now 22, so I have lived with them half my life. And when it first started, every boy in the class wanted to be Bart. It was a pain.

Many note how media-saturated their memories are. "Media is an ever-changing portrayal of the world we live in and the many ways we see it and interpret it" and "By hearing an old song or seeing a TV program we can retrace the souvenirs of our mind to remember the history of our lives." "I have been influenced in what I wear, what I eat, how I act, favourite catch-phrases and accents. I have a love/hate relationship with characters, scheduling their lives into mine" (students from each stream).

The sociological "truths" of gendered play expressed in the performances are deepened in later autobiographies:

> If you are a girl you like Barbie, Rainbow Brite and Care Bears. Pink frilly programs with cute animals. Everything has to be pink. Boys like Transformers, GI Joe, and Ninja Turtles. This is the great truth about New Zealand early childhood. (Louise from journalism)

What is striking is the affectionate observation of their social behavior related to former tastes:

When I was 5, I saw an advert for a Ninja Turtle toy. From that moment my life seemed to glide to a grinding halt as everything became unimportant. The toy became my reason for living. (Tom, radio)

At 6, I discovered early hip-hop. I wanted to be black and have a cool haircut and began to call my friends honkys. (Paddy, radio)

My Little Pony screened at 3:30 pm . . . extremely happy events happened to pretty pink and purple colored ponies and the moral always was 'be kind to EVERYONE'' (*sic*). (Penny, journalism)

They comment, in an almost anthropological sense, on how the rights of passage between "stages" of maturity are signaled by shifts in media consumption:

Everything cool like *My Little Ponies* club were suddenly swept under the carpet and out came *Girlfriend* magazine which taught you how to dress at the school discos (that we didn't have) and kiss boys (that we didn't know), and be fans of *New Kids on the Block*. (Mary, radio)

I started watching horror way too young, probably as a way of being tough to no-one in particular. (Rod, radio)

Finally, they were able to bring a wry and observant eye to their social environment and its attitudes to media consumption:

I am the first child of two school teachers who were, and still are, painstakingly sensible about always rationing television viewing. (Chrissie, television)

In adolescence, I was tragically engulfed by soaps like *Shortland Street* [a local soap], *Spin City, Friends* . . . it enabled me to go to school and discuss anything about them and many people would be instantly interested in what I was saying. (Sarah, journalism)

CAREER CHOICE

The autobiography also asked them to reflect on what drew them to the applied broadcasting degree. Some students were charmingly candid ("I love to talk, so radio was for me"). But most responses fell into two sets of discourse: the first being, "my first taste of radio/television/newsrooms was like a sugar fix, or an itch I just had to scratch . . . " and the second being, "I wanted a job that isn't just a job but a passion, a hobby and a varied fun way to spend my time with different personalities, ideas and opportunities." There was little realism about the tough times existing in the deregulated media environment in New Zealand.

WEEK ONE, SEMESTER TWO: REFLECTIONS ON MEDIA MEMORIES IN LIGHT OF CRAFT LEARNING

Second semester drags them away from their "beloved" craft equipment and immerses them in a course designed to explore the political, economic, and cultural context within which the local broadcasting and media industries operate. At the beginning of this more theoretical semester, they are given back their "cached" autobiographies to read, and are subsequently invited to write to their younger selves.

It is striking that, if anything, the craft experiences confirm their career choices. Typical of comments are: "I aspire even more to enter this exciting industry." "There are so many jobs I didn't know existed." "I'm getting there!" "I enjoyed reading my autobiography, it made me realize how much I had learnt this semester." "Last semester was the best few months of my life. I was doing what I want and I have enjoyed fulfilling my dreams."

Their memories do not shift either:

> I do not think that my memories have changed, just become more precious. These memories are from afar, from another time, detached from the hustle and bustle that are the rigours of craft. (Kelly, television)

> My autobiography is a bit cheesy but I stand by it. (Tim, radio)

And if they view the media differently now, it is because:

> I wonder if the need to understand the realities of the media industry crossed my mind as I wrote my autobiography. (Diana, radio)

> My media habits have changed. I hadn't realized until this exercise. (Jason, television)

> Now I don't take it for granted. I ask "why?" I am much more critical of what I see and hear. (Karen, journalism)

I cringed when I read the autobiography you returned to me, journalism has made me question what I am told. (Suzanne, journalism)

There is a general tone of delight at having been permitted behind the "magic curtain" of production, being taught the "tricks of the trade" and pride in being able to make informed craft judgments. Janet in radio comments: "It's interesting that children we touched through 'Radio Pop' may remember radio more vividly than I do because of it."

There is also a new respect for the craft disciplines behind the product and the constraints of equipment, craft expectations, industrial newsroom deadlines, production budgets, editing equipment, and advertising revenue. Adrian in television describes the "iceberg" of preproduction needed to produce "even one element" of a children's show. Pip comments:

> Previously I saw television as an entertainment outlet only. . . . I was surprised how it shaped things . . . it wasn't the rugby officials who decided when the game began . . . it's the television director.

Angela, a radio student observes:

> I now listen to radio in a very critical way, I look for mistakes, and errors of programming, and I listen carefully to the announcers to see if they really are as good/bad as I previously thought.

But there is also a growing number who express a sense of disillusionment as they understand their role in the media machine:

> I now understand the concept of demographics and psychographics and I find it almost disturbing how I fitted into these "slots" so well. (Ines, radio)

> Commercial radio is about money. I just hope that I won't be another person in the industry that is money hungry and driven by a pay check. I want my passion for radio to survive. (Jenny, radio)

> I feel that I have lost my innocence about the media industry. I love it . . . but . . . the hard work, disappointments and victories of the last semester came as a little surprise. (Peter, television)

Interestingly, there is also a sense of growing professional ethics. Hannah comments:

As a journalist I have to be an idealist of sorts. I really think it is not dramatic to see the journalist as one of the last few bastions of the good and the just.

And Rick from television probes deeper, commenting:

Just what does professionalism mean in today's world? To tabloids, a professional job is getting the article no matter what—getting that ultimate scoop of Robbie Williams kissing Rachel Hunter is showing great professionalism. So, in a world where the tabloids and mainstream news collide, just what does professionalism mean for me?

EXERCISE THREE: FINAL REFLECTION IN LIGHT OF THEORY COURSEWORK

The final formal element of reflection occurs at the end of twelve weeks of institutional, economic, and political background to the media. The "theory" course is designed thematically to explore the media from the perspective of both audiences and producers. So, for example, in the history theme, broadcasting students each contribute an oral history recorded with someone over forty five years of age, and these are cleared ethically for sharing on the web. The passion with which the older informants talk of their treasured media memories provide anecdotal color for subjects as diverse as radio dedications during the war years, radio soaps, the arrival of television, top 40 hit radio, mods versus rockers, the moon landing and Hendrix in Vietnam. Anna from television offers her grandpa's memory from 1924:

It was a bit of a community gathering as the men of the town would sit around his Aunt's radio and listen to Awarua radio. It was not a radio station as such with music and talk . . . it simply broadcast ships' messages from all over the world.

But some of the most important recollections for students relate to social changes brought by the arrival of "new" media:

The whanau [family] used to stick around whoever brought the guitar and sing. That all changed when the telly arrived in 1962. (Manu, male)

Retired broadcasters share their "radical" times with students. One guest, a founder of the pirate radio station on a boat that played the first top 40 in New Zealand, challenges students to reinvent "radical" and "creative" for their generation. Thus, dry institutional and political analysis is brought to life. A two-day workshop on the history of the Treaty of Waitangi (the founding document of the bicultural relationship between Maori and colonial settlers in New Zealand) has a profound impact on students who have monocultural backgrounds and little exposure to colonial history. As one student puts it candidly:

> I am speaking from experience of growing up with a sometimes racist parent, thank you for the enlightenment.

A core element of the course is to bring "cultural margins" to the center of concern through a range of exercises: group tasks of media content analysis that are posted to the web, further interviews and presentations from guests (often Maori or Pacific Island graduates) who talk about new visions and frustrations with the present politics of broadcasting. Again, this is challenging for students who have not thought deeply about their culture before. Sometimes it presents an assault on previous media judgment or even their sense of personal identity. It also raises questions about their own professional agency:

> I do not think of Maori because I find that Maori programs are in ghetto-slots.

> I was embarrassed looking at television in an analytical way [counting content]. (Megan, television)

> The course highlighted that being "in the majority" we were blissfully unaware who had no place in media representation. (Jenny, radio)

Each guest speaker, reading, case study, and real-life scenario is intended to provide yet another angle, another resource to take into consideration when thinking about past and present media constructions. They also, hopefully, suggest a new range of cultural "possibilities." Possibilities are important to keep as a focus of attention when the message about the future is that much is changing in the wake of digital convergence and global marketing. How successful this is as a strategy is less clear-cut as their final "reflective" exercises illustrate.

There is a divide between those who believe that there will be new opportunities for complexity and flexibility (the opportunities for bottom

up niche innovation, or the 'Peter Jackson did it' scenarios) and others who
are daunted by the evidence that points to insecure and poorly paid
employment on the margins of the casual economy.[3] A growing awareness
of the speed of change is the most unsettling subtext of the course, because
it raises concerns about the fate of national media institutions and their
chosen professional futures:

> The course taught me that my future role in the media is to be as
> multi-skilled as possible.

> Now I realize I have to think interactive games, associated merchan-
> dise, rights, international appeal to get investment. I have to think
> about the expense to local culture of making commercially viable
> products.

> I find it quite scary that my career path is in the centre of change. (stu-
> dents from each stream)

CONCLUSION:
ENGAGING THE SOCIOLOGICAL IMAGINATION

This chapter has explored how reflective thinking was used to enable
highly focused and practically minded students find space in which to
review and integrate their experiences. This process focused not only on
their current media practice in a converging digital world, but also on the
implications of their own highly mediated cultural histories, tastes and values for their future practice. As one student puts it at the end of the
course:

> I found the course thought provoking and at times scary. In my
> February autobiography I failed to grasp how important and influential
> the media was on my childhood. (Rachel, television)

The students quoted in this chapter were born after *Star Wars* first hit the
screens but before computers and text messaging became preschool play-
things. They share a very particular but intense media literacy in the artifacts of popular culture during the decade and a half from 1984 to 2002.

    The objective of the described reflective exercises was to excite what
Mills calls a "sociological imagination," the ability to "grasp history and
biography and the relations between the two within society" (Denzin,

1999, p. 93). My hope was for students to make connections between memory and fandom, the industrial processes of "making media" and the overarching transnational political economic and technological forces shaping future creative work places. In the words of one of the students:

> In my autobiography there were all the facts but I didn't think hard about them. Now I do (Sam, Radio)

I also hoped that students would learn to generalize from their particular media experiences in order to better appreciate how institutions, politics, and economics shape formative cultural experiences for all generations. Such insights might then enable them to consider their moral and social responsibilities to the next generation as broad/narrow/web/media producers/writers/composers—whatever their place in the evolving media environment.

The student response to the exercises I designed demonstrate that the shared media memory of a cohort of students presents both pedagogical opportunities and challenges for media teachers. It is a resource that is charged with emotion for students and therefore engages them, but it is also a resource that they can find difficulty gaining critical distance from. At its most potent, this shared memory can be used, as Lewis puts it, in "a more anthropological sense" in order to reflect on how media content has shaped their cultural perspectives, relationships with other generations, and peer group passions (Lewis, 2001, p. 320). The setting of reflective exercises at the end of craft immersion provides the opportunity to remind students of how much they have learned about production processes. It also offers them a chance to reflect on how they once talked about media content simply as fans and audiences. At best, these craft experiences trigger important reflections on the production processes that shaped their shared memories. These, in turn, can later be related to present and future global political-economic themes.

It is, however, in comments made at the end of the theoretical course that we can see how critical pedagogy walks a knife-edge. Such a course has the potential to be radical in the way it inspires new visions and possibilities for the future, but it may also potentially rob some students of their sense of focus and ambition as it relentlessly drives home the dour political-economic magnitude of the media machine. As Jo from television puts it:

> The magic has gone that was there in my first autobiography. In the craft course I became the magician. In the theory course I realized that I was a puppet.

If "hope" might be characterized as the playful openness to possibility, then any course that wishes to enable creative responses to change needs to foster it as a core value. Theory can be used to create this sense of possibilities, and my hunch is that an applied course requires more, rather than less, "theory" in order to provide the means of seeing the world anew. But that requires further pedagogical adventures before the verdict can be given.

NOTES

1. The FCC in the early 1980s, under Fowler, deregulated children's television. This enabled toy manufacturers to offer free associated animations to cable television. Children's programming became, in effect, a promotional window for toys and associated merchandise (Minow, 1995).
2. Four million New Zealanders live in the South Pacific, where culture is shaped by a colonial past and an increasingly hybrid present forged out of a population mix of indigenous Maori (14%) and descendants of the majority European and minority Polynesian and Asian immigrants.
3. Peter Jackson, the producer of the trilogy *Lord of the Rings*, was born and continues to work in New Zealand. He is an inspiration to many of the next creative generations.

REFERENCES

Barcan, R. (2002). Problems without solutions: Teaching theory and the politics of hope. *Continuum: Journal of Media and Cultural Studies. 16*(3), 343–356.

Coldstream, P. (1997). Training minds for the future world of work. Guest opinion. *Capability: Journal of Autonomous Learning for Life and Work, 3*(2), 2–4.

Denzin, N. K. (1999). Biographical research methods. In J. P. Keeves & G. Lakomski (Eds.), *Issues in educational research* (pp. 92–102). Oxford: Pergamon.

Giroux, H. (2000). *Impure acts: The practical politics of cultural studies.* New York & London: Routledge.

Jenkins, H. (1992). *Textual poachers: Television fans and participatory culture.* New York: Routledge.

Kapur, J. (1999). Out of control: Television and the Transformation of childhood in late capitalism. In M. Kinder (Ed.), *Kids' media culture* (pp. 122–136). Duke University Press.

Kinder, M. (1991). *Playing with power in movies, television and video games: From Muppet babies to Teenage Mutant Ninja Turtles.* Berkeley: University of California Press.

Kline, S. (1995). The play of the market: On the internationalization of children's culture. *Theory, Culture & Society, 12*, 103–129.

Lewis, J. (2001). Let's get serious: Notes on teaching youth culture. In T. Miller (Ed.), *A companion to cultural studies*. Cambridge: Blackwell.

McChesney, R. (2002). Children, globalization and media policy. In C. Von Feilitzen & U. Carlsson (Eds.), *Children, young people and media globalization: Yearbook 2002*. The Unesco International Clearinghouse on Children, Youth and Media. Goteborg: Nordicom at Goteborg University.

McKee, A. (2002). What cultural studies needs is more theory. *Continuum: Journal of Media and Cultural Studies, 16*(3), 311–316.

Meijer, I.C. (1998). Advertising citizenship: An essay on the performative power of consumer culture. *Media, Culture and Society, 20*, 235–249.

Minow, N. (1995). *Abandoned in the wasteland: Children, television, and the first amendment*. New York: Hill and Wang.

Seiter, E. (1993). *Sold separately: Children and parents in consumer culture*. New York: Rutgers University Press.

Steinberg, S., & Kincheloe, J. (1997). *Kinderculture: The corporate construction of childhood*. New York: Westfield Press.

Stephenson, J. (1991). *Capability learning*. Paper presented to the British Royal Society, London.

Zanker, R. (2002). Tracking the global in the local. In C. Von Feilitzen & U. Carlsson= (Eds.), *Children, young people and media globalization: Yearbook 2002*. The Unesco International Clearinghouse on Children, Youth and Media. Goteborg: Nordicom at Goteborg University.

4

WHAT KEVIN KNOWS

*Students' Challenges to Critical
Pedagogical Thinking*[1]

Sara Bragg

A few years into my Media Studies teaching career, I found myself wondering where I had gone wrong. I had begun full of optimism about the importance and validity of the general aims and specific strategies of media education. I perceived it as relevant to young people's identities outside education, hoping that my teaching would empower students by engaging with their informally acquired cultural capital in a way that traditional school subjects failed to do (Bourdieu & Passeron, 1977). Moreover, the educational theorists I had read—such as Len Masterman (1980, 1985), Henry Giroux (1992,1994a, 1994b), Henry Giroux and Peter McLaren (1994), and Bronwyn Davies (1993), from their different institutional bases in the United Kingdom, the United States and Australia—assured me that cultural or media studies was an emancipatory practice. They argued that its key "tools of analysis" (concepts and theoretical terminology) would reveal for students the hidden conventions, meanings and values of media texts, or "make the text visible as something constructed from a particular vantage point and with constitutive force and with political implications" (Davies, 1993, p. 174). They would enable students to identify the manipulative ideological intent of media institutions, through answering questions such as "Who produced this text? In whose interests?" (see Bowker, 1991). Teachers would thereby demystify for students the media's role in reproducing social inequalities by manufacturing consent for dominant ideologies such as sexism or racism. Further, these writers argued that once students recognized the injustices the media perpetrated, they would be better placed to transform and challenge it—so media education would contribute to promoting active, critical citizenship in young people. No wonder I had felt confident in my chosen vocation.

Classroom reality, however, proved disappointingly different. Students were bored by my choice of subject matter and approach—analyzing problematic race and gender representations, the news and other high status genres; exposing the concentration and conglomeration of media industries; exploring alternative and "positive images." Our relationship was often marked by sullen resentment on their part rather than the harmonious equality I had hoped for. Because I either neglected the popular media forms and genres they preferred or demanded that they "deconstruct" them, they read my teaching practices as censure of their pleasures. The low grades I gave them for their essays undermined their confidence and seemed to be a dogmatic dismissal of their perspectives. I was painfully aware that I came over as authoritarian and intolerant instead of as the "senior colleague" and "co-creator of knowledge" I had hoped to be. Yet I felt that I didn't have any alternative within the educational approaches available to me. Ideological analysis of topics such as the news was a moral duty if I were to equip students to participate as citizens in the world around them. My negative response to their work rested on a definition of what could count as evidence of understanding and learning. So, for instance, I felt obliged to mark down those students who argued that media portrayals of women simply "reflected" their innate differences from men, because they had failed to understand the constructed nature of representations.

I came to realize that other practitioners and critics shared my dilemmas and had challenged many of the assumptions on which I had based my teaching (see especially Buckingham, 1986, 1990; Buckingham, Grahame, & Sefton-Green, 1995; Buckingham & Sefton-Green, 1994; Ellsworth, 1994/1988; Richards, 1986, 1992; Turnbull, 1993; Williamson, 1981/ 1982). They argued that advocates of "critical" media education often held totalizing and conspiratorial views about how the media operate, seeing them as an "ideological apparatus"—a monolithic and coercive entity set on "legitimizing" conservative worldviews. They criticized them for assuming too readily that meanings are efficacious—that is, able to act on audiences—and for drawing large political conclusions from readings of single films or genres. They pointed out that holding the media to blame for social ills such as racism brought them uncomfortably close to conservative "effects" theorists who condemned the media for other reasons, such as for undermining traditional family structures. "Critical" media concepts, such as the notion that texts have "constitutive" power or that ideology works "behind our backs," often translated into an image of passive, gullible audiences unable to resist omnipotent media.

Critics of these approaches also wrote convincingly about the problems of teaching practice. The notion that "alternative" texts might broaden students' horizons often rested on traditional evaluative hierarchies of "culture" over commerce, the meaningful over the gratuitous, mind (thinking, reflecting) over body (the sensational). Students sometimes resented such oppositions for devaluing their tastes; just as often, they considered them irrelevant (a judgment with which some academics have concurred: see Collins, 1995; Frow, 1995). Concepts such as the "preferred reading" of a text (usually identified with the teacher's or critic's interpretation) led to "guess what's in the teacher's mind" classroom discussions (see especially Chapter Two of Buckingham, 1990). The narrative of enlightenment through media education was problematic in that it figured the teacher (and his/her "tools") as hero and made media education a negative enterprise focused on saving young people from themselves. It thereby held a "deficit model" of young people, implying firstly that they had little knowledge (either through naiveté or perhaps willful disavowal) of how the media operate and secondly, that they lacked the kind of critical discourse which was necessary if they were to "protect" themselves from media manipulation. Nor did critical pedagogues document in any detail what went on in classrooms and what students might have learned from their teaching. Some have questioned how far critical media education marks a significant departure from longstanding practices. Ian Hunter, warning against the "moral magnification" of debates about teaching strategies, suggests that critical pedagogy offers what the state has, historically, always required of mass education—the shaping and disciplining of populations in an environment of moral supervision. And as such, he notes, its practices are inevitably regulatory rather than liberatory (Hunter, 1988, 1994, 1996).

These critiques of critical media education, however, still tended to be written from the perspective of the teacher and to overlook what might be learned from students' "subjugated knowledges." My desire to learn from young people eventually led me to full-time doctoral research, based on classroom observations, interviews with students, and analysis of their written and practical work. I worked with a young white woman teacher

(Kate) whose political and ethical commitments were similar to mine. Kate had moved from a middle-class school that selected students according to ability to a post as Head of Department in a school with a poor academic reputation in a suburban working class area, where she hoped to "make more of a difference" to students to whom she was intensely loyal. Her teaching aimed to recognize and value their existing knowledge and interests by covering topics such as sport, soap opera, and pop music, as well as to promote newly politicized identities and understandings and to introduce less familiar ideas and experiences by studying documentary, feminist film, African cinema, and so on. I recognized aspects of my own past as a teacher in Kate; in analyzing her practice I could also explore dilemmas I myself had encountered. I also admired her "way of being" as a teacher, as she handled her multiple daily tasks—dealing with troubled parents, supporting students in need, managing unruly classes, and so on—with grace and skill. Yet, she also expressed anxieties about how well she understood the "theory" that both exam syllabi and "critical pedagogues" prescriptions required her to impart to students. Although her concerns were doubtless intensified by my presence as an academic researcher, they made me wonder whether radical educational practices overemphasize theory at the expense of valuing what else teachers offer their students, and how we might develop forms of analysis that would do justice to her work. Finally, Kate's teaching practice was more innovative than mine had been, in that the experience of practical media production was as important in her courses as textual analysis. I briefly return to the significance of this point in the conclusion to this chapter.

In the rest of this chapter, I want to consider an exchange between Kate and her mainly white, working class, sixteen-year-old British students in their first term and first year of postcompulsory education. In Britain, media is now recognized as a subject area within the National Curriculum, and is an accredited subject specialism at upper secondary, further, and tertiary education levels; the students here were following a two-year Advanced Level qualification in Media Studies. My research focused specifically on the teaching of horror films in schools, which I chose as a topic partly to engage with debates about "violent" media and their audiences (Bragg, 2000, 2001b). Cultural Studies critics often hold that horror films exemplify postmodern culture (e.g., Brophy, 1986; Pinedo, 1996), which led me to consider what a postmodern media education practice might be like.

Kate taught horror as part of a module on film genre. She began the course with textual analysis, and as Morgan (1996) found in his Canadian-based research, textual analysis continues to be the "reigning pedagogical genre" in secondary school media education. She screened extracts from films students would know (such as *Nightmare on Elm Street* [1984] and

Silence of the Lambs [1991]) and other "classics" they might not (*Frankenstein* [1931], *Night of the Living Dead* [1968]), raising questions about themes, characters, narrative structure, iconography, and point of view and positioning created by editing. Students went on to study the workings of the film industry, to research horror audiences, and to produce a short horror sequence on video. Such approaches are typical of much Media Studies pedagogy, and as mentioned above, Kate's choice of the horror genre was precisely because she was aware of the important role it played in students' lives outside school and wanted to value it. The extract below is taken from the first part of the course, in a lesson attended by four young women and ten young men. Kate is leading a classroom discussion of a scene from *Nightmare on Elm Street* (dir. Wes Craven, 1984) in which the "final girl" (Clover, 1992), Nancy, falls asleep in the bath and Freddy Krueger's knife-fingers emerge from the water:[2]

1   Teacher: The bath scene, then? Why do we have the scissors, the razor blades coming up between her legs?
2   Kevin: Cause it's dirty, cause Freddy's dirty
3   Teacher: **Freddy's** dirty -?
4   Kevin: Freddy's a dirty old man, yeah
5   Teacher: When she's sitting there in the bathtub, she's **filmed** in the bath with her legs open, anyway, / I don't know -
6   Kevin: Most probably, it's probably just like, it depends, what come up through the bath, miss, it's probably just like to spice it up a bit and make it ( )
7   Teacher: But you can't deny, it did look very phallic ( ). When I talk about phallic, when I say it looks a bit phallic, do you know what I mean? (*Silence*). If something's phallic, you might, it's, it's meant to, sort of symbolize the penis
8   Steve: Oh yeah, Miss Hobbs kept going on about that! (*others agree, laughing*)[3]
9   Kevin: Saucy!
10   Steve: She kept going on about it in Clint Eastwood's films
11   Teacher: // So a phallus is basically, it means penis, but, so, a phallic symbol is something that represents a penis ( ) - no, not genitals
12   ?: Oh right
13   Neil: Yeah I know but what's that got to do with that girl? She hasn't got a penis!
14   Teacher: She hasn't, no, **but**, /
15   Kevin: Is that like (? the dictionary meaning)?
16   Teacher: Yes. // So if something is phallic (*Writes on board—phallus— phallic*) people often say

17   that **guns** in cowboy films are kind of phallic symbols because they rep-
     resent umm / men's penises, cowboys' penises, so the bigger the gun, in
     theory ( )—and other people might say that camera lenses might be
     seen as a bit phallic. So something that is phallic represents or symbol-
     izes the penis. So can anyone think of any other examples? (*Boys laugh*)
18   David: Russell's head! // (*more laughter*) ( )
19   Teacher: Often phallic symbols are supposed to represent, not just male
     sexuality but male **power** as well, umm, the bigger the camera lens, the
     bigger the gun, the more **power** you have (. . .)
20   Kevin: Is that like medallions?
21   Teacher: In some ways, I mean, yeah it can be extended to thinking
     about macho symbols, // umm, // masculinity, yeah
22   Neil: My pen! (*holding it up*)
23   Teacher: // Yeah, so when you said it looked a bit rude, you were kind
     of suggesting something like all those razor blades might hurt, so these,
     Kevin, I mean, you were almost making the assumption there, that they
     were kind of **phallic**, / weren't you?
24   Kevin (*in a mock-meek tone*): Yes, / I was miss
25   ?: I don't agree with this
26   Teacher: I don't know, maybe I'm not, maybe it's just **me**, just, reading
     things into it, but when you
27   look at the actual **frame**, you had the girl with her legs open—sshh—//
     the girl with her legs open and this kind of hand in between, // ( ) it's
     almost as if she's almost going to be raped by him, by Freddy's hand, is
     Freddy going to ( ), you don't know. // Umm. // So that's, that's a new
     word
28   Kevin: I'd just like to say -
29   Neil: ( ) and then when she, he just sort of pulled her under, sort of
     thing, he doesn't rape her or /, but they wouldn't, like, show something
     like that, I think they probably put that in just for a bit of fun
30   Teacher: A bit of fun?
31   Neil: I bet this bloke, the director just said, oh we'll do that, it'll make
     people laugh
32   Teacher: Did it make you **laugh**, that bit?
33   Kevin: That's what I said miss, I said, they wouldn't have ( ) on the bath,
     they thought, oh, just to make it a bit more / funny, it's quite funny,
34   ?: Yeah, more like *Jaws*—
35   Kevin: - put it up between her legs, just to make it a bit more outrageous
36   Teacher: So it's just about outrage? ( )
37   David: Cause if they'd had the camera on her shoulder, you wouldn't
     have been able to see ( )
38   Teacher: It wouldn't have been as exciting—or / titillating, titillating in
     the sense that—
39   David: You wanted to see it, like see him, to see that he was there, but ( )

40   Kevin: Exactly (*several voices talking at once*)
41   Teacher: Would you have wanted to see him do something, kind of sexu-
      ally violent towards her? ( )
42   Kevin: It's too -
43   David: - rude (*laughter*)
44   Teacher: But did you like, you kind of liked, you almost liked the antic- ,
      the pleasure in it, the possibility that maybe he's going to—( ) (*boys
      laugh awkwardly*). Am I being—Is that true or not?
45   Kevin: Yeah—Steve thought so (*pats his back*)
46   Teacher: You thought they put it in for fun // (*boys laughing*). Louisa what
      did you make of that / that bit, with the razor blades coming out of the
      bath?
47   Louisa: It was horrible (laughs) //
48   Teacher: Did you think it was, did you kind of, fear, feel frightened at that
      stage or not?
49   Louisa: // It was just //
50   Kelly: Sick
51   Louisa: Sick, (*laughs*) yeah //
52   Teacher: Do those sort of scenes make you feel angry? // (*Kelly laughs*)
53   Louisa: No
54   Teacher: Not really // ( ) Sorry? ( ) You said it was a bit disgusting
55   Steve: It was the same in, er, Dracula, the last one, / did you watch the
      same bit as us? Yeah, did you see that bit where, with the women in the
      bed?
56   Teacher: No, we didn't watch that bit (*boys chorus together 'oh!' gearing
      up to describe it, teacher hushes them*)
57   Steve: one of the women vampires like goes towards his /
58   Kevin: Miss why didn't we watch that bit miss?
59   Steve: and she goes to bite his—/ goes to bite his—/
60   ? (male): not his neck! (*laughter*)
61   Neil: What film?
62   ? (male): *Bram Stoker's Dracula*
63   Teacher: So one of the vampires goes towards his—// phallus
64   ? (male): ( ) Sharp teeth
65   Teacher: So what you'd imagine then is something quite painful
66   Russell: And then it changes to pleasure
67   Teacher: So do you see his face?
68   ? (male): Well you see her go towards him but—
69   ? (male): and then it changes like, he's enjoying it and then -
70   Steve: And then you see Count Dracula come in and tell them to stop
71   Teacher: So do you think that in a lot of horror films, sex is // implicated,
      a lot of them, perhaps the monsters are perhaps umm sexually motivat-
      ed or frustrated even
72   Neil: They're all 18 aren't they, so ( )?

73   Teacher: // Would you enjoy it if they didn't—I mean, / Russell, you said
      that if the hand blades were on her shoulder, or David you said it, if it
      was on her shoulder, you wouldn't get quite as scared
74   ?: No but that makes it better
75   Kevin: It just makes it more interesting /
76   Kelly?: it gets you more (?worried)
77   Kevin: ( ) nice and gradual
78   Teacher: So you can fantasize (*slightly scandalized laughter*)
79   Kevin: Well no ( ) (*more laughter*)
80   Teacher: Let's move on then
81   Kevin: Let's do that miss

Kate's opening move is to ask why the image is constructed in a certain
way—"The bath scene then? Why do we have the scissors, the razor blades,
coming up between her legs?" (1). The question "why" is perhaps the question *par excellence* of the modernist institution of education, looking
towards a space of abstracted rationalistic explanation. In critical media
analysis, it suggests both a determining intention on the part of media producers—that is, a theory of power as a property securely possessed by the
media—and that there are meanings already in the text. Nothing is innocent, especially Freddy's knife-blade hands: but these meanings operate
deceptively, behind the backs of audiences. Hence they must be unmasked
by being translated into other terms supplied by the teacher or critic. Kate's
"translations" of meaning here are informed by feminist and psychoanalyt-
ic film theory. At points she expands the meaning of the image—the knife-
fingers, like guns, stand in for a whole system of patriarchal oppression of
women (19). Elsewhere she contracts it, rendering the metaphorical liter-
al: it may look like scissors, but actually, it's a penis (7); you may think it's
a laugh, but in fact, it's a rape (27). Either version, however, valorizes
expert or specialized knowledge over the everyday knowledges of students.
    The analytic perspectives Kate draws on do allow for multiple read-
ings, but only in reaction to what is already there. Thus, while Kate does
not raise the issue of gender difference directly, it is carried in the phrasing
(and relative number) of questions to male and female students. Many
analyses position men as the more interested and thus more interesting
viewers of horror, which may help explain why she poses more questions
to the male students. She asks whether they find the scene "titillating" (38),
whether they want to see Freddy "do something kind of sexually violent"
towards Nancy (41), to "fantasize" (78), or are seeking an outlet for their
frustration (71). These questions construct male viewers as misogynist
voyeurs taking vicarious pleasure in women's suffering through identification with a killer. Women audiences, by contrast, are considered capable of

taking one or both of two positions. They are thus asked whether they identify with Nancy and "feel frightened" (48), or if they reject the values of the film, read it "oppositionally" and get "angry" as feminists do (52).

Kate's questions position her as a persuader and command assent. She comments on what students say as if to reveal what lies just beyond their comprehension or to incite confession of what they are unwilling to admit: "you can't deny" (7), "you were making the assumption . . . weren't you?" (23), "you almost liked" (44), "is that true, or not?" (44). To be a "good student" in these exchanges involves taking on the teacher's terms, reflecting them back to demonstrate that students too have achieved self-knowledge and reached the same destination (as Kevin does: "yes / I was miss," 24). There is little room for genuine dialogue or reciprocity in this approach: it *knows already who students are* and has mapped out in advance the positions they can take up, the responses they can give. Despite critical media education's declared aims of connecting with students' knowledge and competences, it cannot be truly interested in what students may have to say, because meaning has already been decided elsewhere, by experts or by the teacher.

Such an approach also sees audiences as innocent victims or dupes, whose pleasures and reactions have been produced "for" them by the powerful media. It is interesting, then, that in this class no one takes responsibility for the desires held to circulate within the text. Kevin accepts that the image is sexual, but the motivation is Freddy's—he is "dirty" (2, 4). Others attribute it to the director or a behind-scenes "they" (31, 33, 37), although they simultaneously exculpate them from devious motives; it is "just for a bit of fun" (29), to "spice it up" (8), "make people laugh" (31), "make it more outrageous" (35), or create suspense (35-37). They adopt the role (the "missionary position," as McWilliam [1997] terms it) of passive spectator, being outraged, made to laugh or worry, rather than actively participating in making meaning. When Kate asks them directly about their pleasures, Kevin displaces them on to others ("Steve thought so," 45). For her part, Kate refers to the anonymous structures of the text—how the scene is filmed (5) "the actual frame" (27)—and eventually takes refuge in a teacherly identity, in which she offers novel information ("that's a new word," 27), disavowing any personally invested interpretation or flirtatious intent.

But students also tell a different story about themselves as audiences, about their emotional investments in popular culture and how they manage their media environment. They do not "answer from the place to which they are called" by this practice and thus assert discontinuity (Ellsworth, 1997, p. 109). Louisa may initially give a gender-appropriate response to the question of how she felt, by saying it was "horrible" (47). Yet she refuses the "angry feminist" position; calling it "sick" may not be gender-specific and indeed may be a term of approval. As for Kate's male students, if they are the sadistic subjects the theory tells us, they are not letting on. Most obviously, what they thrill to is not the prospect of rape, but the collective memory of a deliciously endangering fellatio (55-70). Steve's comparison of Nancy and *Dracula*'s Jonathan Harker ("it was the same . . . ," 55) suggests that what they share is not gender, but a situation—of nakedness, vulnerability, exposure, and explicit genital threat. Both are available to viewers for a fantasy that is all the more enticing because it is unfinished and unsatisfying (Nancy is only "pulled under," 29, and Dracula cuts short Harker's pleasuring, 70). Neil, in holding up his pen (22), is self-mocking rather than aggrandizing (if what is bigger signifies more power, as Kate has just said, then his potency is rather limited; and it may be relevant that he is dyslexic).

Certainly, despite over eighty years of psychological effects research that attempts to prove otherwise, it seems that in the encounter with so-called "violent" texts, these young people at least care more about *being done to*—sucked off and sickened—than *doing to* others. Further, telling Kate what something "means" by telling her what it is "like" points to a valuable learning strategy. Students draw on texts they already know—*Jaws* (34) or *Bram Stoker's Dracula* for example—in order to try to "place" the meaning of the one they are now exploring. Their comparisons between *Nightmare on Elm Street* and these films shift what each might signify. They indicate that meaning can never be definitively pinned down, for it depends on its position in relation to something else, and different frames of reference change both texts and reading subjects (cf. Bennett, 1983).

Thus, although there are socially assigned meanings to which we can point (guns and cameras for male power), there are others that we cannot know in advance. When David offers "Russell's head" as one example of a phallic symbol (18), he refers to what is evident, in front of him, and in the public domain, not to what is hidden and needs to be exposed. He does not report on a meaning already existing out there in the world, but brings new ones into being by an "inappropriate" pun. His strategy is more ludic than serious, embodied and personal rather than abstract, because such associations are by their very nature motivated by individual desires, needs, partialities, and feelings. It thus permits the humor that makes the classroom a seductive space to be, but it exceeds rationalization and is necessarily unpredictable. It works to the extent that it identifies relevant attributes that enable comparison and make us look at both Russell's head and phallic symbols in a different light—but you have to *be there* to know what these might be. Hence to you as readers it may be largely incomprehensible, although perhaps evocative, and even to me as observer it was ambiguous. It may be verbal (Russell is a dickhead?), but perhaps—if we are indeed dealing with a generation "more attuned to spectacle than narrative"

(Sconce, 1993, p. 112)—it is aesthetic and visual (a comment on the fact that Russell is red-haired, that his head is close-cropped, disproportionately small . . . ?).

To develop "postmodern pedagogies" that respect the specificity and context-dependence of meaning, perhaps we should begin to consider how we could work with these students' everyday poetics of association, relation, comparison, and substitution, rather than through critical pedagogy's abstract logic, revelation, rules, and application of a language the teacher supplies. There is an issue of social justice here. A demand to know what a text means and why may exclude those who feel less comfortable with abstract, academic discourses. Asking instead of any text, "what is this like? what does it remind you of?," inviting students to tell us about the relational frames of reference through which they place and make sense of texts might produce insights for both them and their teachers into the resources they already possess. In turn, this might suggest that media audiences are not crippled by their lack of an overall interpretive framework as critical pedagogy implies; when audiences need *something to think with*, what they have already to hand (or sitting next to them) serves them well enough.

Moreover, power here is equivocal, never firmly possessed (still less abandoned) by teacher or students, media texts or audiences. The students resist Kate's assumption of the phallic position of the one who knows, at points overtly, at others more subtly. In his words ("Yes, / I was miss," 24), Kevin appears submissively to accept her argument. But through his tone, the timing of his pause, and his (habitual) tag "miss," underscoring the hierarchy between them, he manages to extract a self-accusing confession from her in her turn ("maybe it's just me," 26). David, too, apparently responds obligingly to her request for contributions. Yet for Kate to call the phallus a penis is not neutral. It can act as a cruel unveiling, because as Dyer states, "the penis can never live up to the mystique implied by the phallus" (1992, p. 274). But offering "Russell's head" allows David to claim power for himself, to reassert his "hardness," challenging her authority to talk about (his) privates in public.

This is not therefore the utopian, harmonious learning community of shared values about which many critical pedagogues write so romantically, and which indeed I hoped to find in the classrooms where I taught. But learning can and does go on, in a form that is collaborative, two sided, and accountable to others (cf. Billig, 1987; Shotter, 1993). A response like "Russell's head" partly menaces Kate's authority, but it resists her from within, by taking up her terms, and it simultaneously sustains classroom interaction. Further, David can only gauge the success of his joke from the reaction of his classmates. Their laughter provides a warrant for the comparison, but by showing they "get" it in this way, they reveal their own implication and intimate knowledge of the situation. Here lie the seeds of an *ethical* educational practice, focused on what becomes possible within the collective space of the classroom. Instead of dreaming of "critical autonomy," media teaching would do better to acknowledge that learning and change always require others—whether the textual others we draw on as tools to think with, the other people around us whose attention tells us what we know, or the "other" within us, the unconscious, that connects our thoughts in surprising, unintended ways. Such a view of learning allows something more into the classroom, or, more accurately, allows us to acknowledge the something more that is already there: human kinship and social relationships. If we focus only on the theory that teachers offer students, we lose what was most obvious to me: that the teaching here worked primarily because Kate and her students cared, quite a lot, about each other.

Finally, I want to argue that this exchange conveys something of what I (and some of Kate's students) experienced as her seductive power as a teacher, and that Kate uses it as a strategy for her own survival and sustenance in the classroom. McWilliam cites a definition of seductive power as "the power to achieve authority and to produce involvement" (McWilliam, 1997, p. 227). It is, however, underanalyzed and too little discussed, because as she comments, many official discourses about teaching, including anti-abuse lobbying, deny teachers "the possibility of any claim to seductive power or their own embodied pleasure in the pedagogical act" (p. 227).

Although Kate was extremely committed to her students, she inevitably also frequently felt drained and exhausted by the demands of her work, and no doubt wished to be loved by her students as a reward for the love she showed them. Although I think that this "dream of love" is structured into the pedagogic relation, it may provoke particular dilemmas for the feminist woman teacher, who balances a desire to give against a reluctance to fall into an asexual and nurturing role. Perhaps Kate finds a solution to this problem in her use of ideological critique. Whatever the theoretical inadequacies of a conventional feminist analysis of horror, "doing" feminism here enables Kate to position herself as sexually knowing, powerful, and agentic (a woman who talks about penises and male fantasies) rather than maternal and benign. Through her provocative "difference" from her students she achieves authority and arouses their interest and desire to learn and participate, while caring for herself enough to wrest the pleasures of the erotic from her daily teaching grind.

This is not to suggest that the teaching here is beyond reproach. Women students were largely silent, and not just because they were outnumbered. However, it does bear out the importance of attending to pedagogy's own mode of address—who it thinks students are and who it wants them to be (Ellsworth, 1997). Unlike many critical pedagogy strategies,

Kate does not demand that her students speak only in a serious voice, as concerned and rational citizens; and it is this flexibility that makes her male students, at least, keen to join in. In the process they articulate their perhaps more scandalous investments in the pleasures of passivity and surrender—but equally importantly, they have some fun.

CONCLUSION

This chapter has argued not only that we should take seriously the pleasures and the learning that the mainstream media offer, but also that by listening to young people and recognizing what they already know, we might understand how to work with rather than against them in our teaching. My analysis has attempted to show how everyday life can be a realm from which knowledge emerges, rather than one which should only be the object of critique. Similarly, rather than see the media as sources of ideological domination, we should see them as *resources*—"contributors to our variable capacity to make sense of the world" (Silverstone, 1999, p. 2). Although the media are undoubtedly pedagogical, in that they offer ways of reading the world and positions in relation to knowledge and power, we should not assume we can know in advance how audiences take up and play with those terms. In turn, we should attend to the social relations and identities the teacher's address to students cultivates and brings into being. We should develop forms of pedagogical analysis that are sensitive to its psychic complexities, which can articulate the role of care, interestedness, and even love—but not selflessness—in the classroom (Gore, 1993).

If media education often underestimates what audiences can already do, it needs also to be more modest in its claims about what teaching might achieve. Not least, it might be more reflexive about the mediating effects of pedagogic "games" that constitute texts as objects of study (Morgan, 1996). The teaching discussed here did not import a meaning from elsewhere that it then held up for scrutiny; instead it was a performance that itself constructed meaning, momentarily and provisionally and in relation to the specific power struggles and investments of its location. We might therefore rethink how we approach textual analysis, particularly our demand to know what a text "means." I have argued that Kate's students negotiate their way around their media environment by rearranging what they already know to make it mean differently or to understand what is new. If teaching aimed to help make this process more visible, rather than to oblige students to concur with a predetermined interpretation, it might enhance young people's critical thinking skills by enabling them to make more of their existing understandings and insights.

However, we should also consider less teacher-centered pedagogic strategies. Kate's students spent more time making their own horror videos than analyzing professional texts, and I would point briefly to the potential of practical media production as a means of learning. It broadens the range of identities available to students, from those of dutiful pupil or earnest citizen to more powerful and pleasurable identities of producer, director, and creator. Asking students to construct representations within genres with which they are already familiar values and mobilizes the implicit, unofficial knowledge they have acquired from growing up in a media-rich world instead of prioritizing explicit and consciously articulated critique. The results, as many teachers have found, belie claims that young people are unable to negotiate media meanings without educational input (e.g., Bragg, 2001b; Buckingham, Grahame, & Sefton-Green, 1995; Grace & Tobin, 1998; Grahame, 1995). The learning process does not cease when the product is complete, however. Reflection on the finished text, using analytical approaches derived from Cultural Studies, can lead to nuanced and thoughtful responses (Buckingham, 1986; Buckingham & Sefton-Green, 1994). The teachers' role at this stage might be to construct contexts for "thinking and being together" (cf. Readings, 1996), in which this work is made available for joint reflection on its sources and its significance both for its producer and for other audiences (Bragg, 2002). Finally, it is worth noting that here, the students' horror video work was the first of three practical productions, which together would constitute one third of their final grade. This pragmatic concern with access to educational qualifications attempts to redefine "cultural capital" or literacy away from traditional print forms, which might favor already privileged students, and thus to offer a small adjustment in the power relations of education (Buckingham, Grahame, & Sefton-Green, 1995). Such small-scale, limited reforms of curricula are worthy of far more extended discussion than they are given in debates about media education.

Taken together, these suggestions do not lead to recipes for guaranteed success in the classroom. They aim to progress a debate about "everyday life pedagogies," which I would define as those that enable critical agency—speaking back, thinking or acting otherwise—within the terms available to students, rather than supplanting them with knowledge delivered from above.

NOTES

1. This article draws on material previously published as "Perverse and Improper Pedagogies: The Case of Freddy's Fingers and Russell's Head"(2001a).

2. The following conventions are used in this transcript:

( )	Undecipherable words or phrases
(?)	Approximate transcription
e.g.: *(laughs)*	Contextual or non-verbal information
/	Pause of less than two seconds
//	Pause of more than two seconds

Conventional punctuation marks are used to indicate ends of utterances or sentences, usually indicated by slight pauses on the audiotape.

Bold	Indicate stressed words
–	Indicates interrupted utterances

3. Steve and some of the other students were taught separately by Miss Hobbs two out of four lessons a week.

REFERENCES

Bennett, T. (1983). Texts, readers, reading formations. *Bulletin of the Midwest Modern Language Association, 16*(1), 3–17.

Billig, M. (1987). *Arguing and thinking: A rhetorical approach to social psychology.* Cambridge: Cambridge University Press.

Bourdieu, P., & Passeron, J.-C. (1977). *Reproduction in education, society and culture* (R. Nice, Trans.). London: Sage.

Bowker, J. (Ed). (1991). *Secondary media education: A curriculum statement.* London: British Film Institute.

Bragg, S. (2000). *Media violence and education: A study of youth audiences and the horror genre.* Doctoral dissertation, Institute of Education, University of London, London.

Bragg, S. (2001a). Perverse and improper pedagogies: The case of Freddy's fingers and Russell's head. *The Velvet Light Trap, 48,* 68–80.

Bragg, S. (2001b). Just what the doctors ordered?—Media regulation, education and the "problem" of media violence. In M. Barker & J. Petley (Eds.), *Ill effects: The media/violence debate* (pp. 87–110). London and New York: Routledge.

Bragg, S. (2002). Wrestling in woolly gloves: Not just being "critically" media literate. *Journal of Popular Film and Television, 30*(1), 42–52.

Brophy, P. (1986, Jan.-Feb.). Horrality—the textuality of contemporary horror films. *Screen, 27*(1), 2–13.

Buckingham, D. (1986). Against demystification. *Screen, 27*(5), 80–95.

Buckingham, D. (1990). *Watching media learning: Making sense of media education.* Basingstoke and Bristol, PA: Falmer Press.

Buckingham, D., Grahame, J., & Sefton-Green, J. (1995). *Making media: Practical production in media education.* London: English and Media Centre.

Buckingham, D., & Sefton-Green, J. (1994). *Cultural studies goes to school.* London and Bristol, PA: Taylor and Francis.

Clover, C. (1992). *Men, women and chainsaws: Gender in the modern horror film.* London: British Film Institute.

Collins, J. (1995). *Architectures of excess: Cultural life in the information age*. London: Routledge.

Davies, B. (1993). *Shards of glass: Children reading and writing beyond gendered identities*. NSW, Australia: Allen and Unwin.

Dyer, R. (1992). Don't look now: The male pin-up. In M. Merck (Ed.), *The sexual subject: A screen reader in sexuality* (pp. 265–276). London and New York: Routledge.

Ellsworth, E. (1994/1988)). Why doesn't this feel empowering: Working through the repressive myths of critical pedagogy. In L. Stone (Ed.), *The education feminism reader* (pp. 300–327). New York and London: Routledge.

Ellsworth, E. (1997). *Teaching positions: Difference, pedagogy and the power of address*. New York: Teachers College Press.

Frow, J. (1995). *Cultural studies and cultural value*. Oxford and New York: Oxford University Press.

Giroux, H. A. (1992). *Border crossings: Cultural workers and the politics of education*. New York: Routledge.

Giroux, H. A. (1994a). *Disturbing pleasures: Learning popular culture*. New York: Routledge.

Giroux, H. A. (1994b). Doing cultural studies: Youth and the challenge of pedagogy. *Harvard Educational Review*, 64(3), 278–308.

Giroux, H. A., & McLaren, P. (Eds). (1994). *Between borders: Pedagogy and the politics of cultural studies*. New York, London: Routledge.

Gore, J. (1993). *The struggle for pedagogies: Critical and feminist discourses as regimes of truth*. London and New York: Routledge.

Grace, D. J., & Tobin, J. (1998). Butt jokes and mean-teacher parodies: Video production in the elementary classroom. In D. Buckingham (Ed.), *Teaching popular culture: Beyond radical pedagogy*. London and Bristol, PA: UCL Press.

Grahame, J. (1995). Original copy: Re-selling sounds. In D. Buckingham, J. Grahame, & J. Sefton-Green (Eds.), *Making media: Practical production in media education*. London: English and Media Centre.

Hunter, I. (1988). *Culture and government*. Basingstoke and London: Macmillan.

Hunter, I. (1994). *Rethinking the school: Subjectivity, bureaucracy, criticism*. St Leonard's, NSW: Allen and Unwin.

Hunter, I. (1996). Four anxieties about English. *Southern Review*, 29(1), 4–18.

Masterman, L. (1980). *Teaching about television*. Basingstoke and London: Macmillan.

Masterman, L. (1985). *Teaching the media*. London: Comedia.

McWilliam, E. (1997). Beyond the missionary position: Teacher desire and radical pedagogy. In S. Todd (Ed.), *Learning desire: Perspectives on pedagogy, culture and the unsaid*. London and New York: Routledge.

Morgan, R. (1996). Pan textualism, everyday life, and media education. *Continuum* 9(2),14–34.

Pinedo, I. (1996). Recreational terror: Postmodern elements of the contemporary horror film. *Journal of Film and Video* 48(1-2), 17–31.

Readings, B. (1996.) *The university in ruins*. Cambridge, MA, and London: Harvard University Press.

Richards, C. (1986). Anti-racist initiatives. *Screen*, 27(5), 67–79.

Richards, C. (1992). Teaching popular culture. In K. Jones (Ed.), *English and the national curriculum: Cox's revolution?* London: Kogan Page.

Sconce, J. (1993). Spectacles of death: Identification, reflexivity, and contemporary horror. In J. Collins, H. Radner, & A. P. Collins (Eds.), *Film theory goes to the movies*. New York and London: Routledge.

Shotter, J. (1993). *Cultural politics of everyday life*. Buckingham: Open University Press.

Silverstone, R. (1999). *Why study the media?* London, Thousand Oaks, New Delhi: Sage.

Turnbull, S. (1993). The media: Moral lessons and moral careers. *Australian Journal of Education, 37*(2),153–168.

Williamson, J. (1981/1982, Autumn-Winter). How does girl number 20 understand ideology? *Screen Education*.

5

CRUELTY, COMPASSION, COMMONSENSE AND CRITICAL MEDIA LITERACY

Bill Yousman

I like to think music can shape people's minds and feelings about their own humanity.

Bruce Springsteen, 1988

You see a shot waist up and waist down but you don't know that you're looking for jeans, you could be thinking that it's a commercial to sell capitalism or something . . .

"Lindsey"—18 year-old college student, 2000[1]

INTRODUCTION TO THE PROJECT

From a Gramscian (Gramsci, 1971; Williams, 1977) perspective on hegemony as a continually contested and evolving process, the products of the popular culture industries are best understood as sites of ideological warfare, where domination is both naturalized and challenged in a struggle over what will be enshrined into a nation's "commonsense." In this study, audience responses to popular texts are analyzed in regard to issues of resistance to, and acceptance of, "commonsense" notions about class mobility, poverty, and the American "underclass." The texts utilized in this study are: (a) a commercial for Levi's that depicts a young woman stating that not everyone is deserving of equality, that those who work hard are entitled to "extras," and that she does not expect any handouts because she works for what she wants, and (b) a video for the hit song, *"What It's Like,"* by the rap artist Everlast. Contrary to the Levi's advertisement, the lyrics and images of the song suggest that we should have compassion for those who are in desperate economic and social circumstances. Moreover, they implicitly challenge notions that the poor can best be helped by the withdrawal of social support, an idea that has been naturalized as "commonsense" in the last thirty years (Reed, 1999). This chapter contends that in addition to the overt functions of advertising and entertainment that such texts fulfill, they can simultaneously be regarded as moments of cultural pedagogy, in that they offer claims that inform current debates about public policy and the problems of poverty and the underclass.

A critical media literacy perspective thus must address a number of questions. To begin, if television functions as a powerful form of cultural pedagogy, to what extent can media education counter its efficacy as the primary storyteller in the society (Gerbner, 1999)? The question here is whether or not having access to the alternative discourses that critical media literacy provides would give audiences the necessary tools to read media messages with greater critical distance, as advocates of media literacy education often presume.[2] Specifically, this project explores the following questions: Do those who have been exposed to a critical media literacy curriculum interrogate the implications of media texts differently than audience members who do not have this critical discourse to draw upon? Do these audiences then transfer their knowledge about the way the media system works into a perspective that allows them to challenge the overall notions of commonsense that television naturalizes?

THEORETICAL CONTEXT

This study begins with the premises of the encoding/decoding model of television production and reception (see Hall, 1980; Katz & Liebes, 1985; Morley, 1980, among others). This model suggests that a given text has certain preferred meanings encoded within it during the process of production and that these preferred meanings are powerful but not guaranteed determinants of how an audience member will interpret the meaning of the text; viewers still manifest the ability to read the text in a number of variant ways: accepting the preferred meaning, negotiating with that meaning, or opposing that meaning entirely.

Although subsequent research and critique of this model (Hall et al., 1994; Lewis, 1983; Morley, 1992) have pointed out some of the pitfalls and problems associated with the original conceptualization, the encoding/decoding model still provides a useful theoretical framework to guide inquiry into audience interpretations of texts such as the advertisement and video under consideration here. Nonetheless, while the polysemic nature of media texts is thus acknowledged, this study also draws insights from Condit (1989), who emphasizes the limitations on polysemic readings imposed both by the codes invoked in the texts and by the potentially limited range of alternative discourses that audience members may draw from. As suggested above, one of the central questions of this study is how audiences decode ideologically loaded music videos and advertisements and to what degree the positions on class that are implicit in such texts are accepted or rejected. As such, attention is focused on whether the alternative discourses provided by a critical media literacy education empower certain members of the television audience to challenge the flood of hegemonic words and images they encounter everyday, and to recognize, embrace, and take pleasure in the counterhegemonic moments that occasionally flicker briefly before them.

Furthermore, as Jhally and Lewis argue in their discussion of media literacy, "To appreciate the significance of contemporary media, we need to know why [messages] are produced, under what constraints and conditions, and by whom" (1998, p. 111). This study is therefore also concerned with whether this insight into the media also promotes an insight into the ideological myths of contemporary society. Are students who learn to be critical readers of the media also able to question and resist the commonsense notions that inform and shape our perspectives on issues of race, class, gender, sexuality, aging, power, allocation of resources, democracy, equality, freedom, and so on?

ADVERTISING AND MUSIC VIDEOS

When we turn to the specific texts utilized in this research study, the role of advertising and music video in contemporary American society must first be discussed briefly. Certainly the primary function of advertising is to try and manipulate viewers and readers to buy certain products, or simply just to buy, buy, buy. Music videos are themselves advertisements for the recordings and artists that they promote. As Gow (1998) points out, the primary function of any music video is to sell the performer and the song. However, it is misleading to suggest that simply because the overt function of a media text is to promote a commodity, this means that other specific messages are not also simultaneously being communicated. Yes, the advertisement and the video being considered here are sales pitches, but what they are selling goes far beyond jeans and compact discs.

For example, as McChesney (1999) points out in his analysis of this Levi's commercial, advertising is the messenger of the rich and powerful, delivering to the masses the words handed down from the corporate mountain top: "Behind all the hoopla is the cold fist of class power, of corporate power. Ultimately the message you're getting is always about class domination and corporate rule." In this particular case the message is unusually undisguised—we owe the poor nothing, they are merely obstacles on the sidewalk. Don't look down and don't let them distract you from your ascendancy up the financial ladder. Although McChesney is correct when he points out that the bitterness and arrogance of this advertisement is particularly intense, the argument can be made that these messages of individualism, consumerism, and greed are consistent with the metanarratives of advertising specifically, and the vast majority of television programming in general. Several scholars, for example, have documented how U.S. television tends either to ignore or ridicule the poor and the working class while representing upper-middle-class lifestyles as "normal" and admirable (Butsch, 1992, 2003; Cantor, 1990, 1991; Ehrenreich, 1995; Jhally & Lewis, 1992; Mantsios, 2001; Moore, 1992; Parenti, 1992, 1993; Scharrer, 2001).

Furthermore, the visual imagery of the advertisement—a young girl dressed in funky clothes with lots of bracelets, shuffling and stammering just a bit as she hangs out in a dimly lit alleyway—is a prototypical example of advertising's use of "hip" or "cool" imagery (see Frank, 1997). In this manner, signifiers that appear to stand for rebellion or dissent can be put to work in the service of messages of conformity and confederation with the powers-that-be.

Turning our attention to the music video for "*What It's Like*," textual analysis of both the lyrics of the song and the visual images utilized in the video suggests that, beyond its primary function as an advertisement for Everlast's compact disc, this video is in many ways a counterargument to the messages of the Levi's commercial. Instead of individualism, consumerism, and greed, "*What It's Like*" presents messages of compassion, empathy, and social obligation to those whom television more often ignores completely or demonizes as members of the "underclass"—the homeless and unemployed, unwed mothers, drug addicts, and dealers. Thus, this video can be read as a counterhegemonic argument against the prevailing "commonsense" notions that the poor are responsible for their own misery and we have no obligation to provide them with economic or social support. The song and video also present a subtle indictment of class barriers in lines such as: "You know where it ends, yo, it usually depends on where you start," and the powerful closing images of a white, upper-class family in a store window, dining and laughing, oblivious to the pained expressions on the faces of the multicultural crowd of homeless people and workers gazing at them from the other side of the glass.

THE INTERVIEWS

In order to investigate the research questions noted above, six focus group interviews were conducted during the early part of 2000. Eighteen women and eight men, ages eighteen to twenty-six were interviewed. Interviews took place in two New England towns, one a mid-sized urban center, the other a small college town. Both areas include a mix of working-class and middle-class residents and tend to be relatively liberal, Democratic strongholds. Individuals who participated in this study reflected the general economic mix typical of the two geographical areas.

Three of the groups, designated the "media literacy" groups for the purposes of this study, consisted of students from a large New England state university who have taken a series of courses grounded in a critical media literacy approach. These courses included material on the history, structure, and political economy of the broadcast industries, the powerful influence of advertising and public relations in U.S. society, the social impact of media on audiences, the ideological tendencies in popular culture, and the like. In general, the courses these students were exposed to embodied the sort of contextual media literacy approach advocated by Jhally and Lewis and alluded to above:

> Media literacy, in short is about more than the analysis of messages, it is about an awareness of why those messages are there. It is not enough to know that they are produced, or even how, in a technical sense, they are produced. To appreciate the significance of contemporary media, we need to know why they are produced, under what constraints and conditions, and by whom. (Jhally and Lewis, 1998, p. 111)

The other three groups, perhaps misleadingly labeled "non-media literacy" for identification purposes only, were made up of individuals of roughly similar ages who had not been exposed to any sort of codified media literacy education at all. All respondents were shown both texts and then asked a series of questions intended to spark a group discussion.

Although a great deal of differentiation in interpretations of the Levi's advertisement and the Everlast video was apparent among respondents in this study, there was not a clear and rigid distinction between those respondents who had been exposed to a critical media literacy curriculum and those who had not. Members of both subgroups came up with what could loosely be described as preferred, negotiated, and oppositional readings of the conflicting messages about class, poverty, and the poor invoked by these texts. In fact, the most critical response to the Levi's commercial was articulated by a young woman who has not had a formal education in media literacy. Here, Amelia hones in on the messages of individualism encoded in the Levi's commercial and rejects them with vigor and passion: Group Two (Non-Media Literacy)

> Amelia: When I saw the commercial . . . I was like oh, oh . . . it was just kind of like fuck you . . . no . . . that just seems very selfish, you're not on this earth, you didn't make it as far as you did all on your own, sorry! Like, no matter what you think . . . you had people helping you every day and every way . . . people helped you, people paved the roads, you know? I mean like other people make the Levi's for you, you just don't like make them for yourself and feel proud about it . . . grow the cotton and dye it and all that shit. So you know, I didn't like the commercial at all.

On the other hand, the most oppositional reading of the Everlast video came from a young man in one of the media literacy groups. Victor both acknowledged that there was a political message encoded in the closing images of the video, and simultaneously struggled to resist the implications of this message:

Group Five (Media Literacy)

> Victor: It was just a lame attempt to shock you at the end . . . it showed like that white family having fun and ignoring . . . it's basically like they were in their own world, ignoring the outside world. Like with everybody on the outside looking in. . . . I don't know it had a good message I guess but it just didn't float my boat (laughs).
>
> Interviewer: What about the ending scene didn't you like?
>
> Victor: I don't know. I couldn't take the song seriously and that kind of tried to make the video seem real serious. . . . I just thought the song

.... I have a hard time with that . . . like I just think it's a bad song and incredible how you can make money off of it. Two chords . . . I don't know it just doesn't appeal to me. . . .

At this point in the interview, Victor is avoiding the political implications of the video and expressing his resistance by saying that he couldn't take the video seriously and it was a bad song, and so forth. Later in the interview, however, his resistance becomes clearer:

> Victor: They made that family appear evil . . . like why can't a family be like that? Like there might be problems but . . . I couldn't think of a better word than evil, but it shouldn't be wrong, you know? Like maybe some people probably know a lot of families like that . . . that shouldn't be wrong . . . like a wife . . . they weren't divorced, they had two kids, they were happy, that shouldn't be looked down upon.

Still later, Victor expressed his resentment of homeless people who ask him for money and quietly acknowledged that he identified more with the messages in the advertisement than those in the video.

A simplistic hypothesis that the respondents who were introduced to a critical media literacy education during their college careers would be highly resistant to media texts, while the non-media literacy respondents would passively absorb whatever messages they were exposed to, should be dismissed. This does not mean that no differences whatsoever were found between the media literacy and the non-media literacy groups. Indeed, differences did exist, albeit they were subtle and ranged across a wide assortment of responses to the texts. Analysis of transcripts of the interviews revealed three broadly conceptualized levels of response that emerged during the conversations. Each of these levels is discussed below, along with the particular themes associated with them and examples of respondents' comments.

ABSENCE OF CRITICISM

An absence of a critical perspective was by far the most common occurrence throughout the interviews. The label "absence of criticism" is meant to convey the idea that in these responses there was a noticeable lack of perspectives that challenged media images or conventional notions of commonsense. If media literacy education is designed to encourage a critical distance from the media-saturated environment that young people in

Western cultures grow up in, the relative absence of these sorts of responses is a discouraging sign. However, it should be noted that although these uncritical discourses were articulated across all of the groups of respondents, they did seem to appear more frequently and with less negotiation in the non-media literacy groups. Discourses that are associated with this category of response include the following:

1. *Naturalizing class inequality:* This discourse appeared repeatedly, throughout both the media literacy and the non-media literacy groups, usually in response to a question about the opening line in the advertisement: "I mean I'm not going to run around being like everyone should be equal. . . ." This discourse is exemplified by these samples of conversation:

Group Five (Media Literacy)

Michaela: (To Victor) I agree with you, it's not going to happen. In an ideal world we would all have equal opportunity regardless of race and sex and whatever but, it's not going to happen.

Georgette: I don't think I could imagine everyone having the same amount of money, I just think it wouldn't work.

Michaela: No, it wouldn't.

Aretha: No.

Victor: Communism.

Michaela: Yeah, exactly. (They all laugh).

Group Three (Media Literacy)

Erna: . . . we're just going to admit to ourselves and everybody else that we're going to be unequal and it's just like a fact of our society . . .

Viki: . . . something we have to live with.

Admitting that we live in a society that is not equal might be the beginning of a progressive critique of social structures that create and enforce that inequality. However, based on these excerpts, that is obviously not the direction in which this discourse goes. Rather, inequality is rationalized in the name of inevitability. Georgette's comment is particularly interesting here. She says that she can't even *imagine* everyone having the same amount of money. This is a clear example of how commonsense notions of the world make alternative ways of thinking difficult to even imagine. As Erna says, we are just going to have to admit that inequality is inevitable, just a fact of our society. After all, facts cannot be challenged because they are . . . facts. Then Viki chimes in with the (non)policy implications: we are just going to have to live with it. It's important to note again that this discourse occurred throughout the interviews, regardless of the respondents' exposure (or lack of exposure) to a critical media literacy curriculum.

2. *Don't judge others:* Another discourse that was prominent throughout the interviews occurred primarily in response to a question that asked what the Everlast video was about. Respondent after respondent said that the video's message was not to judge other people. Although this response does reflect the message of compassion that is encoded in the song and video, it also serves to inhibit a more political reading of the song. This is best illustrated through this excerpt from one of the non-media literacy groups:

Group Six (Non-Media Literacy)

> Ellen: I think that maybe they're trying to get you to think, the next time you're walking down the street and you see a homeless guy and he asks you for some change, they're not saying you have to definitely go up to the guy and give him change, but they're kind of saying you can't just look at this guy unsympathetic and want to kick him or something. . . .
>
> Lindsey: . . . they're saying that we should just accept it . . . not really accept it, but you know, you can do some changes but they're not saying to change it, they're saying to accept the people for who they are . . .

Thus, a discourse of "don't judge" slides into a discourse of "accept the situation," a position that leaves the respondents unable to articulate any response to poverty except "don't kick the homeless." Again, this discourse, the most common response offered in regard to the Everlast video, appeared in both the media literacy and the non-media literacy groups. The frequency with which this discourse appeared suggests that, as far as the viewing and listening public goes, and contrary to the possible reading offered in the introduction to this chapter, this is the key to the preferred reading of this video.

However, if this is indeed the preferred reading of the video, it is a reading that drains any sort of critical perspective from the text. Moving from "don't judge" to "accept the situation" allows one to be completely comfortable with a laissez-faire approach to problems of poverty, homelessness, and the like. In this manner, even texts that have the potential to encourage a critical position on social issues can be read in such a way that any critical potential is nullified. Although the textual analysis of the music video and advertisement offered earlier in this study suggests that the messages encoded in each are completely opposed to one another, the apparent "preferred" reading of the Everlast video is actually consistent with the messages of the Levi's advertisement.

3. *The undeserving poor:* This discourse articulated the commonsense notions that the poor are responsible for their own misery and that poor people don't want any help. In these statements all of the stereotypes of the underclass were activated through anecdotal evidence:

Group One (Non-Media Literacy)

> Roberto: . . . some bums just want to be bums, some of them do. . . . (He then tells a story about a homeless man that he knows who earns seven hundred dollars a week panhandling.) I'm not going to go out there to work for you, you know, I'm not going to work and give you my check.

Group Six (Non-Media Literacy)

> Lindsey: . . . I don't really know if I agree with the welfare system that much because there was a lot of trouble with it in my town. We lived in this nice area except there were like three sections of welfare that they kept building . . . the kids that would come to our school were always the trouble makers and they'd always cause fights and everything and I don't know why, and I'm not going to be like biased or anything, but I don't think that it's working because they're not . . . maybe because the parents are on it, they're not making the children want to make anything of themselves because they're just showing them that this is an easy way out . . . .

This type of discourse occurred primarily in the non-media literacy groups. Although there were traces of the "undeserving poor" discourse in some of the conversations with the media literacy groups, these tended to be more muted than the sharp attacks offered by the non-media literacy respondents, both male and female, Latino and non-Latino, and working and middle class. When it did appear in the media literacy groups, it was hedged by some statements of support for social welfare programs and was usually articulated by individual respondents but not picked up on or advanced by the group as a whole.

In fact, the only respondents who expressed complete support for welfare and public assistance were from the media literacy groups. When the interviewer introduced the term "welfare" into the non-media literacy groups, the negative associations attached to this word were immediately activated in the respondents. Only respondents with a media literacy background were able to challenge this connotation of the word and express a "pro-welfare" attitude. Without prompting from the interviewer, several of these respondents attributed their position on this issue direct-ly to information that they had learned in their media criticism courses about the ways in which politicians and the news media in the United States have articulated welfare to a purely negative connotation; as a "handout" for the lazy rather than social support for the unfortunate. This was one of the most obvious, and not politically insignificant, ways that the media literacy groups differed from the non-media literacy groups in their responses.

4.   *Conflating images and ideologies:* The power of visual imagery to influ-ence how a message is read was quite evident in responses to a question about whether the advertisement and the video were similar or different. As alluded to above, there was a tendency among most of the respondents (regardless of their media literacy background) to concentrate on similari-ties in visual style. For example:

Group Five (Media Literacy)

> Interviewer: Do you think that the commercial and video were similar or different?
>
> Aretha: They were similar. I was thinking that before but . . . it was kind of, not shocking I don't want to say, but they were both somewhat interesting, caught your attention, ummm, not the normal kind of commercial and it wasn't the normal kind of video. They were both kind of drab, like no bright colors or anything.

In the non-media literacy groups in particular, the focus on stylistic ele-ments seemed to inhibit recognition of difference in the ideological posi-tions articulated by the texts. For example, the interviewer asked if Everlast and the young woman in the commercial would agree or disagree with each other if they were to have a conversation:

Group One (Non-Media Literacy)

John: I think they'd agree.

Interviewer: What do you think they would agree about?

John: Everything . . . she'd probably tell him, I like that music and he'd probably tell her, yeah I like them jeans (Laughs).

Roberto: Yeah, I could see them agreeing because as much as Everlast is saying don't judge other people, he's working hard, trying to get his money so he could get the extras.

Oscar: Yeah, they're definitely going to agree.

Again, we see that any potentially political implication of the Everlast video is pushed into the background as questions of consumerism and style are foregrounded in this discourse. If popular culture is a battle, clearly the ideological weaponry wielded in the Levi's commercial is winning here.

In another dialogue that occurred in a non-media literacy group interview, the power of visual imagery to overwhelm verbal messages can be seen in what initially seems to be just a misreading of the ideological stance of the woman in the commercial:

Group Six (Non-Media Literacy)

Ellen: . . . and it seems like, ummmm, she's just a bitter feminist type girl . . .

Here, Ellen must be basing her belief that the young woman is a feminist on visual cues and signifiers, because there certainly is no indication of a feminist position in her verbal message. Other respondents in this group went so far as to state that the woman was promoting an anticapitalist message. In this sample from their conversation, their articulation of the Everlast message as "just accept things the way they are" is melded to their perception of the woman as an anticapitalist radical in a way that reverses the messages of the two texts:

Lindsey: I would think that she would take more of a stance because she's against the whole capitalism, or whatever, so I'm sure she would be like, we have to take care of the poverty situation, blah blah blah, and I think that Everlast isn't saying that, theyre saying that umm, we should just accept it, not really accept it, but you know . . . you can do some changes but they're not saying that you . . . they're not saying to change it, they're saying to accept the people for who they are . . .

Ellen: . . . and not how much money they have . . .

Lindsey: They're not saying to give them money and not accept the situation . . .

Ellen: Yeah definitely, I think that the girl would just start talking about how "society has killed so many people" (says this with a mocking tone). . . .

Mary: I think that she would take a stand and say this is what we can do to help, this is what we can do to make things better and then Everlast would just be like, well that's their choice and we should just be able to accept it and understand that that's what they want to do and if they want to change then they can change themselves, because a lot of homeless people don't want help from people.

A number of crucial points come together in this dialogue. Clearly, the visual signifiers in the commercial (the youth of the woman, her clothes and somewhat awkward manner, the dim lighting, the alleyway) have encouraged these respondents to identify the woman as "alternative" —a term that came up in other groups. This label was then associated with a feminist and anticapitalist ideology despite the directness of the verbal message. Thus, images of "dissent" are put to work in favor of a conformist message. Then, the move from "don't judge" to "just accept the situation," examined above, is utilized, along with a stereotypical representation of the poor, in order to justify a laissez-faire attitude. This is not simply a misreading of both texts. Rather it is a reading that foregrounds visual style to such an extent that the verbal messages are completely abandoned or, in this case, reversed.

The tendency to regard the advertisement and video as similar because of their visual styles also occurred frequently in the media literacy groups, but in these groups there was a tendency for this to be tempered by an acknowledgment that the ideological positions advanced by the text were opposed to one another. Some of the respondents in the media literacy groups were also able to take this one step further by acknowledging that the images and words of the advertisement were contradictory:

Group Four (Media Literacy)

Melanie: I don't know, it just seemed like an alternative commercial, it just had on like this girl, or this woman, the way she was and her ideas didn't seem like anything different or alternative.

Kathy: Yeah, she dressed kind of simple and just looked kind of ordi-
nary and plain and she was talking about how she likes material things
and it just didn't seem to fit her.

5.   *The American dream, class mobility, and agency:* Unlike the subthemes
identified above, this discourse did sharply differentiate the non-media literacy from the media literacy groups, perhaps more clearly than any other
theme identified in this study. In this discourse, which appeared only in the
non-media literacy group interviews, a position that fits nicely with the
messages in the advertisement was often articulated through an oppositional reading of the line in the Everlast song, "You know where it ends
usually depends on where you start." This is perhaps the most political line
in this song, and we will see that in the media literacy groups it evoked an
acknowledgment of class barriers and class struggle. In the non-media literacy groups, however, the implications of this line were rejected and
notions of class mobility, individual choice, personal agency, and the
American Dream were called upon to bolster this oppositional response to
the lyric:

Group One (Non-Media Literacy)

Interviewer: Do you agree? Where you end depends upon where you
start?

John: Oh no, no, I don't agree with that. Where you begin is where
you end up? No, I don't believe in that. I know a lot of kids that started in [a local poverty- stricken area], now they got money, they work,
live in [a suburban, upper- middle class town], they took the right
road. . . .

In the following excerpt from Group Six (also a non-media literacy group),
the commonsense notions of individual agency and the work ethic are so
strong for all of the members of this group that it is virtually impossible for
them to imagine anything different. This is apparent in Lindsey's initial
response to the question when she says she agrees and then immediately,
and without seeming to be aware that she is doing so, contradicts herself.
The others then chime in to support her in what becomes a paean to individual effort:

Lindsey: ummm, I agree because you could start from many different
positions, you could start upper class, lower class, but if you start with
the right attitude also you can take yourself wherever you want to go
pretty much.

Mary: I think if you apply yourself you're going to go anywhere. If you use what you have you can do anything, if you have the idea I want to be this I want to be that, I think you have the ability to go out and do it.

Ellen: You can overcome your origins. If you are born into poverty, umm, and you are a hard worker, and you're intelligent, and you do well in school, then you can get scholarships and go to great places and you can overcome what you started out with and become this incredible whatever, and be successful and maybe wealthy, and maybe not wealthy, but you can make something of yourself if you have the motivation and the drive.

Although these discourses that have been grouped together under the label "Absence of Criticism" were the most prominent in the interviews, they were not the only discourses present. There was some, if limited, evidence of a critical approach to both these texts and media in general, and even some criticisms directed at the class structure of American society. Both of these levels of response are discussed briefly below.

MEDIA CRITICISM

Both the media literacy groups and the non-media literacy groups showed some evidence of a critical perspective based in an understanding of the American media system as a commercial one that is driven primarily by the profit motive, although it should be noted that this type of response appeared quite infrequently. One rare example of this sort of discourse is offered here:

Group Four (Media Literacy)

Melanie: . . . if Levi's . . . had her say something, like, different or something that wasn't mainstream it couldn't be on television. If she said something like anti-capitalist or anti-material goods she probably couldn't . . . the commercial wouldn't be on television, I think.

Perhaps the most surprising result revealed in this project was that the respondents who had had exposure to a critical media literacy curriculum did not articulate a critical perspective on the media more often. In fact, the non-media literacy groups were just as likely to articulate a critical response to the media as the media literacy groups were. For example:

Group Two (Non-Media Literacy)

> Amelia: You might think your hair is just fine until you see fifty commercials over the span of two weeks telling you your hair is nasty, you know?

> Interviewer: You said that's what TV is all about?

> Amelia: Yeah, that's why the shows are there, so that you watch the commercials, not the other way around, and the commercials pay for the shows.

CRITICISM OF THE AMERICAN SOCIAL STRUCTURE

Where the ability of the media literacy respondents to draw on their educational background was more apparent, interestingly, was in their criticisms of the U.S. class structure. Somewhat in contradiction to the hegemonic perspectives that were articulated in the examples of non-critical discourses offered above, acknowledgment of class barriers and rejection of the "those who work hard get rewarded" myths espoused in the Levi's advertisement occurred with surprising regularity in the media literacy group interviews. As demonstrated in the excerpts of dialogue provided below, these respondents also often directly acknowledged that the perspectives that they were articulating had been influenced by their course work.

Group Four (Media Literacy)

> Nancy: People who work hard don't get the most money, like I just learned in Professor Smith's class, he pointed out people who have the most fun and interesting jobs get paid the most and the people that have, like, the tedious jobs that no one wants get paid the less, you know?

> Kathy: My roommate is like an absolute genius, she writes amazingly and she applied for the Boston Globe internship, they took one person

out of 200 and this girl, this random girl that doesn't even, is not even interested was like, "Oh my dad publishes the *Boston Globe* and I could have gotten that internship if I wanted it," and we both just looked at her like, that's who's going to get it! Someone like her is going to get that internship as opposed to my roommate who has no connections, but she's a genius, and it's like that's when you realize it's who you know it's really . . . you work so hard, but . . . .

Group Five (Media Literacy)

Interviewer: Do you agree with that idea that where you end depends on where you start?

Victor: I'm learning this in a class right now—Professor Lopes' 297F class barriers (laughs).

Interviewer: Tell me what you mean by that. What is he talking about that you think is relevant?

Victor: Well just the situations they're put in, like, it's almost impossible for people at the low end to succeed. Like there's one example with education, they can't get the proper . . . how some tests might not be, umm, made for them . . . like the SATs might be specifically geared at white kids while a black kid who went to high school as well might not have learned the same stuff, like an impossible situation to get out of where you start. The rags to riches story, they might seem possible because you hear about them on TV all the time but it's probably like point zero, zero, zero or whatever, one percent of people that happens to.

In both of these excerpts, students acknowledge that U.S. society is divided by class barriers, and they explicitly call on information from their media coursework to provide evidence and persuasive power to their arguments. It is important to note that the respondents brought up their courses without prompting from the interviewer.

Also important, however, are the limitations on how far the ability to call on their media literacy background can take these respondents. By way of example, Victor, who is quoted above, is the same young man who was quoted earlier in this study being completely resistant to the potentially progressive messages of the Everlast video. In another part of his interview he also expressed agreement with the tone of the Levi's advertisement. This suggests that although Victor is able to call on specific information from his media literacy courses in regard to specific contexts, he is not apt to apply this knowledge during his daily encounters with the world of media and popular culture.

CONCLUSIONS

As stated above, the results of these interviews do not reveal a simple bina-ry opposition between those who have been exposed to media literacy education and those who have not. In other words, this research project did not find that those who have a media literacy background were insightful critics of the texts they viewed whereas those without this background were complete cultural dupes. Subtle disparities, however, did exist between the groups of respondents.

Overall, the media literacy groups did show a tendency to question commonsense notions about the underclass in their acknowledgment of class barriers, their support for the message that there is a social obligation to help the poor, their stances on welfare, and so on. In generating these critical responses to the status quo, the individuals in the media literacy groups often explicitly invoked information that they had picked up from their course work. However, this critical stance was limited in its range and intensity. First, it should be noted that the level of discourse that has been labeled "the absence of criticism" in this study was the most prevalent throughout the interviews, regardless of respondents' exposure or lack of exposure to a critical media literacy curriculum. As suggested above, in the hegemonic battle that is waged within popular culture, ideologies of criti-cism and resistance to "commonsense" notions about poverty and the poor seem to be losing. Contrary to the formulations of theoreticians like Fiske (1989), who argue that audiences are constantly and continuously engaged in resistance and reconstruction while reading popular texts, it was much more common for the respondents in this study to embrace messages that reinforce and naturalize the status quo.

Furthermore, when critical perspectives were advanced, it seemed that respondents in the media literacy groups were invoking somewhat rote dis-courses that could not quite be sustained enough for them to be able to apply the insights of these critical positions to either the specific texts that they had viewed or to the ways that these texts either reinforce or challenge the dominant tendencies in American media and popular culture. This rais-es questions about whether these respondents are able to transfer the knowledge that they use in examinations and classroom discussions to their lives outside of the classroom. The lack of critical discussions about the media system in general is particularly relevant in regard to these questions.

Whereas three levels of discourses were noted above—the absence of criticism, criticism of the media, and criticism of the American class struc-ture—what might be considered a fourth level, at least in potential, was missing in these conversations. This fourth level might be identified as a full integration of a critical perspective. This hypothetical discourse might be described as a cognitive space where the respondents articulate full awareness of how the media system works to naturalize, reinforce, and, in some cases, construct power and resource inequities in society and are able to apply this understanding to the specific institutions and texts they encounter daily, thereby challenging the "commonsense" notions advanced by those texts and institutions. This would represent a position of true semiotic power that could potentially lead to an increased level of political activism and collective struggle. The absence of this sort of discourse in the conversations reported above suggests both the strong limitations of, and the exciting challenges for, a contextual critical media literacy project.

It is possible that the limitations of media literacy education noted here are related to the limitations of higher education in general, where students may often seem unwilling or unable to transfer the knowledge and skills they acquire in the classroom to their daily lives. This suggests two important considerations that any educator involved in critical media literacy will have to reckon with. First, media literacy education should ideally be as experiential as possible. Students must learn how to connect their classroom experiences with the world outside the classroom. Traditional models of information delivery are limited in terms of their efficacy in this regard. A hybrid model of education that introduces students to challenging ideas and then allows them the space to work on materials and projects in a way that brings the instructor's lecture to life may be the best way to accomplish this goal.

Second, and perhaps most important, educators, parents, legislators, and others must realize that critical media literacy education should begin as soon as exposure to media begins. If we first expose our young people to media education in college or even high school classrooms, we have come late to a battle that in many ways has already been lost. For children who are born into a media environment and are therefore exposed to literally thousands of hours of mediated sounds, images, and stories before they ever set foot in a classroom, there is no such thing as an intervention that comes too early. If we are careful to teach our children to be wary of strangers long before they ever encounter a stranger, why are we not as vigilant when it comes to surrendering them to the strangers who control the world's media and cultural industries?

NOTES

1. All the names of respondents have been changed.
2. The term *discourse* is used in this chapter to indicate both particular perspectives that are conveyed through language, and in the sense of verbal expressions of thoughts and ideas.

REFERENCES

Butsch, R. (1992). Class and gender in four decades of television situation comedy. *Critical Studies in Mass Communication, 9*, 387–399.

Butsch, R. (2003). Ralph, Fred, Archie, and Homer: Why television keeps recreating the white male working-class buffoon. In G. Dines & J. M. Humez (Eds.), *Gender, race and class in media* (2nd ed., pp. 575–585). Thousand Oaks, CA: Sage.

Cantor, M. (1990). Prime-time fathers: A study in continuity and change. *Critical Studies in Mass Communication, 7*, 275–285.

Cantor, M. (1991). The American family on television: From Molly Goldberg to Bill Cosby. *Journal of Comparative Family Studies, 22*, 205–216.

Condit, C. (1989). The rhetorical limits of polysemy. *Critical Studies in Mass Communication, 6*(2), 103–122.

Ehrenreich, B. (1995). The silenced majority: Why the average working person has disappeared from American media and culture. In G. Dines & J. M. Humez (Eds.), *Gender, race and class in media* (pp. 40–42). Thousand Oaks, CA: Sage.

Fiske, J. (1989). *Reading the popular.* Boston: Unwin Hyman.

Frank, T. (1997). *The conquest of cool: Business culture, counterculture, and the rise of hip consumerism.* Chicago: The University of Chicago Press.

Gerbner, G. (1999). Foreword: What do we know? In J. Shanahan & M. Morgan, *Television and its viewers: Cultivation theory and research.* Cambridge: Cambridge University Press.

Gow, J. (1998). Mood and meaning in music video: The dynamics of audio visual synergy. *Southern Communication Journal, 63*(4), 255–261.

Gramsci, A. (1971). *Selections from the prison notebooks.* New York: International.

Hall, S. (1980). Encoding/decoding. In S. Hall et al. (Eds.), *Culture, media, language* (pp. 128–138). London: Hutchinson.

Hall, S. et al. (1994). Reflections upon the encoding/decoding model: An interview with Stuart Hall. In J. Cruz & J. Lewis (Eds.), *Reading, viewing, listening* (pp. 253–274). Boulder, CO: Westview.

Jhally, S., & Lewis, J. (1992). *Enlightened racism: The Cosby Show, audiences, and the myth of the American dream.* Boulder, CO: Westview.

Jhally, S., & Lewis, J. (1998). The struggle over media literacy. *Journal of Communication, 48*(1), 109–120.

Katz, E., & Liebes, T. (1985). Mutual aid in the decoding of *Dallas.* In P. Drummond & R. Paterson (Eds.), *Television in transition* (pp. 187–198). London: British Film Institute.

Lewis, J. (1983). The encoding/decoding model: Criticisms and redevelopments for research on decoding. *Media, Culture and Society, 5*, 151–169.

Mantsios, G. (2001). Media magic: Making class invisible. In P. S. Rothenberg (Ed.), *Race, class, and gender in the United States* (pp. 563–571). New York: Worth.

McChesney, R. (1999, April). Unpublished speech given at the 3rd Annual Schmio Awards, New York.

Moore, M. L. (1992). The family as portrayed on prime time television, 1947-1990: Structure and characteristics. *Sex Roles, 26*, 41–61.

Morley, D. (1980). *The "nationwide" audience.* London: British Film Institute.

Morley, D. (1992). *Television, audiences and cultural studies.* London: Routledge.

Parenti, M. (1992). *Make-believe media: The politics of entertainment.* New York: St. Martin's.

Parenti, M. (1993). *Inventing reality.* New York: St. Martin's.

Reed, A. (1999). *Stirrings in the jug: Black politics in the post-segregation era.* Minneapolis: University of Minnesota Press.

Scharrer, E. (2001). From wise to foolish: The portrayal of the sitcom father, 1950s-1990s. *Journal of Broadcasting and Electronic Media, 45*(1), 23–40.

Williams, R. (1977). *Marxism and literature.* Oxford: Oxford University Press.

6

GLOBAL TEENS

Marketing, Politics and Media Education

Barry Duncan[1]

Marketing to youth in North America is a hundred billion dollar business. That is why teens are described as a hot demographic. Theirs is the largest generation of teens in history and the one with the most disposable income. In 2000, teenagers spent a total of US $155 billion in discretionary income (Quart, 2003). To capitalize on this phenomenon, popular brands with their powerful imagery and magical appeal have become the new rock stars. It's no wonder, then, that forging a sense of identity in today's media-saturated consumer culture constitutes a real challenge for today's typical teen.

Since the 1950s, there have been numerous pedagogical approaches to media analysis and media education based on historical, social, political and even aesthetic considerations.[2] Very few, however, have dealt with the negotiation process that takes place between teenagers and consumer culture, and fewer yet have looked at school-based projects that encourage resistance. Naomi Klein's ground-breaking and best-selling work *No logo* (2000) makes the important connections between the role of corporations, new marketing paradigms, the erosion of public space, and the important role of resistance and protest. Much of this essay is inspired directly by her work.

The first half of this chapter describes the new models of global teen marketing (including the power of branding and the use of "cool" hunters) in order to provide context. Then, based on many years as a media educator, I intersperse throughout this discussion a number of class exercises that I have found useful in expanding young people's critical thinking skills. In particular, I examine how they can creatively cultivate points of resistance—through "culture jamming" for example—despite the massive marketing efforts being directed at them. The second half of the chapter endeavors to explore media education within a framework of critical pedagogy. I suggest methods that foster a democratic classroom and a "global perspective," and discuss impediments to exchange and dialogue as well.

CONNECTING THE GLOBAL ECONOMY AND "GLOBAL EDUCATION" TO MEDIA EDUCATION

In 1991, U.K. educator Len Masterman asserted at a media education conference held in Guelph, Ontario, that a new paradigm of "critical marketing" had to be addressed by media educators. He pointed out how advertising and public relations' practices were converging, and subsequently wrote: "The primary function of commercial media in Europe is the segmentation, packaging and segmenting of audiences to advertising" (Masterman, 1997, p. 67). In making that statement, he foreshadowed developments we now associate with globalization, including free trade, transnational marketing, branding, deregulation, and privatization, or what Herbert Schiller aptly described in the subtitle of his important book *Culture Inc.* as "the corporate take-over of public space" (Schiller, 1989). Building on these assertions, I contend that there are several major media and cultural challenges that educators must address:

- The corporate take-over of public space embraces everything from shopping malls to the changing role of art galleries and museums. Sponsored culture is now commonplace. For example, in Toronto, the *History of Santa Claus* exhibition at the Royal Ontario Museum in 1993 was sponsored by Coca Cola. We have witnessed increased commercialization in our schools through media such as Channel One and advertisements in textbooks: the curriculum is now being brought to you by Lever Brothers.

- Corporate merger mania and concentration of ownership and control profoundly influence our choices in entertainment, both locally and globally, including our sources of news. That CNN is often the main source of international news in the developing world is very troubling, indeed.
- The public relations industry has created spin doctors, skillful lobbyists, image consultants, and crisis managers for governments and corporations. The war on terrorism has made the notion of "manufacturing consent" for government positions critical to sustaining this propagandistic endeavour.[3]
- Today, business has shifted from selling products to building brands.

Due to ever-increasing competition in the global economy, marketers and social engineers have colluded to target youth as a multibillion-dollar market segment. In response to this reality, in 1992 the Ontario's Teacher's Federation adopted a new pedagogical concept:

> A global perspective in education can be defined as an approach or framework to education which will help our young people gain the knowledge and develop the values, attitudes and skills to be effective participants in a world rapidly becoming more interdependent and interconnected. (Lyons, 1992, p. 2)

Within the context of global education, media education is concerned with helping students develop a critical understanding of how the media work, how they construct meaning, how they can be used, and how to evaluate the information presented by them. Media education is closely associated with critical literacy and cultural studies, where media texts are examined in terms of their social, cultural, geopolitical and historical contexts.

Media education, then, is involved in analyzing media texts for the representations of both local and global events and the issues and ways in which these representations help to shape the meanings we assign to them. It involves understanding the ways in which ideology and values can be constructed and defined in the media and asking questions about who benefits from the constructions. It also involves examining the ownership and control of media and technology and asking questions about the impact of current policies and practices on access, choice, and range of expression. Finally, it includes an examination of the Western media for the way relationships between the North and the South are defined, and for the positions of dominance and oppression that may be reinforced through them.

GLOBAL MALLS AND GLOBAL TEENS

Before examining youth marketing more deeply, I would first like to consider the typical setting for today's commerce and the favorite hangout spot for North American teenagers—the shopping mall. In a culture of consumption, the mall (or "Temple of Mammon"/"Cathedral of Consumption," as the critics call them) assumes an important symbolic place in the lives of youth. Precisely because of their importance, I have conducted field trips with both high school students and media teachers to several shopping malls in metropolitan Toronto.[4] The goal of these field trips is to share perceptions about the pleasures and liabilities of this pervasive North American institution. And getting students to think about who owns the mall is a good way to introduce students to the notion of public versus private space. For example, many teens who think they have rights in this logo-driven environment are shocked when security guards evict them from the premises for alleged loitering. Meanwhile, however, the merchants of cool can be found conducting research and brainstorming marketing plans with the aim of persuading young people to purchase the next hot Nike sneakers, cool Ray Ban sunglasses, and trendy Tommy Hilfiger clothes.

Below is a sampling of questions and issues I have raised with high school students and other media educators when conducting a "mall crawl:"

- How does the layout/structure of the shopping mall influence people's behavior? Your behavior?
- How does this mall compare with other malls? Which one(s) do you prefer and why?
- To what extent, the mall a gendered experience? Critics have noted that much of the mall content is aimed at women. Citing examples, agree or disagree.
- Briefly interview several people, ideally representing the mall's different constituencies: shop keepers, regular shoppers, tourists, downtown workers, teens, seniors, and occasional visitors. How is each group benefiting from the mall? Account for their likes and dislikes.
- What are the differences between the way we experience television and the way we experience the mall?
- What are some current pop culture trends reflected in the mall? How are they marketed? Consider current ad campaigns and the use of posters.

- Malls are privately owned but publicly used places. What are the differences between main streets and shopping malls? Malls are increasingly becoming outlets for a small number of stores with global distribution, from Gap to Polo Ralph Lauren. What problems—cultural, economic, and social—do these stores present?
- If you were to film the mall either as a celebration or as a radical critique of consumer culture, brainstorm an outline for a film.

THE IMPORTANCE OF BRANDS IN THE WORLD OF MARKETING

The 1990s witnessed a major tactical shift in corporate marketing as advertisers began to realize that strong images and emotional meanings could be attached to products and services—that is, branding. Although not a new idea, the intensity of this brand-oriented marketing changed the face of advertising. Today, corporations may manufacture products but consumers buy brands. The brand is the essence of a corporation and advertising is the company's way of conveying their ethos to the consumer. To cut through the clutter of messages and products, a brand needs to do more than identify a product; it must give it a personality. Through our allegiance to certain brands, we say something about ourselves. For example, Nike CEO, Phil Knight, announced in the late 1980s that although Nike is indeed a "sports company," its mission is not to sell shoes, but rather to "enhance people's lives through sports and fitness and to keep the magic of sports alive" (quoted in Klein, 2000, p. 28).

Another significant change in marketing practice has been the rise of product placement and sponsorship. A good example of this phenomenon is the teenage cast of the TV drama *Dawson's Creek*, who were outfitted for the show first by J. Crew and later by The Gap: they also appeared on the cover of the J. Crew catalog in January 2003. Important branding opportunities also come with/from celebrities, from film and TV stars—especially those appearing on MTV—to the superheroes of sports culture. For product placement, the undisputed king has been Michael Jordan who, according to Phil Knight, helped Nike become "the world's best sports and fitness company" (quoted in Klein, 2000, p. 51)

In this consumer culture, product logos are ubiquitous, from the restaurant chains in which we dine to the branded and logo-ed clothes we wear.[5] Understanding how various logos resonate with teens is the first step in exposing their consumer codes, including to themselves. The following investigations can open up this territory and provide teachers with valuable insights.

- What logos do you and your classmates wear? List them and discuss the results.
- What logos do your parents wear?
- What do you like and/or dislike about logos and designer clothing? Give some examples.
- In groups, brainwave the creation of a new product or a new venue (e.g. a restaurant) and try creating an effective brand image.
- Include some examples of how you would create synergy by arranging extensive contra-marketing deals (TV, magazines, radio, and sponsorships).
- Working in groups, determine the characteristics of a good logo as well as an ineffective logo.
- Try creating an original brand and then devise a suitable logo for your brand image. Share your examples.
- Check out the official web sites of several major brands. How do corporations effectively maintain their brand image?
- For students to reflect on themselves, as distinct from deconstructing popular culture, ask each student to create a collage reflecting his or her values, interests, and identity. Although it may use some media references, including written text and pictures, there should also be some original work that is personal to the student and written by her or him.
- Following from this, ask students to create another collage in which they convey their views, both positive and negative, about mass media and popular culture. They should be expected to include examples of brand images.

After doing these projects, each student then summarizes his or her personal insights about media and branding and the challenge of exploring personal identity. Students can express their views on brands and logos through writing a poem or lyrics for a song. They should be encouraged to use plenty of brand names, exploring the many layers of associations and meaning. This could be in the form of a parody.

COOL HUNTING AND THE ART OF BEING COOL

For teens, the appeal of cool people and cool consumer goods gets to the heart of their evolving identities as they try to be their coolest selves. This kind of marketing has gained a great deal of publicity in recent years because of the role of professional "cool hunters." Although the term is loaded, it becomes, like the discussion on logos, a valuable way to learn about marketing to teens and their personal investment in popular cultural texts. One can talk about the phenomenon at a safe distance through discussing their choice of bands, posters, movie stars, and places to visit. "Cool hunting" is all about tapping into the interests, mindsets, and perspectives of teens in order to predict the next big trend. Once discovered, it is exploited as a marketing breakthrough or used to rebrand an existing product that is experiencing slumping sales. For example, the soft drink Sprite was given a new life with teens when it was aligned with hip-hop culture. Cool hunters observe teen behavior and try to make sense of new trends before they enter mainstream culture. To do this, they seek out trend setters in order to try and obtain some kind of peer influence. The challenge with "coolness," however, is that it is always in a state of flux. Once it's been pinned down, cool moves on to the next big thing.

Naturally, cool hunters reject criticism that they are collecting data about teens in order to manipulate them into buying new products. Instead, they argue that their role in the marketing process is valuable because it allows them to take the best ideas from teen culture and help manufacturers produce products that will satisfy the needs and desires of the teenage market segment. In spite of cool hunters downplaying their role, students might discuss in class to what extent they believe they are being exploited. To test some of the above observations, they might be directed to look at several lifestyle magazines, especially those aimed directly at teens, such as *Teen People*, and determine how the advertising throughout uses the power of cool to sell products. The 30-minute documentary *The Merchants of Cool* (2002)[6] is particularly relevant here, revealing cool hunters and targeted teens in action, making the students' marketing insights concrete and experiential.

MEDIA IDENTITY VERSUS PERSONAL IDENTITY

Cool stuff may seem to provide an identity for young people, especially when it helps them fit in with friends who share some of the same consumer goods. However, what is crucial is to encourage them to differentiate between buying an image that is subject to constant change and exploring their own values as emerging adults. Although identity may be fluid and evolving, it is much more than just listening to a new band or feeling good in new clothes. What youth are consuming may give them high status and the "right look" but that is merely an image and not an identity. We might begin to work with students in the classroom by posing questions such as: "Does coolness simply mean being true to yourself or is it all about hearing the same music and dressing as everybody else?" Crucially, how can we reconcile the contradictory views that teens are quite prepared to attack the media yet still feel they have to conform and buy the newest fads?

After class discussion and debate, it is important to work through perspectives on marketing to youth by following the suggestion of Paulo Freire in *Pedagogy of the Oppressed (1970)*. The logic he describes starts with awareness and dialogue, moves to reflection, and culminates in appropriate action. I have found culture jamming to be especially useful, specifically focusing on the art of creating parody collages following *Adbusters Magazine*'s "subvertising" model. Kalle Lasn, cofounder of the magazine and the Media Foundation, says somewhat hyperbolically:

> ... the challenge for the new millennium activists is to find the courage to let go of all their old orthodoxies, "isms" and sacred cows, and to commit to a "ruthless criticism of all that exists." And after that, the big challenge is to bring revolutionary consciousness and contestation back into the modern world by standing up and boldly announcing to the world what Parisian rebels declared some thirty years ago: "We will wreck the world." (Lasn, 1999, p. 69)

The legacy of increased globalization on today's global markets is those highly visible corporations that speak to us directly. For many protesters— including a surprising number of teens—corporate culture has become an ideal target. Some of the more compelling protests focus on the activities associated with "culture jamming." As defined by activist Mark Dery, culture jamming is "anything, essentially, that mixes art, media, parody and the outsider stance" (cited in Klein, 2000, p. 283). Culture jamming has grown out of the dissatisfactions of consumers with brands, celebrities, trendy fashions, and big ticket entertainment. The corporate spectacles that surround us are, according to Lasn, to be "uncooled" their products "demarketed." The activist messages of his magazine, he claims, will "jolt post-modern society out of its trance. . . . We reverse the spin cycle. We demarket our news, our entertainments, our lifestyles and desires—and, eventually, maybe even our dreams" (Lasn, 1999, p. 18). Working in small groups, students can intercut ads and photographs from magazines in order to make collages with some telling juxtapositions for parodic purposes ("Calvin Swine" modeled from Calvin Klein, and "Joe Chemo" from Joe Camel are two examples: see www.adbusters.org). However, aside from provoking some laughter through having well-known brands parodied, this activity should be seen as a stepping stone for raising further critical thinking or for producing more advanced creative output.

For media educators, there are other important benefits in this kind of project. U.K. researcher and educator David Buckingham observed an intriguing school project in which students created parodies of sensationalist TV dramas. Besides opening up issues around gender and sexuality, the project offered the students "an opportunity to speak the unspeakable and to unleash the 'unpopular' and subversive things that are normally restrained by the institution of the school" (Buckingham, 1998, p. 31). Ideally, the best "subvertising," like the best of any satirically directed work, should amuse us but at the same time make us feel uncomfortable. It should be noted that comedy simply seeks laughter as an end in itself. Naomi Klein points out, however, the potential limitation of subvertising and much culture jamming activities. "It is harmless satire, a game that exists in isolation from a genuine political movement or ideology" (Klein, 2000, p. 309).

To see how we can potentially rise above these limitations, I would like to comment briefly on the work of Richard Slye, a professional Toronto collage artist whose work has appeared in art shows and in the form of book and magazine covers. Slye's work is in the fine tradition of German artist John Hartfield who, in the 1930s, created some satirical and very subversive collages featuring Adolf Hitler, until such art became too dangerous and Hartfield had to flee the country. Slye has a huge stock of magazines and photographs, an amazing image bank to access for creating his collages. One of his favorite themes concerns the recurring motif of our favorite fast food icon—the hamburger—which he places in bizarre settings, each time gathering many layers of meaning. Here are some examples:

- Slye uses the famous Norman Rockwell painting of the nuclear family at their dinner table smiling warmly—not, however, at the traditional Thanksgiving turkey, but rather at a two-foot size Big Mac.
- Poking fun at our obsession with fast food delivery, the artist shows us beef cattle in a field, their flanks bulging with ready-to-serve hamburgers.
- Hamburgers made into airplanes and stuffed with American consumer goods such as TVs and stereos successfully invade a Third World country.

Slye's most controversial work comprises a giant Big Mac inserted into the middle of Mecca—the holiest site for devout Muslims—with its thousands of supine pilgrims at prayer. Questions and activities we might work on in class include:

- Is it possible to be a "good" Muslim but still enjoy the satirical humor of this provocative collage? To what extent are our responses to this kind of art influenced by political correctness?

- Why might some Muslims be offended but others not?
- Compare Slye's collage with the scene in the Monty Python film *Life of Brian*, in which Brian is hanged from the cross.
- Brainwave other ideas drawn from popular culture for their potential use of satirical juxtaposition. Using the content of a variety of magazines, create your own satirical collages. Your goal is to make a humorous but critical statement that stretches beyond the most obvious laughs. After the class has established criteria for effective satirical collages, each student's work should be assessed through peer evaluation.

What focuses the various sites of struggle in this essay for closer scrutiny are the issues raised by the need for a suitable pedagogy. Before the "critical pedagogues" such as Giroux (1992), Simon (1992) and McLaren (1994) emerged with sociopolitical critiques and oppositional readings, Len Masterman published *Teaching the Media* in 1985. In spite of some criticism, Masterman's insights about the sociopolitical dynamics of class discussions are of paramount importance to media educators seeking to empower students through carefully managed dialogue and the appropriate use of reflective skepticism. Masterman contends that the ultimate goal is to create critical autonomy whereby:

> Dialogue involves a genuine sharing of power—even if differential power relationships exist outside of the dialogue. Participants need to maintain an attitude of reflective self-criticism upon their thinking and actions within the dialogue in order to eradicate manipulation. It is genuinely a group process (rather than something which is engaged in by a number of discrete individuals) in which members recognize the power which can be generated through co-operative learning, group action and reflection. . . . Through dialogue it is possible to develop dialectical thinking which recognizes the internal contradictions and tensions which exist within the group and within each individual, and which understands that such contradictions are inherent in all situations which the group explores. . . . Dialogue does not attempt to dissolve contradictions into consensus, but seeks contradictions out as the motivating power for change. . . . Finally, dialogue is oriented towards action. Using and intervening in the media are important parts of any media education course. (Masterman, 1985, p. 33)

Subvertising exercises, creating satirical collages, and engaging in discussions about the role of satire, parody, comedy, and irony inherent in media culture today demand a thoughtful kind of critical teaching that, as Masterman argues, is grounded in effective dialogue. Extending some of Masterman's ideas, it is evident that they are theoretically compatible with the critical processing of media associated with the American-dominated "critical pedagogy" discourses. I agree with most of the critiques of critical pedagogy in the anthology *Teaching Popular Culture: Beyond Radical Pedagogy* (Buckingham,1998), which point out that critical pedagogy is often too dense in its vocabulary and syntax to be accessible. Critical pedagogy repeats buzz words like "citizen" and "democracy" without providing concrete examples and it makes too much of big problematic global issues without first addressing the local environment. Bill Green's essay (Buckingham, 1998) confronts these deficits and, together with Roger Simon, provides a definition of the critical pedagogy territory:

> [A] practice within which one acts with the intent of provoking experience that will simultaneously organize and disorganize a variety of understandings of our natural and social world. It is therefore a practice, a mode of working on and with aspects of material existence, on the part of the teacher, in interaction with a learner or a community of learners, that simultaneously seeks to order and disorder the latter's experience, as one moment within a larger social and cultural movement of (re)production, renewal, change and transformation. (Green, cited in Buckingham, 1997, p. 188)

How can the examples of marketing and parodic collages which have been presented thus far be interpreted within and beyond a postmodern critical pedagogy? The critical pedagogy discourse applied here requires thoughtful audience research that addresses the negotiation of meaning, students' subjectivities, and the nature of difference. I am thinking here mainly of reception theory, which, among other things, helps us filter our discussions through the framework of gender, race, and class. Teaching these rich, provocative media texts demands dealing with the uncertainties of creativity, ambiguity, complexity of thought, and inevitable contradictions. Masterman's concern that dialogue be seen "as the motivating force for change" is crucial. The key factor missing is agreeing on suitable empowerment strategies for action. These observations are especially pertinent to the response of educators, especially American media educators, after the events of September 11. An article in the *New York Times* on September 19, 2001, by Richard Rothstein, asserted that very few teachers were doing an adequate job of bringing the necessary critical thinking to this multilayered topic. Unfortunately for these crucial teachable media moments, no immediate study guides are available.

In my experience, having students study sharply focused satirical collages by politically committed artists in a course with similar models and exercises helps to lay the foundation for more complex analysis. Subsequently, when students then create their own works, debating their aesthetic tactics with their peers, they can claim ownership in the process. Obviously, this is not a magic formula, but I trust there are important elements here for media educators to ponder.

Teenagers have a fragile and evolving sense of self, which is contested by media narratives; our consumer culture offers them instant identities, thanks to cool hunters and their successful marketing tactics. Unfortunately, today's youth are being addressed not as citizens but as consumers. In this site of struggle, media teachers should know the dangers of trivializing and co-opting students' popular culture and be aware of their vulnerability to peer pressures to acquire the latest consumer goods. The white boy in the suburbs or in a small town in Saskatchewan can listen to rap music and say "Yo" to his buddies and eagerly consume the latest gossip about black rappers. This phenomenon could provoke critical inquiry for media educators seeking clues to understanding postmodern youth.

MEDIA ACTIVISM AND STUDENT ACTION

Critical pedagogy raises issues about democratic access and participation in the media. U.K. educator Robert Ferguson writes: "For media education to be more than a mere inventory of media provision, it must be socially, aesthetically, politically involved. Media researchers and students, like any other intellectuals, are implicated in the societies of which they are a part" (2001, p. 20). Media educators must face the challenge of deciding what kinds of activism are appropriate for their students, and for themselves perhaps. Fortunately, there is a new face to protest today that was not apparent in the predictable 1960s images of long-haired radicals throwing Molotov cocktails (Falconer, 2002). The Summit of the Americas in Quebec City in 2001 and the war in Iraq are perfect examples to demonstrate (a) how the goals of protest have been reconceptualized; and (b) how the mainstream and the alternative media covered these events. New materials such as *Challenging McWorld* (Clarke & Dopp, 2001) offer a stimulating range of activities for encouraging students. There are many important targets for resistance. Many of our public institutions—sometimes discussed under the heading of public space—have undergone major changes because of corporate influences. Schools now have soft drink franchises; companies such as Lever brothers and computer companies such as Apple and IBM offer schools attractive prepackaged school curriculum. We are all aware of sporting events sponsored by companies such as Rothmans and Molson. All of these trends need to be examined and debated in the media classroom. Otherwise, educators will be politically naïve, insular, and culturally irresponsible.

Our relationships with the corporate world are complex and often contradictory, and it is difficult for an individual to make a difference. Dissatisfaction as well as praise for corporate and government actions can take many forms, and it is perhaps easiest to think of our democratic choices as a range of possibilities, each one containing different degrees of commitment. We might register our criticism or pose important questions by starting with a letter writing campaign. The Canadian Broadcasting Corporation claims that one phone call praising or criticizing a program is the equivalent of 1,000 citizens. We may also need to contact various advocacy groups, all of whom have their own web sites. Possibly the most successful Canadian one, The Council of Canadians, claims to be "the unofficial opposition in Canada," taking aim at the perils of free trade treaties. For example, the Council has been successful in mobilizing people to persuade governments to abandon treaties that would limit the rights of citizens.

CONCLUSION

The ways in which the media and popular culture more generally are involved in offering ready-to-wear identities through clever marketing to young people should compel media educators to address this important site of struggle through dialogic methods, innovative ways of encouraging student resistance, and the use of the most effective aspects of critical pedagogy. This is a challenging task, because at stake, is how well we create the democratic classroom, clarify our values, and define our role as citizens.[7]

NOTES

1. Some material is in the introductory paragraphs of this essay first appeared in Wilson and Duncan (2001).
2. See the works of Masterman (1985, 1997, 1998); Ferguson (2001); Buckingham (1990, 1998); Tyner (1998).
3. See Herman and Chomsky (1994).
4. For more information see Duncan et al. (1996, pp. 110 118).
5. Surely one of the world's best known commercial symbols is McDonald's golden arches.
6. Available through www.PBS.org.
7. My colleague Carolyn Wilson, a media teacher and the president of the Association for Media Literacy, has written about global studies (Wilson & Duncan, 2001) and presented at conferences her rich experiential curriculum

for her students. They all benefit from her action-based learning in the context of her media and global studies class. These include: following some corporate logos such as Nike to their origin in Asian sweatshops; placing her students in global studies for one week every year with a live-in family in the Dominican Republic; and taking students to the School of Americas in Columbus, Georgia, the site where counter terrorists have been trained, for an annual event of protest and remembrance.

REFERENCES

Adbusters Magazine, 1243 West 7th Ave., Vancouver, B.C. V6H 1B. www.adbusters. org

Buckingham, D. (Ed.). (1990). *Watching media learning.* London: Routledge.

Buckingham, D. (Ed.). (1998). *Teaching popular culture: Beyond radical pedagogy.* London: Routledge.

Clarke, T., & Dopp, S. (2001).*Challenging McWorld.* Ottawa: Canadian Centre for Policy Alternatives and Resources.

Duncan, B., D'Ippolito, J., Macpherson, C., & Wilson, C. (1996). *Mass media and popular culture. Version 2.* Toronto: Harcourt-Canada.

Falconer, T. (2002). *Watchdogs and gadflies: Activism from marginal to mainstream.*Toronto: Penguin.

Ferguson, R. (2001). In defence of media education. *The International Journal of Media Education, 1*(1), 21–22.

Freire, P. (1970). *Pedagogy of the oppressed.* New York: Seabury.

Giroux, H. (1992). *Border crossings.* London: Routledge.

Herman, E. S., & Chomsky, N. (1994). *Manufacturing consent: The political economy of the mass media.* London: Vintage.

Klein, N. (2000). *No logo: Taking aim at the brand bullies.* Toronto: Random House.

Lasn, K. (1999). *Culture jam: The uncooling of America.* New York: Eagle Books.

Lyons, T. (1992). *Education for a global perspective.* Toronto: Ontario Teachers' Federation.

Masterman, L. (1998). *Media education in 1990's Europe: A teacher's guide.* New York: Manhattan Publishing Company.

Masterman, L. (1997). A rationale for media education. In *Media Literacy in the Information Age.* New Brunswick, NJ: Transaction.

Masterman, L. (1985). *Teaching the media.* London: Routledge.

McLaren, P. (1994). *Critical pedagogy and predatory culture.* London: Routledge.

Merchants of cool. 30 minute video (2002) and teaching notes on-line. Order from www.pbs.org

Quart, A. (2003). *Branded: The buying and selling of teenagers.* Cambridge, MA: Perseus Books.

Schiller, H. (1989). *Culture inc. The corporate take-over of public expression.* New York: Oxford University Press.

Simon, R. (1992). *Teaching against the grain: Texts for a pedagogy of possibility.* New York: Bergin & Garvey.

Tyner, K. (1998). *Literacy in a digital world: Teaching and learning in the age of information.* Mahwah, NJ: Erlbaum.

Wilson, C., & Duncan, B. (2001). Global studies and media education. *Telemedium,* 47(3), 3–13.

7

SPRINGING UP
A REVOLUTION

Media Education Strategies for Tweens

Salina Abji

Ever since the girl power phenomenon of the 1990s, the tween market has captivated the interests and spending dollars of marketing strategists, media producers, advertisers, and retailers. Tweens are the preteen children of an aging baby boomer population and, in Canada, they boast an estimated $1.5 billion per year in spending dollars (Global Television, 2003). Although preteens have always been considered a niche market by media producers and advertisers, the girl power phenomenon of the 1990s demonstrated the ability of the tween market to influence the tastes of the broader culture. Many studies have documented, for example, tweens' growing influence over the spending habits of their families, or "pester power" (Global Television, 2003). And, as Giese surmises, the fact that most of us can name a favorite Spice Girl is ample proof that "13-year old girls rule the world" (Giese, 1998, p. N1).

The increased media attention on tweens brought about by the girl power phenomenon has received mixed reviews from feminist theorists, activists, and media educators working with this age group. Although the emphasis of girl power on recognizing the strengths, capabilities, and achievements of young women is arguably better than more stereotypical representations, many feminists have questioned the viability of this new brand of "feminism lite" (Giese, 1998, p. N12). As music writer Ann Powers observes: ". . . at this intersection between the conventional feminine and the evolving Girl, what's springing up is not a revolution but a mall. . . . Thus, a genuine movement develops into a giant shopping spree" (Klein, 2000, p. 114).

In November 1999, MediaWatch Canada began conducting focus groups with tweens aged 11-14, in Burnaby, British Columbia, and Toronto, Ontario. MediaWatch is a national nonprofit feminist organization that seeks to transform the media environment from one in which women and girls are either invisible or stereotyped, to one in which they are realistically portrayed and equitably represented in all their physical, economic, racial, and cultural diversity. By researching the impact of increased media attention on tweens, MediaWatch's aim was to determine if and how media affects the self-esteem and body image of young girls and to produce a resource that would raise public awareness as well as assist in the development of effective media education strategies for this group (MediaWatch, 2000, pp. 2–3).

Although results of the MediaWatch study confirmed what feminists have been saying all along —that sexist media representations have a profoundly negative effect on the self-esteem and body image of girls—the research also raised a number of important questions regarding the efficacy of contemporary media education strategies. For example, the study indicated that the ability to read and critically analyze advertising messages did not prevent girls in this age group from experiencing negative effects, such as decreased self-esteem, as a result of media consumption. Similarly, the study found that girls' ability to name a variety of strategies for challenging sexism in advertising did not translate into social action: in fact, the majority of respondents had never engaged in these types of activities, despite being able to catalogue an "impressive" list (MediaWatch, 2000, p. iv).

This chapter discusses the implications of MediaWatch's research for feminist theorists, activists, and media educators working with tweens. Not only do contemporary media education strategies underestimate girls' ability to read and critically analyze media messages, they also overestimate the power of "critical viewing" alone as a strategy for empowering girls. Furthermore, emphasis on consumer-based activism does little to address the problematic corporate practices behind ads, or the everyday experiences of tweens living in an increasingly branded world. MediaWatch's findings therefore challenge feminist theorists, activists, and media educators to develop new strategies for resistance and resiliency—strategies that incorporate, rather than alienate, the opinions and experiences of girls.

THE MEDIAWATCH STUDY

Although the sample size was small (37) and limited to two geographic regions in Canada, the strengths of the MediaWatch study lie in its qualitative focus. The methodological approach of the study, for example, was highly participatory and allowed tweens to express their opinions and experiences in a variety of mediums: through semistructured group discussions, hands-on group activities, self-reflexive diary writing, and self-directed collection of media images for discussion. Focus groups were organized by age (11-12 year olds and 13-14 year olds) and limited to 8-10 participants, in order to encourage and facilitate discussion. Participants were also assured that their identities would be kept confidential and were provided with notepads and pens to take notes throughout the project, as well as incentives (food coupons, T-shirts) after both sessions.

A community center in Burnaby and a public school in Toronto assisted with the recruitment of tweens for the project. The 11-12 year old Burnaby group was composed of tweens who attended the same school and were familiar with each other. This group was "very animated, vocal and forthcoming" (MediaWatch, 2000, p. 3). The 13-14 year old Burnaby group, however, were less familiar with each other and attended a secondary school that is the largest in Canada. These tweens live in an economically disadvantaged area and were "very reserved, self-conscious and cautious" (MediaWatch, 2000, p. 3). Respondents from both Toronto groups attended a school for the arts and were selected as "potential leaders among their peers" (MediaWatch, 2000, p. ii). Although there appeared to be very little difference between the 11-12 year old and 13-14 year-old Toronto groups, the 13-14 year olds demonstrated better overall communication skills and knowledge of social issues.

The research team consisted of specialists from a wide variety of sectors, including academic, market research, and health and social services professionals. MediaWatch's Executive Director and project lead, Melanie Cishecki, brought over ten years of experience in qualitative research to the project, as well as her experience working with youth. The content and format of the sessions were developed by The Health Communication Unit (THCU) at the University of Toronto's Centre for Health Promotion. A counselor from an eating disorder center in Toronto moderated the sessions.

Prior to the first focus group session, tweens were asked to collect images from the media that caught their attention. During the first session, tweens were asked to comment on the images they brought in and on their experiences with media literacy and social action. Tweens were also asked to record their thoughts in a media journal during the four-week interval between sessions.

The discussion of the first session influenced the development of the discussion for the next session (MediaWatch, 2000, p. 4). Specifically, the research team identified several issues that required more exploration, including "positive" and "negative" images and their perceived effect(s); social action options; suggestions for resource design and development; and evaluation of public service announcements (MediaWatch, 2000, p. 4). These issues were discussed by tweens during the second focus group session. Participants were also asked to submit their media journals at the conclusion of the second session.

Transcripts from the focus group sessions and content of media journals were then analyzed by the research team and categorized into five major themes with additional subthemes: media consumption, media influence, media literacy, suggestions for resource development, and any additional issues brought forth by tween respondents (MediaWatch, 2000, p. 4). A final report, entitled *"Media Environment: Analyzing the 'Tween' Market,"* was subsequently published by the Centre for Health Promotion at the University of Toronto in May 2000.

HEARING WHAT WE THINK: MEDIA EDUCATION STRATEGIES AND TWEEN AGENCY

One of the major lessons that can be drawn from the MediaWatch study involves the critical thinking skills and agency of tweens. A large body of literature produced during the 1980s and 1990s saw girls as particularly vulnerable to media messages—young women, it was assumed, do not have the critical capacity to resist or challenge negative media messages. In fact, literature on the impact of negative media messages on girls focused almost exclusively on *content* analysis, whereas the process by which girls interpret, appropriate, and/or resist media messages was largely ignored (see Duffy & Gotcher, 1996; Hesse-Biber, 1996; Parker et al., 1995, for example).

A good example of this can be found in Duffy and Gotcher's (1996) in-depth analysis of the teen magazine *YM*. Using symbolic convergence theory, Duffy and Gotcher demonstrate how teen magazines reinforce stereotypical notions of femininity through the creation of a shared "rhetorical community" among young female readers (1996, p. 36). However, central to their thesis is the notion that girls are being manipulated without their knowledge: "the editors cynically exploit young women's intense desire for belonging, connection, and answers to puzzling life questions with a caricature of friendship. This is the ersatz affection of a salesperson whose devotion is fuelled only by the desire to sell" (Duffy & Gotcher, 1996, p. 43). Furthermore, any express use of cosmetics or other beauty products by girls is ample proof that they have been "unwittingly duped." As they conclude: "exposure results in [girls] incrementally forming new attitudes or reinforcing existing attitudes *without being aware* of having been persuaded" (p. 45, my emphasis).

Far from being "duped" by media advertisers, however, tween respondents in the MediaWatch study were well aware of the bottom line of media advertisements, and, moreover, exhibited excellent critical thinking skills and media savvy. As noted in the report, "the variety, quantity and depth of comments clearly reveal the desire and ability of tweens to critically analyze the messages that surround them" (MediaWatch, 2000, p. 10). Many of the respondents, particularly those in the 13-14 year old group, were able to identify contradictory messages in advertisements and expressed skepticism regarding proposed product results. As one tween noted:

> I think that when you are reading a magazine, it's just one contradiction over another, because you're reading it and they're going "you should accept yourself and everyone's beautiful" and then you turn the page and [they're showing] all these models with gorgeous, skinny bodies and stuff, and then you turn the page again and they're showing food ads.
>
> *Toronto respondent, 13-14 age group*

Similarly, tweens in the 11-12 year old group spoke passionately about the "false advertising" of cigarette ads, arguing that advertisers misrepresent the reality of smoking as a health and environmental hazard. One participant, for example, noted the "irony of placing a nature backdrop on a tobacco advertisement and cited the number of cigarette butts that would ruin this type of scenery" (MediaWatch, 2000, p. 10).

Tweens were also aware of the negative impact of sexist media representations on girls' self-esteem and body image. Stories of eating disorders among their families and friends were brought up by several tweens during the sessions. Respondents were critical of ads for weight loss and cosmetic surgery aimed at their age group and recognized the pressures associated with these advertisements. As one respondent commented about the use of a 12-year old model in a dieting ad, "I don't think it is positive, because they are trying to make you worry about yourself . . . it makes [girls] feel self-conscious" (Burnaby respondent, 11-12 age group). A similar response to weight loss ads was expressed by another tween: "You are not supposed to diet when you are that young, because you are still growing. [The ad] is preying on the fact that . . . we apparently haven't found ourselves yet, like, we are still changing and everything . . . just to make money" (Toronto respondent, 13-14 age group).

MEDIA LITERACY INITIATIVES

The notion of girls as passive victims of media manipulation was subsequently taken up by media literacy initiatives in the 1980s and 1990s. The focus of media literacy training, for example, revolved around teaching girls how to read media messages, identify stereotypes and recognize the persuasive intent of media producers. Given the critical thinking skills and media savvy demonstrated by girls in this age group, it is not surprising that tween respondents in the MediaWatch study were wary of attempts to educate them. Presentations by media "experts" for example, were described as frustrating for tweens, who felt both silenced and unable to relate to the often didactic, top-down approach utilized:

> Do you want to know why we hate it when guest speakers come? Because we are not allowed to say what we think. . . .
>
> Ya, you have to agree with them. . . .
>
> Like, they don't want to hear what we think. Like, the teachers are there and if you say that their ideas are bad . . . you get in trouble.
>
> *Burnaby respondents, 11-12 age group*

> If you have an older person come in and talk about something that never really affected them in their lives, coming in and telling you how it would affect you . . . I always think, "if you can't relate to us, then who are you to come and tell us what to do?'"
>
> *Toronto respondent, 13-14 age group*

Tweens were also critical of media education strategies that singled them out as girls. As one respondent commented: "There is so much stuff for girls. . . . Like, I am not saying that it's bad or anything. That is great. But why don't guys have any stuff like that? Why don't they say, like, 'you need help with your self-esteem?'" (Burnaby respondent, 11-12 age group).

During the second focus group session, tweens were asked how they would design a more effective resource aimed at their age group. By far, tweens favored peer-to-peer strategies where, for example, stories of kids their age who had overcome obstacles would be shared and discussed. Other guidelines suggested by tweens included ensuring confidentiality, welcoming all opinions, and involving people their own age in resource development and delivery (MediaWatch, 2000, p. 17). As one tween described: "I think what we can do is, like, what we are doing right now, talking about [our experiences]" (Toronto respondent, 11-12 age group). This type of discursive space—where tweens can discuss, engage, and share opinions and experiences—was clearly lacking in the lives of tween respondents, who not only felt silenced by media literacy experts within their schools, but who also reported a lack of venues to discuss media messages with family or friends (MediaWatch, 2000, p. iii). The MediaWatch findings therefore draw attention to the need for media education strategies that not only recognize tweens' agency, but provide opportunities for young women to discuss, share opinions and experiences, and develop their own strategies for resistance and resiliency.

BUT I STILL SUBSCRIBE: UNDERSTANDING AND CHALLENGING MEDIA EFFECTS

> I flip the glossy pages looking at beautiful women. People I want to be. I learn make-up tips and read articles all judging me, telling me who I am, who I want to be. I'm angry and depressed as I close the magazine and place it by my side. I hate it. I never hated anything more. But I still read it. I still subscribe.
>
> *Excerpt from media journal entry,*
> *Toronto respondent, 14-years old*

Although the MediaWatch study found that tweens are active consumers of media who possess excellent critical thinking skills and media savvy, the study also confirmed that sexist media representations have a profoundly negative effect on the self-esteem and body image of girls. As noted by the researchers, tweens "readily acknowledge that the most common images of women in the media are unrealistic and unhealthy. However, this understanding has not prevented them from criticizing themselves in light of the images they condemn" (MediaWatch, 2000, p. 21).

During the first session, for example, tweens were encouraged to discuss images from the media that they had collected or taken note of prior to the session, as well as a selection of images provided by the research team. As indicated previously, tweens were critical of media images that featured unhealthy representations of women. One tween noted, for example, the problematic use of anorexic models on Fashion TV: "You look at the girls and they are so skinny . . . and they don't look healthy. It is only their ribs. Like, they have no stomach . . . are they trying to make them look like hangers?" (Toronto respondent, 11-12 age group). The ability to identify negative representations, however, did not prevent tweens from comparing themselves unfavorably to images of beauty portrayed in the media. A respondent from the Burnaby group, for example, explained how girls often feel when confronted by super-thin models in fashion ads: "Girls [our age] are like, OK, that is a tight shirt, like that is going to look good on me! (sarcastic). It looks good on her; she is really a hot looking babe" (Burnaby respondent, 11-12 age group). Similarly, a Toronto tween describes her own feelings of lowered self-confidence: "You see that there are all these other girls, tall and skinny and gorgeous. And I look at myself, and I am going, you know, I'm really self-conscious about myself" (Toronto respondent, 13-14 age group).

The cultural mandate to be beautiful, as portrayed in the media, was further reinforced by parents, teachers, and peers. This "combined influence" has been well documented, in fact, by a number of studies examining adolescent self-esteem and body image (see Dunkley et al., 2001; Currie, 1999, for example). As students in a school for the arts, respondents from the Toronto groups brought forth numerous examples of the pressures exerted by teachers, coaches, and parents to maintain an ideal body type:

> Her [skating] coach kept telling her that she needed to lose weight in order to get like, double or triple jumps. . . . She had to go to the hospital and it was really bad.
>
> *Toronto respondent, 11-12 age group*

> They have to stick to that diet, and if they don't, they get kicked out. [The modeling school] is saying "no, you have to be skinny."
>
> *Toronto respondent, 13-14 age group*

> Even the [ballet] teacher is encouraging you to lose weight, and that was really unhealthy.
>
> *Toronto respondent, 11-12 age group*

Tweens from the Burnaby groups detailed the pressures they faced with respect to their male peers. Respondents described how, for instance, male students would hang sexually provocative images of women in their school lockers and regularly comment on the physical attributes of the models. As one tween explained:

> Guys look at the singers and stuff and go "ooh, she's so hot, I like the
> way she is dressed" and all that, "it shows her boobs" and everything.
>
> *Burnaby respondent, 13-14 age group*

This in turn made some tweens feel added pressure to change their own
appearance:

> The more guys who have [models] up on their locker or whatever; you
> try to be like that, eh . . . (Another) if girls want guys then they try to
> be like that . . . they want to look like [the models in the ads].
>
> *Burnaby respondent, 13-14 age group*

No doubt, the everyday experiences of girls as they interacted with teachers, parents, and peers reinforced the notion that although standards of
feminine beauty portrayed in the media may be unrealistic, "the cultural
mandate to be beautiful conveyed by these texts is real" (Currie, 1999, p.
245). This complexity is observed by a tween in the following quote:
"People may not say it outright, that people should be skinny, but that is
what they think, because that's what stereotype is shown" (Toronto
respondent, 13-14 age group).

It is not surprising, then, that the large majority of tweens expressed
feelings of dissatisfaction with their body shape, weight, or with specific
parts of their bodies such as thighs, breasts, nose or stomach (MediaWatch,
2000, p. 8). This "self-critical view of the body" has also been documented
in other studies (see Currie, 1999; Thompson & Hirschman, 1995, for
example). In many cases, comments about bodily dissatisfaction were
made without reference to media influence or any other influences
(MediaWatch, 2000, p. 8). Rather, the desire for a more ideal body, as
exemplified in the following statements, often formed the subtext of larger group discussions:

> I don't like my stomach, and I always wanted to lose it.
>
> *Burnaby respondent, 13-14 age group*

> When I look at my legs and there is like, fat hanging off my knees, and
> I think "God, that is disgusting."
>
> *Toronto respondent, 13-14 age group*

> It's that part where you get pregnant, that part, that part is like, the big
> part on me. When I sit down I've always got to like, put my hands there
> or something.
>
> *Burnaby respondent, 13-14 age group*

> I want to tone my body . . . I don't want to be thin, I want to be muscular.
>
> *Toronto respondent, 13-14 age group*

The complex experiences and conflicted emotions of tweens, as identified by the MediaWatch study, indicate the need for a more nuanced understanding of media "effects"—one that takes into account the agency of tweens while situating tweens' experiences within the broader sociocultural context. Results of the MediaWatch study also caution against overestimating the power of critical viewing strategies. Rather, if media education is to have a truly significant impact on girls in this age group, it must move beyond content analysis to address the lived experiences of tweens.

How then can feminist theorists, activists, and media educators develop new paradigms for understanding and challenging media effects? In their 1995 study of consumer practices and self-conceptions, Thompson and Hirschman draw upon poststructuralist notions of power and subjectivity in order to provide a more nuanced account of media effects. For example, in their analysis of interviews with thirty consumers (male and female between the ages of 6 and 54), Thompson and Hirschman observe the same "self-critical view of the body" expressed by tweens in the MediaWatch study. In the following passage, an 18-year-old female provides a detailed inventory of the relative attractiveness of different parts of her body:

> I am pretty content with my hair because I have good hair. I have good eyesight (laughs) so I don't have to wear glasses or anything. . . . My hands are pretty square. I have a kind of a big butt. Then, I don't have that great of a stomach. I like my arms. They're not flabby, like you see a lot of people with flabby arms.

The self-critical view of the body observed in the study was not limited to young women, but was also exhibited by men and women across the age spectrum. In the following excerpt, for example, a 40-year old male respondent expresses dissatisfaction with an aging body:

> I don't know how to describe it, it's like, sort of over the sides of my hips. I feel like there's more flesh than there used to be, and I don't like it. So when I put on pants sometimes, can sort of feel that, you know, oh well, I don't really like that. And abdominal, you know, like the lower abdomen, it's just harder to kind of keep tight. (Thompson & Hirschman, 1995, p. 147)

Instead of positioning these findings as ample proof that consumers are (passive) victims of media manipulation, however, Thompson and Hirschman utilize a poststructuralist theoretical paradigm that takes into account the agency of consumers while situating consumer experiences within the larger sociocultural and historical contexts. The self-aware subject, Thompson and Hirschman explain, is "simultaneously *subject to* a multitude of sociocultural influences" (1995, p. 142). Thus, although consumers make choices and engage in activities based on individual needs, preferences, and personal desires, these behaviors are rendered "intelligible" through shared systems of cultural meaning. Furthermore, media advertisers and producers operate within the same sociocultural context and hence draw upon shared cultural beliefs, assumptions and normative values "in the search for novelty and the need to reach new markets" (Gallagher, 2000, p. 76).

In accounting for the self-critical view of the body expressed by consumers, therefore, Thompson and Hirschman demonstrate how mind/body dualism (a major structuring concept in Western thought) renders intelligible the notion of the "body" as a material object in need of constant surveillance, criticism, and maintenance. As they explain:

> For those socialized in a Western worldview, it seems self-evident that each of us has a "mind" (or an immaterial self) that is housed in a material body. This mind observes its body, critiques its appearance and form, and engages in activities—such as exercise, surgery, dieting—to transform the body into a more desired form. (Thompson & Hirschman, 1995, p. 139)

Concepts such as the "mind," "body," and "self," Thompson and Hirschman clarify, are viewed by poststructuralists as social constructions, rather than reflecting inherent characteristics of reality. The notion of the body as a material object has powerful currency within our consumer culture, where multibillion dollar cosmetic, diet, and fitness industries have an explicit body focus (Thompson & Hirschman, 1995, p. 139). Be it the "mind over matter" philosophy commonly espoused by diet and fitness industries, or the plethora of objectified, idealized bodies (and body parts) used in advertising, television, and magazines—all of these are salient illustrations of how concepts of the mind, body, and self are "formed, perpetuated and transformed through cultural discourses" (Thompson & Hirschman, 1995, p. 143). Thus, although tweens were critical of media images that portrayed super-thin models and instead preferred depictions of healthy, active women, what went largely unacknowledged was the underlying social/moral obligation to observe, critique, and engage in activities to improve the body-as-object.

The poststructuralist paradigm used by Thompson and Hirschman has further implications for media education as pedagogical practice. Instead of simply teaching girls how to read so-called "positive" and "negative" representations in the media, a poststructuralist approach to media education examines the deeply held cultural beliefs, assumptions, and normative values underlying surface representations, as well as the way that these beliefs are (or are not) taken up in our everyday practices. As such, the role of media education shifts from teaching tweens critical viewing skills towards providing discursive spaces where tweens can instead engage in critical cultural studies.

A good example of this pedagogical shift involves tweens' discussion of a popular ad campaign for milk that features celebrities with milk moustaches. During the focus group discussions, tweens expressed differing opinions about the perceived influence of this ad campaign. As one tween suggested about the use of celebrities in these ads: "Maybe you'll start to drink milk yourself because Britney Spears is also very pretty, you want to be like her, so you drink the milk" (Toronto respondent, 11-12 age group). Conversely, other tweens insisted that enjoyment of the ad had little influence over milk consumption: "If somebody doesn't like milk . . . because they might not think it tastes good, so [the ad] is not going to make them want to drink milk" (Toronto respondent, 11-12 age group). In either case, tweens' understanding of media "effects" involved the persuasive influence of the ad campaign on individual consumption patterns. In other words, to drink more milk because Britney drinks milk was to be "affected" by media; to base milk consumption on personal tastes was to stand unaffected. Furthermore, because milk is the product being advertised, any perceived influence is understood as positive: "I'm not saying that [milk advertising] is all that bad, because milk is good for you" (Toronto respondent, 13-14 age group).

A critical cultural studies approach to media education, however, would take as its point of analysis the very notion of milk as that which "does a body good" and the underlying cultural beliefs, assumptions, and normative values that render the notion of "good" foods (which can be freely consumed) and "bad" foods (which pollute the body) culturally intelligible (Thompson & Hirschman, 1995, p. 145). This social construction of "good" and "bad" foods, for example, becomes particularly apparent when examining the history of nutritional and medical discourses, which have, as Thompson and Hirschman document, been marked by "many reversals and changes in received opinion" (1995, p. 146). Within the context of media education, therefore, tweens would be encouraged to use media content as a starting point for examining competing discourses of health, nutrition, and medical science and the way "culturally sanctioned" knowledge claims are taken up and reinforced by media advertisers. The everyday practices and personal desires of tweens, who actively choose to consume or not to consume, would therefore be situated within a historically specific socio-cultural framework.

ADDRESSING PROBLEMATIC CORPORATE PRACTICES

Media education strategies developed in the 1980s have come under greater scrutiny in recent years for their failure to address the problematic practices being carried out by increasingly sophisticated corporations (see Gallagher, 2000; Klein, 2000, for example). As the girl power phenomenon of the 1990s demonstrated, today's corporate marketers are producing ads that not only adopt the same techniques as culture jammers (irony, mood, emotional nuance), but which also have the ability to "absorb, accommodate and even profit from content critiques" (Gallagher, 2000, p. 66; Klein, 2000, p. 292). In her ground-breaking work *No Logo*, Klein documents the blatant hypocrisy of corporate policies and practices behind closed doors. In 1998, for example, Nike developed a popular ad campaign, "If you let me play sports," which challenged discrimination on the basis of race and gender and formed part of Nike's new corporate mythology as a brand that embodies the very "spirit of sports" (Klein, 2000, p. 51). At the same time that Nike was profiting from the language and ideals of feminism and anti-racism, however, the company adopted a "brands, not products" philosophy that, as Klein documents, severely disempowered young female laborers in developing countries. "Although girls may indeed rule in North America," she notes, "they are still sweating in Asia and Latin America, making T-shirts with the 'Girls Rule' slogan on them and Nike running shoes that will finally let girls get into the game" (Klein, 2000, p. 123).

Tweens in the 13-14 year old Toronto group indicated some awareness of Nike's practices during focus group sessions. As one tween commented about Nike ads: "I felt like they were using people with disabilities and stuff in their ads, to make people want to buy it, but they're also using kids . . . children working for them in their factories and stuff. . . . I never, never buy anything [from Nike]" (Toronto respondent, 13-14 age group). The majority of tween participants, however, indicated little awareness of the problematic practices behind corporate advertising. This finding makes sense given the fact that for the system to function, laborers who produce goods must remain hidden from those who consume goods and vice versa (Klein, 2000, p. 347). Part of the task for media activists and educators, therefore, becomes "making visible those practices and realities that are routinely kept out of sight" (Gallagher, 2000, p. 69).

The "Brand Boomerang," for example, is a strategic tactic used by activists to expose the problematic corporate practices behind positive ads by bringing evidence of "the riches of the branded world" to goods-producers in developing countries, and evidence of "the squalor" of goods production to "blinkered consumers" in the West (Klein, 2000, p. 347). By making connections between the goods tweens consume, and the global, economic systems that underlie the production of those goods, tweens can bring a new level of analysis and resistance to their engagement with complex media messages.

A second problematic corporate practice that is particularly relevant here involves the "tremendously expanded role" that corporate advertisers are playing in our culture (Klein, 2000, p. 335). A 1997 study conducted with young adults in the United Kingdom, for example, found that although young people are active, sophisticated consumers of advertising, they frequently feel "unable to escape it" (Gallagher, 2000, p. 94). Klein documents a similar sentiment among Canadian university students who, in the late 1990s, suddenly discovered commercial advertisements in "every nook and cranny" of their campuses, including in public washrooms. As Klein describes: "The bathroom ads made it unmistakably clear to a generation of student activists that they don't need cooler, more progressive or more diverse ads—first and foremost, they need ads to shut up once in a while" (2000, p. 293).

What made 1990s branding different from previous attempts to market to students, however, was the increasing movement of marketing activities from private into public spaces. As Klein explains, 1990s-style branding seeks to take positive brand-associations "out of the representational realm and make them a lived reality" (2000, p. 29). In other words, the goal of 1990s branding is "not merely to have child actors drinking Coke in a TV commercial, but for students to brainstorm concepts for Coke's next ad campaign in English class" (2000, p. 29). The brand "invasion" of public space is particularly problematic, Klein points out, in its redefining of the traditional (and regulated) relationship between companies and consumers. "As more and more companies seek to be the one overarching brand under which we consume," Klein explains, "the entire concept of public space is being redefined . . . [and] options for unbranded alternatives, for open debate, criticism and uncensored art—for real choice—are facing new and ominous restrictions" (2000, p. 131).

So, for example, marketers have slowly begun moving into school curriculum by producing free curriculum kits that feature the brand's logo and include brand concepts within curriculum content. The Hostess Potato Chips "count your chips" math supplement, for example, challenges students to calculate the number of potato chips a person eats in a year, given the daily average (Clarke & Dopp, 2001, p. 40). Scholastic Inc. has also developed a limited number of "sponsored" curriculum materials for corporations such as AT&T, McDonald's and Chrysler (Clarke & Dopp, 2001, p. 41). Similarly, as cash-strapped schools look for new sources of revenue, the Canadian education system is witnessing a growing number of school-business partnerships, where corporations provide much needed funds and equipment in exchange for increased access to a captive youth audience (Clarke & Dopp, 2001, p. 40). One of the more widely-known partnerships is the Youth News Network (YNN), which offers schools an average of $150,000 worth of computer equipment, a television set for every classroom, a satellite dish, an internal distribution network, and a fully stocked computer lab, in exchange for direct access to students (Clarke & Dopp, 2001, p. 36). As part of the contract, schools must broadcast a daily 15-minute "news" show developed by YNN, which includes 2.5 minutes of commercials. In order to ensure a "return on investment," YNN has access to school attendance records that indicate the number of students who are present during "news" broadcasts, and, should the contract be terminated after a six-month trial period, the much-needed funds and equipment are promptly removed (Clarke & Dopp, 2001, p. 36). Although YNN has, to date, met with lukewarm reception in Canada, the more successful American version, Channel One, currently has access to 8.1 million students in the United States every day (Clarke & Dopp, 2001, p. 36).

The steady loss of unbranded spaces in our public education system is particularly troubling given the fact that, as indicated by the MediaWatch study, tweens already lack venues to discuss, engage, and develop their own strategies for resistance and resiliency. Part of the task of media activists and educators, therefore, involves providing and protecting nonbranded spaces (both virtual and real) within schools and local community contexts. Tweens must also be included in public discussion and debate around the increasing role of corporations in curriculum development and school funding partnerships. As Clarke and Dopp suggest: "There is no reason why high school students could not become involved in developing a set of guidelines or rules for governing school-business partnerships, [and] organizing campaigns to build support for such alternative rules among parents, teachers and the community at large" (2001, p. 137).

ONE LITTLE PERSON WHO DOESN'T WANT TO WATCH: SOCIAL ACTION STRATEGIES FOR TWEENS

Perhaps one of the most troubling findings of the MediaWatch study involves the feelings of disempowerment expressed by tweens in the face of media producers, advertisers, and decision makers. Media literacy initiatives developed in the 1980s sought to empower young people through social action strategies such as writing letters of complaint, boycotting products, creating ad spoofs (or culture jamming), and raising awareness about the harmful effects of sexism in the media (Gallagher, 2000). The MediaWatch study, however, indicated that 11-14 year old girls were well aware of strategies for social action. During the MediaWatch focus group sessions, for example, tweens were asked to brainstorm as a group "ways they could react to offensive media" (2000, p. 12). Despite having little or no formal media education, the tween respondents were able to catalogue an "impressive" list of strategies, including:

- Write to the company
- Tell store not to supply it
- Confront advertisers
- Petition
- Try to get more people to send letters/e-mails

- Boycott
- Ignore/change channel
- Form committee
- Don't buy there
- Get friends/family not to buy

- Protest/raise awareness
- Violent protest/ vandalism
- Realize it's not real
- Look away/throw it out
- Write article in flyer, magazine, newspaper

The study also found, however, that girls' ability to name a variety of strategies did not translate into social action. Part of tweens' reluctance to engage in social action involved the belief that as young people, they could not do anything about an image they were uncomfortable with, or, if they did take action, there would be no result (MediaWatch, 2000, p. 11). During focus group discussions in Burnaby, for example, tweens were critical of the sexualized portrayal of women wrestlers on television. However, when asked how they could respond, tweens felt their opinions would be ignored or disregarded by media producers, who are simply providing what the majority of viewers want to see: "That's why it's on TV, it's respectable, it got voted, or whatever, to go in" (Burnaby respondent, 13-14 age group). A more effective coping strategy, according to tweens, was to simply ignore offensive material—change the channel, turn it off, flip the page or throw it out. As one tween recommended: "close your eyes . . . there are like, one million people who want to watch that, and you are just one little person that doesn't want to watch" (Burnaby respondent, 11-12 age group).

But as the steady movement of marketers into school classrooms, textbooks, and even washrooms indicate, the corporate search for "brand ubiquity" is making it virtually impossible for young people to simply turn it off or change the channel. Moreover, far from being ignored or disregarded by media producers and advertisers, the opinions and preferences of tweens are being sought out as one of "the most effective wealth generators in our entertainment economy" (Klein, 2000, p. 261). All this while real live youth—young women working for less than subsistence wages in developing countries, for instance—are "being used to pioneer a new kind of disposable workforce" (Klein, 2000: 261). By bringing these complex corporate practices to the forefront, media education strategies can provide tweens with the raw material they need to develop new strategies for resistance and resiliency: strategies that address their concerns not solely as consumers, but as global citizens within an increasingly branded world.

SPRINGING UP A REVOLUTION

In *No Logo*, Klein describes how a growing number of youth activists—enraged by the colonization of youth culture and identity for profit, as well as the increasing impossibility of simply "turning off" or "ignoring" corporate influence—are leading an emerging international anti-corporate movement. A far cry from the girl power phenomenon of the 1990s, this youth-led movement is raising not a mall, but a revolution. It is, Klein describes, a "war of actions, not images . . . against the control that corporate power as a whole exerts over our spaces and choices" (2000, pp. 124, 189). This has involved developing new strategies for resistance and resiliency, strategies that address the interests of youth as global citizens in a rapidly changing world (Klein, 2000, p. 446). And, as options for unbranded alternatives become fewer and farther between, this anticorporate movement is slowly repositioning itself as more than just a resistance or "anti" movement. Rather, "if youth are going to take control over their economic, social, and ecological future" Clarke and Dopp explain, there is a need "to affirm as well as to resist . . . to anchor these actions in a vision of hope for the future" (2001, p. 136).

The implications of the MediaWatch study take on a greater significance for feminist theorists, activists, and media educators within the context of this emerging youth movement. Instead of simply teaching girls how to read critically or providing a list of consumer-based actions, today's media education strategies must go further to address the complex and contradictory experiences of tweens living in an increasingly branded world. This means recognizing tweens' agency and media savvy through peer-based approaches and venues for discussion and debate. It also involves engaging tweens in critical examination of the deeply held cultural beliefs and problematic corporate practices behind surface representations. But more than that, it involves the fundamental right to unbranded discursive spaces, both virtual and real, where young women can be free to exercise their imaginative capacities, develop viable alternatives, and take control of their political, social, and economic futures.

REFERENCES

Clarke, T., & Dopp, S. (2001). *Challenging McWorld*. Ottawa: Canadian Centre for Policy Alternatives.

Currie, D. H. (1999). *Girl talk: Adolescent magazines and their readers*. Toronto: University of Toronto Press.

Duffy, M., & Gotcher, J. M. (1996). Crucial advice on how to get the guy: The rhetorical vision of power and seduction in the teen magazine *YM*. *Journal of Communication Inquiry, 20*(1), 32–48.

Dunkley, T. L. et al. (2001). Examination of a model of multiple sociocultural influences on adolescent girls' body dissatisfaction and dietary restraint. *Adolescence, 36*(142), 265–279.

Gallagher, M. (2000). *Gender setting: New agendas for media monitoring and advocacy*. London: Zed Books.

Giese, R. (1998, February 14). 13 year-old girls rule the world. *The Toronto Star*, p. N1.

Global Television (2003, April 23). Too fast, too soon: Tweens on Global. 60 mins.

Hesse-Biber, S. (1996). *Am I thin enough yet? The cult of thinness and the commercialization of identity*. New York: Oxford University Press.

Klein, N. (2000). *No logo: Taking aim at the brand bullies*. Toronto: Vintage Canada.

MediaWatch Canada. (2000). *Media environment: Analyzing the "tween" market*. A Report by The Health Communication Unit (THCU) at the Centre for Health Promotion, University of Toronto.

Parker, S. et al. (1995). Body image and weight concerns among African American and white adolescent females: Difference that makes a difference. *Human Organization, 54*(2), 103–114.

Thompson, C. J., & Hirschman, E. C. (1995). Understanding the socialized body: A poststructuralist analysis of consumers' self-conceptions, body images, and self-care practices. *Journal of Consumer Research, 22*, 139–153.

8

MEDIA EDUCATION AND NEGOTIATING BODY IMAGE

Michelle A. Wolf

Kelly Briley

INTRODUCTION AND GENERAL FOCUS

For the past seven years, the first author of this chapter has been posing a series of discussion questions about mass media and body image to heterosexual, gay, lesbian, and transsexual men and women between the ages of 17 and 75. The questions stimulate in-depth exploration of how women and men of different sexual orientations perceive their own bodies, whether they see bodies like theirs and bodies they appreciate in mainstream mass media, and, ultimately, how media contribute to their developing sense of self-conception. The results of this research have been reported elsewhere (see, for example, Wolf, Decelle, & Nichols, 2003).

In this chapter, we explore the pedagogical strategies and outcomes of posing these questions to heterosexual women, ages 18 to 35, who were gathered in various settings in groups ranging in size from seven to roughly 100 (the larger groups included men). They were convened in college classrooms, focus groups, and on a three-day retreat that was videotaped and produced by the second author as a video documentary entitled, *Body Image: The Quest for Perfection.* This documentary has been part of the pedagogy in the classroom settings since January 2001.

We begin by describing the discussion questions and groups and explaining how the pedagogy varied across settings. This leads into a summary of the conceptual framework that guided our thinking and was explicitly (and only) presented to students in the lecture. We then contextualize our instruction as a media literacy effort, summarize and analyze the outcomes of our pedagogy, offer some general conclusions, and review the main limitations of this project.

DISCUSSION QUESTIONS, GROUPS, AND PEDAGOGY

The data and arguments advanced here come from a series of discussions with women who met in the San Francisco Bay Area over the past five years. They responded to the same general questions, grouped into the following four areas.

- Cultural and personal ideals: Based on your experiences as a media consumer, what are the common images of women's bodies in mass media in general? What are the common images of women's bodies in specific media forms/genres?
- Representation/exclusion: Have you seen your body represented in mass media? In what ways, if any, is your body excluded? What is not shown in media?
- Body image feelings: How do you feel about your body? Have your feelings affected (directed) your behavior and life choices? If so, in what ways?
- Sources of body image feelings: What do you think are some of the sources of your feelings about your body? Consider messages from media and other people.

Prompts for each area varied slightly in relation to group size and composition, duration of meeting time, and the environments in which the questions were posed. The most intensive setting was a three-day retreat that was videotaped and produced as a documentary.[1] Less intensive were two-hour focus groups and large lecture classes with female and male students. Because the discussions were natural and free-flowing, some additional prompts emerged in each setting. However, there were no significant deviations from the original questions.

The instructor began all three groups by sharing her personal experience with eating disorders, which dates back to anorexia nervosa beginning in 1971, a hospital stay, and several years of bulimia.[2] The goal here was to use personal experience to encourage a willingness on the part of the participants to self-disclose.

Women from the retreat responded to a notice that was posted online as a call for participants and tacked up as a flyer throughout the San Francisco Bay Area. Respondents completed written surveys with brief questions about demographics, caretakers and siblings, body image thoughts and feelings, and any history of counseling. The group was narrowed down to thirty-three women who were individually interviewed to ensure group diversity regarding ethnic background and self-conception issues/experiences. The final seven participants wrote in journals. At the retreat, they participated in various organized and spontaneous media literacy activities. For example, we brought magazines and asked them to find pictures of women who reflected their ideal body types and women they felt represented them. They also engaged in several noncontrolled group activities such as watching television, shopping for food, personal grooming, relaxing in a hot tub, and preparing for the day. The women were re-interviewed on videotape and via email after the group met. Several stayed in contact after the retreat.

Focus groups participants responded to the same announcements as the women at the retreat. They completed four-page, open-ended body image and media usage questionnaires and wrote two narratives, one on their feelings about their bodies and the other on their experiences with food.

The university lecture classes were offered every fall and spring and typically enrolled seventy to one hundred students. Classes met once a week for two hours and fifty minutes. The four-hour unit began during the second half of one class meeting and continued through the next full class. Again, the instructor began with her personal story, followed by a "participation" exercise in which the students wrote answers to the same set of general questions posed in the focus groups and at the retreat. Data from the three semesters were analyzed for this writing.

After the instructor shared her personal story and students completed the written participation exercise, the instructor introduced and initiated discussion of the theoretical framework and then showed the documentary produced at the retreat. The unit ended with a substantial in-class discussion about the documentary and the student's experiences with and responses to the issues covered. The prompt questions posed during the focus groups and at the retreat were woven into this discussion. Students were given an assignment to record and submit their personal responses to the unit after it ended and they were resurveyed in an optional e-mail assignment about six months after the semester ended. Students were also tested on the unit; despite the large group size, they wrote essay exams on the material. An important part of the pedagogy here was to steer students away from rote memorization and regurgitation of course material and towards a deeper level of thinking and analysis.

Prior to this unit and throughout the semester, students had weekly opportunities to complete other participation activities by writing personal responses to in-class and take-home assignments.[3] These grew out of a locator paper assigned at the first meeting that required students to explore and articulate the values, beliefs, and principles by which they live. Students wrote about social issues that concerned them and articulated their worldview and ideology as members of a series of increasingly larger sociocultural groups. These are important precursors to the body image unit because they reveal a level of personal engagement that is often overlooked in large classes. By the time the students were asked to write and talk about body image, they already had extensive practice using theories to probe and explain their thoughts about the electronically mediated world culture. The body image unit marked a transition in the semester in which students moved from considering broader cultural and political media issues to personally exploring their own self-conception in a world permeated by corporate-produced electronic media and popular culture.

CONCEPTUAL FRAMEWORK

Several theories form the conceptual basis of our pedagogy and serve as lenses through which individuals can analyze and begin to understand how mass-mediated pictures and ideas become internalized as forces that contribute to self-conception. Although these frameworks were used to develop the questions posed to all participants, they were only explicitly incorporated in the classroom instruction.

This research proceeds from the assumption that reality and self-conception are subjective, constructive social processes shaped by human and electronically mediated communication. Self-conception is influenced not only by other people, but also by what Walter Lippmann (1922) refers to as "pictures in our heads," the "medium of fictions" that frame how we adjust to our environment (Kielwasser & Wolf, 1992, p. 352). As memories, these pictures are implicated in our self-conception (Kielwasser & Wolf, 1992; Wolf, Decelle, & Nichols, 2003) and in how we construct our personal and social realities. George Gerbner and his colleagues (2002) argue that mainstream media play an especially significant role in shaping the social realities of heavy media users, characterizing the process as one of *cultivation*. Media tell us the same stories over and over and over again, cultivating common images and bringing diverse individuals into shared ways of thinking.

Our media literacy efforts were designed to encourage women to critically evaluate cultivated media representations by examining images of ideal and real bodies, how these images are presented in mass media, and the extent to which messages in media and communication with other people (who have been exposed to the same mediated images) contribute to the constructive, ongoing processes of self-conception. In the context of this cultivated imagery, we had another theoretical goal; to encourage critical thinking about the role of *social comparison* in the formation of the self-image (Festinger, 1954; Kalodner, 1997). This theory posits that we have a need to evaluate ourselves and that one way we do this is by comparing ourselves to others. Botta (2000) applies this framework to body image disturbance by asserting that "people will compare themselves and significant others to people and images whom they perceive to represent realistic, attainable goals" (p. 146) and "television viewers will compare their looks to television characters" (p. 147). Related to this were several questions designed to encourage the women to think about the impact of other people on their self-conception. We refer to this hereafter as *self conception through other*.

Finally, we wanted the women to more fully understand how their own specific and often very personal ideas about their bodies directed them to perceive mediated representations in distinctive ways. Here we worked from the *distinctiveness postulate*, which suggests that we pay stronger attention to stimuli that we see as different (distinctive) from our environment. Kielwasser and Wolf (1991, 1993/94) apply this to self-conception, arguing that when we see aspects of ourselves as different from other people, we pay special attention to those characteristics we believe make us unique. Several of our questions were designed to stimulate the women to think about how they scan their environment for pieces of recognition (and contradiction) and actively participate in framing their own body image against other women and the idealized bodies represented in mass media.

In the lectures, the instructor explained how to combine these perspectives:

> You enter a room and imagine how the people are seeing you (self-conception through other, social comparison). That shapes how you evaluate yourself. You also imagine that the people are seeing you not just through their eyes, but also through the colored lens of media (cultivation). Because you have a heightened sensitivity to certain

aspects of yourself (distinctiveness postulate), you suspect that other people do as well, so you think they are also focusing on what you believe makes you different (e.g., your flabby stomach). And since your self-conception is based on how you imagine they see you, now the media are implicated in your own self-conception.

This theoretical instruction is of special significance here. As we argue in the rest of this chapter, we believe that this component of our media literacy effort is the key factor that explains the more powerful and lasting impact of the classroom pedagogy in comparison to the others.

In all three settings, our pedagogy functions as a media literacy effort in which analysis and application are of special concern. Our definition of media literacy comes from the 1992 *Aspen Institute's National Leadership Council on Media Literacy Education*, where a group of scholars defined media literacy as "the ability of a citizen to access, analyze, evaluate and produce communication for specific outcomes" (Tyner, 1998, p. 120). A number of widely accepted media literacy principles are explicitly listed in the syllabus used in the lecture class described in this chapter. The body image pedagogy addresses four of these principles: (a) all media are constructions; (b) people construct unique meanings from media messages; (c) media messages are representations of social reality; and (d) media messages have economic, social, and aesthetic purposes. Specifically, women in all groups discussed a range of social, cultural, political, and economic forces that shape electronic media content. They contemplated some of the processes through which they individually and uniquely integrate electronic media into their daily lives and applied a critical sociological imagination to assessing the role of electronic media in the United States.

LEARNING OUTCOMES

Positive learning outcomes were evident across all groups, regardless of size and composition. Although women in the smaller groups had more time to discuss their ideas in more intimate settings, the classroom pedagogy offered students ample and more deeply analytical opportunities to explore their self-conception processes. We believe this is largely due to the explicit integration of theoretical material and the variety of discussion and feedback opportunities offered, including class discussions (in general and in response to the documentary), guided in-class and take-home writing assignments, and private e-mail communication with the instructor after the class and the following semester. With multiple outlets for expression, distinctive stimuli for discussion, and the introduction and application of theoretical lenses through which students came to *understand* their thoughts and feelings, the classroom pedagogy was a stronger stimulus for encouraging critical thinking, bolstering individuals' resilience, and enhancing positive identity formation and self-esteem.

Encouraging Critical Thinking

A central goal for each group was to encourage critical thinking about body image and self-conception. Although critical discussion was abundant in all three settings, students were more deeply analytical than the other participants, moving beyond discussion to more penetrating analysis and understanding. Our best explanation for this centers on the theoretical component of the classroom pedagogy. Although some theories were informally addressed in the other settings—for example in one of the focus groups the moderator mentioned the distinctiveness postulate when a comment about distinctiveness was made—it was only in the lectures that theories were specifically introduced. Theory was presented at the beginning of the body image unit in a lecture/discussion format and supplemented with a handout listing all relevant theories and explanations of each. The instructor made frequent and explicit references to these theories as students shared their thoughts and feelings about the documentary and their own processes of self-conception. Students embraced these frameworks as tools to move beyond discussion to explanation and understanding, and repeatedly noted a direct correlation between the theories they learned in class and their enhanced understanding of media's impact on themselves and their peers. As one woman wrote: "The theories we have gone over continually come up again and again in my life whenever I watch something on television."

Media Representation

The questions about *cultivated media imagery* encouraged all participants to critically evaluate self-conception and media representation. Women in each group described specific mass-mediated body parts that had become points of focus and held special interest for them. Together they lamented this situation. The value of theory became clear when we analyzed this first area of discussion and began to notice that students articulated and extended their thinking in ways that differed from women in the other two groups. The students moved beyond description to a deeper level of analysis and explanation. Whereas most participants described their fascination with the bodies, for example, in music videos, students also clarified things that they said they had not previously deconstructed on their own. Many reported knowing, for example, that they felt "jealous" of real and mediated women. The fact that they scanned *both* their real *and* mediated environments for the very same female body parts was not news to most of these women. Yet finding a way to explain this theoretically and having the opportunity to articulate explicitly how and why they used the unreal women of media as points of comparison were sobering for many. As media students, these women knew that media images are constructed, but they had not really thought through how media images get "inside" them. We did not see this happening in the other settings.

Women in all groups also critically evaluated recurring images of bodies and body parts and common underlying messages and values about ideal bodies in U.S. popular culture. They had implicitly learned what cultivation theory suggests and were acutely aware that narrowly defined images had been cultivated across media genres and forms. They described this variously, as when someone from the retreat spoke of "fat phobia," the ubiquitous media preference for thin women, and the general exclusion of positive images of large women and a full range of body types. Students dug deeper, as in this comment on how narrow media representations of women's bodies reflect a larger and more complex issue regarding cultivated media imagery: "It is obvious that the media focus primarily on the young, thin and Caucasian women. However, women are also portrayed as petty, ridiculous, cruel and somewhat stupid. If this is how we think of ourselves, it is difficult to not be self-critical. This criticism goes beyond our physical bodies."

Critical discussion of media aesthetics also pervaded the groups as participants noted, for example, how camera "tricks," filters, and editing devices are employed to challenge their insecurities. A student wrote: "I know not to compare myself to women in media because women in magazines get corrected and edited before the magazine gets published. Television uses camera tricks to make women look like the goddesses that they are." They recognized that understanding aesthetic devices did not necessarily deflate media impact. Many students spoke and wrote of the incongruity between cognition and affect, between what they *thought* versus what they *felt* about their bodies. For some the gap was painful. Students underscored the tensions here, as one woman wrote: "Even the people in the media who are held to be beautiful have been physically changed by editing and special effects. If this is true, then perhaps no woman in the world is beautiful by media standards."

Media Exclusion

Critical analysis of media imagery pervaded the discussions of media *exclusion*. Representation and exclusion of race raised significant concerns in all three settings, as the women criticized mainstream media for favoring Caucasian women over all other cultural groups. Agreeing that even ethnically diverse women are "watered down" and "whitewashed," participants criticized media makers for featuring Caucasian women who appropriate specific aspects of other cultures, for example braids, as far back as Bo Derek in the film *10*, and the more recent infatuation with collagen lips. An Asian-American focus group participant recalled an article in *Teen Magazine* "about what kind of eyeliner will make my eyes look rounder." When she read this as a teen, she saw it as a solution. Revisiting the memory in the group, she re-evaluated the article as racist and very offensive. Although the distinctiveness postulate was clearly operating here, it was not a point of instruction in this setting. In the lecture, however, where students did learn about this concept, an African-American student evaluated the mixed signals she receives from a community that appreciates her voluptuous curves and media that cultivate an unrealistic, thin ideal. For her, the negative effects of this exclusion undermined the positive reinforcement she received from some members of her community, leaving her feeling only "half acceptable."

Representation and exclusion questions also stimulated critical evaluation of the narrow range of "acceptable" body shapes and sizes. Many women expressed concern about the influence of narrowly *cultivated* media imagery on societal perceptions of body size and shape. Women in all three groups criticized media makers for casting "fat" women in unfavorable roles. A retreat participant described the common images: "They're either oafs, stupid, dumb, mothers, plain, cackling witches, or a background character. Never a lead. Never the romantic partner. Always the butt of the joke." Participants complained that writers and producers use "fat" as a plot device and not a human quality, as is clear from this woman's comment: "If they have a lot of excess fat, they're cast that way for a purpose. Say *Muriel's Wedding*, her weight was an issue. The main character [Kathy Bates] of *Fried Green Tomatoes*, her weight was an issue as well." She went on to argue that large women are "used" in media content because they are big; they are "non-women" because they are "fat." Many students acknowledged the effects of this representation on their own perceptions. As one man noted, "cultural influence in our country has taught me to find something wrong with overweight people."

We include this comment because it is worth noting that critical engagement pervaded the classrooms. In the only mixed gender setting, women reported great appreciation for the opportunity to discuss body image issues with their male peers. After viewing the documentary, nearly all of the men expressed sadness, along with greater empathy for and increased interest in women's struggles. One wrote: "I think I need to take a few women's studies classes. I don't know my female friends as well as I think I do." Men were fascinated by what they learned, commenting that the video and discussion helped deflate stereotypes they had about women and body image. Many men said the documentary and discussion made them question how they spoke to women about their bodies, for example: "I'm never going to give any female a hard time about her appearance again in my life. All these young girls and women are running around trying to change their bodies to conform to the social standard and it is just destructive and downright dangerous to their physical and mental well-being."

The men overwhelmingly agreed that the classroom unit offered them greater insight into their own self-conception and how messages from mass media and other people had impacted their lives. Several criticized the tendency to ascribe body image issues mainly to women, reporting that they struggled mightily with their own body self-acceptance. One student worried that because body image is more often presented as the domain of women, men might hide their own insecurities due to fear of emasculation. Many women were, in fact, surprised to discover that men in the class had real body image concerns not unlike their own. "I was surprised to see that they felt the relevance of the subject and [were] sympathetic because they also have insecurities about their own body images," wrote one woman.

Bolstering Resilience

Women in all three settings engaged in various forms of resisting the cultivated imagery of mass media. They despised the mediated "pictures in their heads" of what is and is not attractive in our culture. Students explicitly referred to Walter Lippmann's (1922) notion of this term to explain this situation. They agreed that media imagery affected their self-conception and assumed that others evaluated them at least in part through the colored lenses of mass media. Women in all three groups recognized what was for some a constant struggle to negotiate the gap between the idealized images they had constructed in their heads and their real bodies. Interestingly, especially in the face of their massive exposure to mass media, most of the women said they did not discuss these images or their body image feelings with other women because they were embarrassed and had to compete with other women, even their closest friends, to "get along" in the culture.

In the end, the women appreciated the opportunity to listen to and share their feelings with other women. A retreat participant captured this sentiment: "Whether we're from the same background, rich, poor, different races, whatever, there's this thing we have in common." This communal thread was liberating for many. Another retreat participant said: "It reaffirmed everything that I felt as a woman. Everything I've tried to discuss with my friends, my family, my boyfriend, questions within myself. I thought I was alone in what I thought. I thought 'are people really accepting the crap that they're dishing us?'" Interestingly, this woman initially assumed that cultivated media images had affected everyone but her. She was surprised and moved to find out that others had the same concerns, and that she, too, was profoundly impacted by media. After the retreat, she began to see a therapist to more deeply explore her self-conception issues. She recently completed a film entitled *Big Fat Deal* in which she explores what it means to grow up "fat" in a society that has so completely bought into the thin ideal.

Most of the women said they were uncomfortable discussing these issues on their own. It became clear to us that it was not terribly difficult for the women to participate in what we refer to as "descriptive" conversations about body image. With various measures of (dis)comfort and the careful selection of conversation partners, they could and did describe some of the things they "did to" their bodies. Yet these discussions were largely superficial; they touched on such things as a new hair dye, a preferred exercise regime, the purchase of a dress that hid the "bulges," or a subscription to the diet of the month. Another goal of our pedagogy—bolstering resilience—was realized as women in all three settings reported that they could begin to break this pattern of discomfort by moving from conversations about what they did to their bodies to explorations of how they felt about themselves and why they had these feelings. Their expressions made them feel vindicated and encouraged them to look deeply into their real lives and, as a woman from the lecture group put it, "see what she could do with them."

Thus, the impact of the lecture unit on body image moved out of the classroom. In the postlecture surveys, a great many women (and men) reported that they used the lecture content and the insights they gained from the theoretical material to initiate discussions with family members, partners, and friends. Many students explicitly stated that they wanted to, and did, share what they learned in class. As one woman attested: "I always revert back to your class. I find myself having to educate these people based on how you have educated me." Students appreciated the value of theory as a way to explain media impact. Another woman wrote: "It's only now that I am fully aware of myself, and my thought patterns, and how they are developing."

Although most students appreciated the opportunity to talk about these issues, some men and women reacted negatively to what one person described as an "obsession with body image." A few students said that thinking about body image was a luxury in a world full of starving people. One student wondered if spending energy on such issues takes away from more pressing social concerns. Although thoughts like these were welcomed and freely expressed in the classroom, many women were enormously disappointed to hear their classmates move the discussion from the personal to the more broadly political. These women were so relieved to have a forum in which to express their disappointment that they explicitly resisted efforts to diminish their feelings. As one woman put it: "I was very angered by the lack of compassion."

Noting that opportunities for such discussion were rare to nonexistent, most of the students argued that no woman could fully escape the feelings of inadequacy, competition, exclusion, and insecurity in our culture. One woman hypothesized that negative reactions to discussing body image might stem from embarrassment in the mixed gender classroom setting. We suspect that some students who were outwardly critical about the topic might have already possessed a healthy body image and therefore gained less personal insight from the body unit. Some students had such low self-esteem that they needed more guidance than a classroom unit could provide. In any case, the vast majority of students were grateful for the opportunity to explore the role of media in the development of self-conception.

Improving Self-Esteem

The women at the retreat agreed that the experience marked the start of a deeper exploration of self. Some students reported using the body image discussions and the documentary to launch unofficial support groups to continue what one woman described as a "catalyst for change." When the smaller group meetings came to a close, the women traded strategies for dealing with body image and self-conception. They spoke of the importance of community support and mentoring young girls and also offered some solutions: for example, teaching children about body image and media literacy; being less critical of other women; becoming more aware of how they feel manipulated by media imagery and other people; and trying to change media programming. These responses demonstrate the pedagogy's effectiveness in moving students beyond analysis and into (re)action.

For some participants, greater awareness of self-conception came with a price. Several women felt enlightened yet saddened by issues that arose and recognized that dealing with new insights can be painful: "I think it's been very beneficial to see several different points of view, but at the same time, I think it's been very hard, because there has been the opening of a deep wound." Other women acknowledged that pain had surfaced but concluded that the discussions made them feel stronger and more capable of dealing with the onslaught of negative media imagery they faced on a daily basis. Students also appreciated that deeper critical thinking and understanding of the forces that shape self-conception do not necessarily bring immediate relief. In an e-mail message to the instructor, a woman disclosed how badly she felt about the impact of other people on her self-conception:

> I continue to crave validation from the outside. I find it difficult, if not impossible, not to feed off the perceptions of others. People only seem to tell you how great you look when you lose a noticeable amount of weight. They don't often tell you how great you look when you are packing a few extra pounds. This closely relates to the self-conception through other perspective and I am afraid this is the theory to which I fall most victim. It seems synchronous with my overall need for validation from outside sources.

CONCLUSIONS

Throughout this chapter we have explored the pedagogical strategies and outcomes of posing a series of discussion questions about mass media and body image to heterosexual women gathered in various settings in groups of different sizes. Here, we summarize the major results of these strategies, offer recommendations for others who engage in similar media literacy efforts, and review the limitations of this research.

The pedagogy explored here varied across several dimensions. As previously stated, the settings differed in terms of size, composition, duration of meeting time, and the texture of the environment. Although the questions were consistent across settings, women at the retreat had substantially more time for discussion and reflection. They also developed intimate relationships as they engaged in their daily routines and personal interactions.

Women in the focus groups felt relaxed and comfortable and spoke freely about very personal thoughts and feelings that many had never shared before. The large, mixed gender setting restricted the amount and intensity of personal interaction so that relative to the class size, a small percentage of the women actually spoke aloud. Although the classroom was less personal, students learned how to use theories to deeply analyze the links between body image, mass media, and their own processes of self-conception. The fact that they were tested on this material reinforced their understanding in a more formal way.

Thus, group size and context affected the quantity and quality of individual expression. Although the smaller groups allowed for more active and personal participation, the classroom discussions were nevertheless effective and powerful stimuli for self-reflection and expression, though not necessarily in the form of talk. Those students who did speak were surprisingly forthcoming in the lecture environment, and their e-mail communication with the instructor was quite intimate. Although it would make

sense to assume that a large classroom would discourage personal participation, the pedagogy described here is uniquely designed to challenge this
assumption. In a published analysis of the teaching strategies employed in
this class, Glenn (2002) argues that Wolf achieves a level of critical student
engagement that is much more common in smaller and typically "safer" settings, attributing this in part to a pedagogy that encourages her students to
feel secure as they critically engage with the course content.

We believe the discussions reported here can be successfully conducted in different environments for educational purposes. In fact, perhaps the
most interesting conclusion is that the pedagogy was most potent in the
lecture settings. We believe this occurred for three main reasons. First, the
classroom instruction began with an overview of conceptual frameworks
through which the students could and did make sense of their learning
experiences. Second, classrooms were the only settings where the documentary was used as an instructional tool. Seeing and hearing other women
discuss body image and self-conception experiences helped students to
focus their thoughts and feelings and to use the experiences of other people as stimuli for their own self-expression. Comments that began as
responses to the documentary became increasingly more personalized as
the postviewing discussion and writing assignments progressed. Third, the
participation activities encouraged critical thinking and gave students a
chance to think independently and to continue this thinking outside of the
classroom. The fact that they were surveyed about their thoughts and feelings after the class had ended suggested to several students (based on comments they made and notes that accompanied the second e-mail survey)
that this sort of continuation of thought matters and, perhaps more important, that what *they* think matters.

RECOMMENDATIONS

It should be clear by now that we believe that our body image media education program has helped many women think more critically about, and
in some cases resist, mainstream mediated representations of the female
body. We have ample evidence to support the argument that our pedagogy
encourages critical thinking, and we have offered a number of explanations
for why we believe this played out differently across the three groups. To
varying degrees women in all of the groups reported that our pedagogy
helped them to think more critically about body image, to develop strategies to resist media imagery, and to feel better about themselves. Given
this, we offer the following recommendations for those who engage in similar media literacy efforts.

- *Create an atmosphere of intimacy.* Although this is more difficult to achieve with a large group, it is still very important when a course is framed around problematic media representations, identity construction, and such sensitive content areas as gender, race, sexuality, age, (dis)ability, and, as elaborated in this chapter, body image. This challenges the instructor for obvious reasons. The lecture environment is by its very nature impersonal; for example, students are typically unknown to the instructor, their learning is commonly assessed through quantitative measures, and they are more likely to cut classes. Establishing intimacy against such odds clearly requires a significant instructional effort.
- *Model the kind of introspection desired and offer follow-up opportunities for application.* There are many ways to encourage participants to open up. The documentary, for example, allows students to respond to experiences of other women before personalizing the material. The discussion questions from the video's study guide help instructors to facilitate increasingly inward thinking. When facilitators share personal experiences, they also model emotional literacy, an important component of media literacy.
- *Integrate theory.* Students used the theories described here to name, normalize, and make sense of their life experiences. Develop an array of assignments that allow participants to use theory in different ways. When possible, use assignments that call for writing, probing, and self-disclosure.
- *Encourage critical engagement.* In the end, a central goal of this pedagogy is to find ways to encourage participants to engage critically with the material. This is of utmost importance. As Glenn (2002, closing thoughts, pp. 11-12) concludes:

> Dr. Wolf's intentional and risky stimulation of her students through explicit cultural critiques and controversial media choices, open and honest self-disclosure, and spontaneous, provocative participation assignments all promoted critical engagement in diverse and particularized ways in her classroom. Likewise, her students' understanding of, and responses to, her intentions and approach seems to indicate that the performance of critical rhetoric, on the part of teachers, offers an alternative to privileging student dialogue while maintaining the ability to nurture students' critical consciousness development. Contrary to critical pedagogy literature that assumes learner-centered dialogue is the key to critical consciousness development, this study seems to suggest alternative, unique aspects of critical engagement in a large class that does not lend itself to critical discussion.

LIMITATIONS

This chapter would be incomplete without some discussion of the limitations of the arguments advanced here. We do not see all the points that follow as drawbacks, yet they are certainly worthy of consideration for those who develop media literacy programs and incorporate ideas presented here.

To begin, we have not assessed the long-term impact of the instruction. Because the classroom responses and retreat follow-up questions were voluntary, this participation was self-selected and included only a subset of the original groups. Nevertheless, the response rate was quite high, as more than half the students wrote something, all the women in the retreat participated in videotaped interviews, and most of the women in the focus group responded to e-mail communication. The women from the retreat and focus groups were also self-selected and thus already interested in the project and thinking about the issues we discussed. Also, at the retreat, the videotaping and the women's awareness that they would be featured in a documentary surely affected the nature and unfolding of self-disclosure. We do not assume the women held back in significant ways; nonetheless, we must allow for this possibility.

In addition to the constraints of the lecture setting itself, the presence of men in the classroom is likely to have discouraged some women from talking. Because the more significant disclosure occurred out of the classroom in personal written communication with the instructor, we do not see this as a major drawback. It is nevertheless a point to acknowledge. Notably, many women appreciated that men saw the documentary and gained some insight into the female body image experience through the video and class discussion.

It is worth mentioning again that because part of the students' course grade was based on written participation, the e-mail responses carried a reward. Because students had many options for such activity, feedback on this particular subject was not necessary to earn the maximum participation points allowed in this class.

We also made some assumptions about depth of understanding based on limited data in any given class. The arguments advanced here, however, should be considered within the broader context of Wolf having taught this and other mass communication theory classes for almost twenty five years to groups of students ranging in size from five (graduate seminars) to over 650.

In closing, we want to make one final point. Understanding how media images get inside our heads does not free us from the corporate media culture or its impact. The development of self-conception in the face of media imagery is a complicated and lifelong process. Media literacy is more than deconstructing and analyzing media images, and being media literate is not a pass to override culture and find liberation from its clutches. We are very concerned about the obsession in U.S. culture with how we look, and therefore strongly support media education pedagogies that teach emotional literacy and provide people with the tools to deconstruct not only their external, but also their internal environments.

NOTES

1. The main documentary objectives were twofold. A primary goal was to stimulate in-depth discussions of media-cultural-personal body image ideals, media representation (and exclusion), feelings about body image and the sources of these feelings. A secondary objective was to produce greater awareness of the forces that shape self-conception in general and body image in particular. A viewing guide with classroom discussion questions and activities was developed to assist teachers who use the documentary as a media literacy tool (see http://www.bodyimagesite.com) and want to stimulate student thinking on self-conception in general and body image in particular. Because the same questions posed in the classroom and smaller group settings were used to frame the documentary, it has helped us in our ongoing re-assessment of the value of these discussion questions for encouraging women (and men) to explore and come to understand how they negotiate their body images in the face of consonant and disparate messages from mass media and other people.
2. We use the term "instructor" throughout to refer to the focus group facilitator and the instructor of the lecture class. This is also the first author of this chapter.
3. For a lengthy analysis of the pedagogy employed in this classroom see Glenn's (2002) published case study of Dr. Wolf's class.

REFERENCES

Botta, R. E. (2000). The mirror of television: A comparison of black and white adolescents' body image. *Journal of Communication, 50*(3), 144–159.

Briley, K. (Producer), & Khani, H. (Director). (2000) *Body image: The quest for perfection* [Videotape]. http://www.bodyimagesite.com

Festinger, L. (1954). A theory of social comparison processes. *Human Relations, 7*, 117–140.

Gerbner, G., Gross, L., Morgan, M., Signorielli, N., & Shanahan, J. (2002). Growing up with television: The cultivation perspective. In J. Bryant & D. Zillmann (Eds.), *Media effects: Advances in theory and research* (2nd ed., pp. 43–67). Hillsdale, NJ: Erlbaum.

Glenn, C. B. (2002). Critical rhetoric and pedagogy: (Re)considering student-centered dialogue 1. *Radical Pedagogy, 4*(1). Retrieved March 10, 2003, from http://radicalpedagogy.icaap.org/content/issue4_1/02_Glenn.html

Kalodner, C. R. (1997). Media influences on male and female non-eating-disordered college students: A significant issue. *Eating Disorders, 5*(1), 47–57.

Kielwasser, A. P.,. & Wolf, M. A. (1991, Feb.). *The sound (and sight) of silence: Notes on television and the communication ecology of adolescent homosexuality.* Paper presented to the Annual Conference of the Western States Communication Association, Phoenix, AZ. (ERIC Document Reproduction Service No. ED 332 242)

Kielwasser, A. P., & Wolf, M. A. (1992). Mainstream television, Adolescent homosexuality, and significant silence. *Critical Studies in Mass Communication, 9*(4), 350–373.

Kielwasser, A. P., & Wolf, M. A. (1993/1994). Silence, differentiation, and annihilation: Understanding the impact of mediated heterosexism on high school students. *The High School Journal, 77*(1 & 2), 58–79.

Lippmann W. (1922). *Public opinion.* New York: Macmillan.

Tyner, K. (1998). *Literacy in a digital world: Teaching and learning in the age of information.* Mahwah, NJ: Erlbaum.

Wolf, M. A., Decelle, D., & Nichols, S. (2003). Body image, mass media, self-concept. In R. A. Lind (Ed.), *Race/gender/media: Considering diversity across audiences, content and producers* (pp. 36-44). Boston: Allyn & Bacon.

Wolf, M. A., Nichols, S., & Decelle, D. (1997, Feb.). *Television, body, self: How women (18 to 33 years) of different sexual orientations relate to television's construction of body.* Paper presented to the annual conference of the Western States Communication Association, Monterey, CA.

9

MEDIA, TEENS AND IDENTITY

Critical Reading and Composing in a Video

Monica Pombo

David Bruce

This chapter chronicles the story of a four-month qualitative research project aimed at documenting the role of critical pedagogy[1] in media studies and video production classes. The collaboration took place between researcher Monica Pombo and teacher David Bruce, and the process involved is described from both of our perspectives. Together, we discuss a classroom-based research project in which students studying media literacy completed exercises exploring their identities through journal and video composition. The chapter concludes by reflecting on the project results and implications, as well as our own collaborative work.

SETTING UP THE PROJECT (MONICA)

The research project involved observing a critical pedagogy teacher in the classroom who would have students create a media journal, detailing their media and the video production processes. Ethnographic fieldwork in David's classroom took place over a period of four months during which I visited the classroom once a week, for a total of twelve trips.[2] As a researcher, I was conscious of my bias toward critical pedagogy, because I practiced it in my own classroom. My teaching practice was informed not only by critical pedagogy writers such as Giroux (1997), McLaren (1994), and Freire (1970), but also by authors who have critiqued the critical pedagogy approach, including Ellsworth (1989), Fine (1993), and Buckingham (1998). Despite my background, I did my best to conduct the fieldwork in the classroom without preconceptions about how critical pedagogy should be practiced or what outcomes I would find in students' journals and their identity videos.

THE PROJECT: STUDENTS' VIDEOS
AND IDENTITY (MONICA)

On my initial visit, I told David the research would involve three aspects. First, I would observe the class. Second, I would collect student artifacts, particularly media journals detailing their production processes and media use as well as the identity videos they created. Third, I would interview both teacher and students during the process. The video production exercise was created so as to leave enough room for teacher creativity, allowing the teacher to demonstrate his or her pedagogy within the parameters of the exercise. The parameters required the videos to deal with students' identities. However, I left the design of the assignment, content, goals, and assessment to David.

Media journals were an integral part of the creation of identity videos, in that students responded to prompts that helped them reflect upon different parts of their identities, the production process and the media's impact on their everyday lives.

I left it to David to make the procedural decisions about the journal, such as students' decoration of the front cover of their notebook, the frequency in which students wrote in their journal, as well as the grading criteria for the videos and journals. All students involved in the research turned in their journals at the completion of the project.

SETTING UP THE CLASSROOM PROJECT (DAVID)

In order to effectively integrate the project that Monica and I had discussed, some of the materials and activities normally included in the semester had to be truncated to accommodate the production time that the students would need to complete their video projects. Nonetheless, before we got to the video production, I devoted considerable class time to journal writing, with topics such as: "What have you learned about yourself, others, and about your project after working with your initial footage?" Once the class had covered the course media literacy principles, students were assigned to create a video in which they would explain their understanding of one of the media principles. The guidelines for the video were: (a) pick a media principle that was of interest to them, (b) explain their understanding of the topic, and (c) demonstrate how their life interacted with that topic. Students included a confessional in which they explained to the viewer how they understood their chosen subject matter, as well as any connection they made between their selected topic and their own perceived identity. Students were instructed to work in groups of two or three. However, a few students who worked on topics that were of a more personal nature opted to work alone.

THEORETICAL FOUNDATIONS (MONICA)

My theoretical framework for this research was grounded by cultural studies theory. As such, my textual analyses of the students' identity videos were based on the work of cultural studies theorists who have written extensively on the issues of identity, media representation, and power. For example, Grossberg (1997) has explained that texts are not isolated and immutable structures. Instead, media texts are in relationship with viewers who become possible creators of media. Hall (1995) has written that ". . . positional identities are narratives, that they are stories we tell ourselves about ourselves" (p. 66). Thus, representations help guide us in how we interpret our subjective positioning in the world, and identity is partially formed by the relationship between how we see the world represented and how we represent others and ourselves. Hall (1980) has also shown how texts are negotiated by audiences, referring to three different levels of audiences' readings of media texts. One is the dominant/preferred reading, the second is a negotiated reading, and the third level is an oppositional reading. In this chapter, these different levels of readings will be connected to how students construct and deconstruct their identities in their videos.

THE PRACTICAL APPLICATION
OF A THEORETICAL MODEL
(DAVID)

In my classroom, I applied Scholes' (1985) concept of levels of reading to how I used media as texts in my classroom. Scholes argues that readers must first *submit* to a text before any other level of understanding can occur. Only after the submission occurs can possibilities for a second level (*interpretation*) of reading happen. Once they have read a number of the same type of texts, readers can move on to the third level of reading, which is *criticism*. With criticism, the reader makes comparative and qualitative judgments regarding the content of the work.

For example, in the first reading of a media text readers will *submit* to it by simply giving it their attention and reacting to it. Submission is the level where most students will naturally be, unless encouraged to read more deeply and widely. The *interpretive* level comes when they start to examine the elements that make up the media text, such as music, edits, camera work, graphics, and so forth. *Criticism* requires students to observe and question how those individual pieces were synergized to achieve the final product, as well as consider and question the cumulative effect those elements had on the viewer. In working with the students to read and create their videos we found that it took a lot of scaffolding to move them from a reading level of submission to criticism.

THE DILEMMA OF CRITICAL PEDAGOGY
(DAVID)

To teach critical pedagogy in the United States is a challenging prospect, essentially because it is considered "radical," and to be radical is controversial, tainted with the suspicion of militancy or extremism. However, studying only the dominant discourses circulating in the media denies students exposure to other valid and valuable layered perspectives. Thus, my main agenda through media literacy is to make students *aware* of perspectives that they might not otherwise have been exposed to, including some issues that might even be uncomfortable for them to consider. I also wanted to encourage students to *resist* those issues that they considered to be harmful to themselves or others. But how can a teacher committed to enlightening students and politicizing the mass media avoid cramming his own subjective beliefs down his students' throats? A fine line exists between inviting students to question things critically and telling them how to think about different issues. Are teachers who practice critical pedagogy also allowing for what Fine (1993) has described as the silencing of those students who disagree?

Also problematic for teachers who practice critical pedagogy is that relatively few opportunities exist in American society for individuals to critically examine mainstream culture, thereby nurturing and expanding the information gained from the classroom. So, the tensions created in a "critical classroom" are mitigated when students walk out of the class and into the barrage of unquestioned media messages within the larger culture.

MEDIA LITERACY PRINCIPLES (DAVID)

As a classroom teacher interested in the composition processes my students use while creating their videos, my biggest concern is that they take ownership of their work. Also, over the years, I have moved from a lecture/discussion format to a more project-oriented approach that allows them to explore the topics under discussion. As Buckingham (1998) states, such an approach "does not specify a set of facts to be learned, [and] identify particular objects of study" (p. 39). Thus, my curriculum is based on information from Bazalgette (1989), Meyrowitz (1998), and materials from the Media Literacy Resource Center in Cincinnati, Ohio. The thematic units are:

- *All media are constructions:* Media are deliberate creations and are carefully crafted, oftentimes by teams of people. Therefore, they do not just come together on their own.
- *All media construct reality:* All media products present a "reality," or a way of viewing the world. Different production techniques including the use of images, sounds, and edited sequences all contribute to the creation of that reality.
- *Audiences negotiate meaning from the media:* Audiences are not passive recipients of the media. They actively make meaning and form connections to other forms of knowledge. Although media consumption does not often engender reflective thought, meaning making is always occurring in the viewer.

- *Most media have commercial interests:* Most media are tied to economic concerns. Advertisements, sponsors, and multinational media companies have interconnected monetary affairs.
- *Media contain ideological and value messages:* Media messages are not innocuous. Rather, they transmit values and ideals, both overtly and covertly.
- *Media have social and political implications:* The dissemination of the mass media takes place in the public sphere and therefore reflects and promotes social and political ideas.

When Monica initially proposed her research project, we considered ways to accomplish her research goals within the context of my course framework, as I approach the six aspects of media literacy in a specific pattern. First, I spend the beginning of the class doing an activity illustrating the principle that we will be covering. Then, I introduce the media literacy principle, define any terms with which students might not be familiar, and explore how the activity was related to the principle. Lastly, I guide students through a few other illustrations of the media topic before assigning a separate activity designed for them to explore an aspect of the topic more fully.

For example, the first idea we studied is that *media are constructions.* In the introductory activity, I divided the class into groups and piled Legos onto their desks.[3] The only instruction was to "build something." They all assembled some sort of structure and when finished, each group shared what they had built. Oftentimes, students created goofy narratives and stories about their model. When all the groups were finished, I informed them that they had just demonstrated the first principle of our study, that media are constructions. Just as their Legos were carefully put together in some semblance of order, so too were the media they consume. Over the next several classes, we deconstructed several commercials, looking at their component pieces (such as camera angles, edits, special effects, graphics, and audio) to examine their constructedness.

To reinforce the principle of the constructed nature of media, their follow-up class assignment was to make a brief video essay. I assigned each production group an abstract topic such as "conformity," "success," or "happiness." These topics encouraged the students to think carefully about what kinds of images, sounds, and texts they could use to construct their video compositions. When viewing each others' work, it was the students who offered suggestions and critiques to their classmates about which images, sounds, and songs they might have included in their videos. This activity also served to teach rudimentary production techniques that were continually refined throughout the course.

Each topic covered in class followed the aforementioned pattern of introduction, explanation, and experimentation. Together, we were able to explore issues such as race, gender, economics, and identity construction.

PRACTICING CRITICAL PEDAGOGY
IN THE MEDIA LITERACY CLASSROOM (MONICA)

One of my research goals was to examine and evaluate what processes and practices were involved in teaching critical pedagogy in a video production and media studies classroom. My assessment is that David effectively used critical pedagogy to teach his students about media content and production and he emphasized the constructed nature of the media, its values and ideological content. He also explored students' lives as they related to issues of power (particularly gender and race) within society. Most importantly, however, he enabled a student-centered classroom whereby teacher and students share and challenge knowledge through dialogue.

David acknowledges that his pedagogy is informed by discourse theory and constructivism, or what I refer to as critical pedagogy, and he explains how this approach manifests itself in the classroom:

> The down side of the whole constructivist, negotiated classroom is that it is very messy and it makes for really difficult days. It is not predictable. You cannot chart it out. The return that comes out of this, though, is amazing. They will own it [the topic]. And in some way they will process their understanding and meaning of it. But only when you take that risk.

David also recognizes that teachers must relate to their students and that different topics will achieve different levels of engagement:

> Different things are going to be triggers for the student and it is getting them to be aware of that. If my class becomes a gigantic crusade to be strictly gender issues they will know that and filter me out. As opposed to the girl in 7th period, who is dealing with bulimia. Body image for her, I guarantee, is what she is going to filter in it. It will be great awareness and it would empower her.

Critical pedagogy involves honest conversation (called dialogue) and the building of a rapport with students. Dialogue, which has a life of its own, depends on students' backgrounds, who speaks, and what points of view are articulated. David, who is critical of lecture-format classrooms where teachers pour knowledge into students' heads and expect them to regurgitate it back to them, prefers to engage with students. He does this by making issues relevant to his students. Also, through dialogue in his class, not only does he ask his students to explain their answers, he also wants to

know *why* they feel a certain way. This process honors his students' experiences and validates their opinions and feelings.

David also invited his students to help co-create the curriculum and
encouraged his students to bring pleasurable media into the classroom.
Thus, for example, a student brought in some records to discuss satanic references in popular music. David, a Christian teacher very committed to his
spirituality, was not afraid to invite such challenging issues into his classroom, despite the risks involved in discussing topics such as satanic
imagery, subliminal messages, and the musicians' use of drugs and alcohol.
David admits that the risk becomes part of the excitement in relating to
students' personal lives. Doing so, he explains, acknowledges the complex
realities that exist in the lives and minds of contemporary youth. To him it
is therefore important not to polarize issues but to unravel the many layers of meaning and relate them to real-life experiences.

ASSESSING THE STUDENT JOURNALS
AND VIDEOS (MONICA)

Part of the class requirements involved students keeping a media journal in
which they responded to written prompts and class discussions. But to
begin, students were asked to create a collage on the front covers of their
journals with images and words, revealing aspects about themselves and
their identity. Of the nine covers created by young men, three contained
pictures of sexy young women in bikinis or sucking a lollipop. Other male
covers focused on cars, skateboarding, and movie stars. Most journals host-
ed mainstream images from the mass media, but many revealed a more
experiential side of students' lives and identities. For example, some had
photos of themselves at parties, images of cigarette smoking, and hard-
liquor advertising. In fact, images of alcohol (beer, whisky, and vodka)
appeared on four of the nine covers. Of the ten covers created by females,
six were composed of images taken from the mass media (i.e., movie stars,
movie posters, clothing and car ads, etc.) and three were composed solely
of images from their private lives. Many had group photos of themselves
with their friends and family and several photos showed young women
engaged in activities. Several shots showed them dressed up for special
occasions such as prom or Halloween. Finally, many of the girls placed their
zodiac signs on their covers.

To get a more layered textual analysis of the representative students'
identity videos it was helpful to analyze the front covers of their journals.
Many students showed within their texts different levels of awareness (and
often contradictions) in their understanding of the implications of their

chosen topics. For instance, they might know what sexism means while at the same time both adopting and challenging traditional gender role representations in their journals and videos. One female student, for example, demonstrated a desire to resist dominant cultural white female imagery, so her front cover showed pictures of young African-American women wearing designer dresses or tough, street-wise, hip-hop clothing. She explained in her journal entry: "I put strong independent women on the cover to symbolize my heroes and idols." Young men on her cover, however, followed more traditional representations of highly masculinized males. She also included affirming words and statements and phrases cut from magazines, including:

- Your hopes, your dreams
- Prove it
- On the edge
- Not every angel needs wings
- All the ways you play; at any given moment you are different—the way you look, feel, think, what you want to do
- Life is a journey and every woman travels her own road
- Each new day offers twenty four hours of possibility and moves you forward; laughter is one way to survive
- There's nothing like looking good, except maybe feeling good
- You and the strength you never knew you had

The content of the journals also demonstrated a high degree of self-reflection on the part of the students. Assigned entries were from one to two pages in length. Across gender lines and regardless of the quality of their videos, students tended to use their journal as a place where they felt it was safe to speak about themselves.[4] For example, in one journal entry, a female student described herself as relating to Ariel from the movie *Footloose* because both have strict dads "that control their every move." Also, when responding to the prompt *"What have you learned about yourself, others and about your project after working on your initial footage?,"* she answered, "I now know I am a strong, smart person and can do anything I want to . . . no one really knows how I feel and what I really care about it."

Students' videos were analyzed based on three criteria set by the teacher: (a) understanding and applying key media literacy concepts to their identity video; (b) articulating those concepts as they related to their identities; and (c) examining how students read and wrote media. This last one involved interpreting their videos through Hall's (1980) levels of reading media texts: the preferred, negotiated or oppositional reading. Almost all of the students (16) completed their video assignments and were able to articulate awareness of one of the six media literacy concepts studied in the classroom. Students tended to mostly detail the two concepts that focused on "all media construct reality" and "audiences negotiate meaning." Merging those key concepts with the notion of identity was relatively successful, as eight students connected key media concepts while also articulating aspects of their identities. Two projects demonstrated an oppositional reading involving the questioning of mainstream ideology.

Student work that involved resistance of dominant media texts created powerful pieces. One video made by Aidan and Seth, for example, contained a series of still images from hip-hop videos showing gender stances (mostly tough, masculine attitudes) portrayed within hip-hop culture.[5] It also highlighted consumer objects that reflected ideals within hip-hop culture such as cars, clothing, and accessories. The still images that opened the video also demonstrated the rewards of belonging to hip-hop culture in which males are surrounded by signifiers such as money and women.

Aidan and Seth's video was highly organized and included students performing raps in the high school cafeteria, students wearing hip-hop styles, brand name clothing, and accessories, the close link between tattoos and hip-hop culture (as documented by numerous examples of students having tattoos similar to their favorite hip-hop artists), and their friends using lingo and phrases found in hip-hop culture. In the conclusion, the producers reflected on the project, ruminating about how the media helped to construct the identities of themselves and their friends. Aidan and Seth understood, contemplated, and articulated the impact of consumer culture, the style it sells to their peers, as well as the media's impact on their sense of identify. By deconstructing media and by constructing their own videos, they were able to see the traces of power embedded in these representations. In interviews, they both understood that their identities were influenced by representations in dominant media images, but also pointed out that in producing the video they were limited in their ability to show the multiplicity and complexity of their own identities in the everyday life of their high school. For them, the school's culture was also a site that helped frame their identities within stereotypical characteristics and specific types such as the jock and nerd. As such, while consumer culture helped them build a one-dimensional character, the school culture reinforced those simplistic constructs.

LEARNING OUTCOMES
(DAVID)

At the completion of the course, Monica and I sat down to assess the outcomes of our collaborative project. Throughout the process, Monica interviewed me on various topics including my teaching philosophy, curriculum, assessment criteria, and classroom assignments. Those interviews had self-reflective moments for each of us, me in my teaching and Monica in her research of critical pedagogy. In our dialogues, we found clear successes from the classroom project while also recognizing shortcomings with it as well.

First of all, the students demonstrated a clear awareness of the media literacy principles taught, and by the end of the semester, I felt pleased that the students had a good working grasp of the foundational ideas we had studied together in class. Students not only identified the media themes, they also paraphrased those messages with their own words and examples. One group of girls explored "media and value messages" as their topic by recording several continuous hours of MTV and then analyzing the public service announcements (PSAs) and the programming content. In particular, they documented and analyzed the content of several antidrug campaigns. Ironically, as they pointed out, these public service announcements were aired between music videos filled with images of drinking and drug use. The girls repeated their analysis for safe-sex PSAs and found a similar disconnect between images shown and messages stated. The girls summed up their research by stating that MTV played by the "do as we say, not what we show" philosophy.

Another success in the project came when students developed an awareness about how their "teen" identity was defined, at least in part, by media representations. The class explored a wide range of teen cultural artifacts (in print, advertising, TV, and movies) and examined how teenagers were portrayed within them. Students then compared those media representations with their own lives, examining the similarities and discrepancies. For example, many of my students worked after school, were involved in school activities, and took their grades seriously, but they saw little reflection of that reality in the media representations of teenagers. Returning, then, to Scholes' (1985) framework, students demonstrated the three levels of reading by going from the initial *submission* of the media text representations of "teenager," to *interpretation* of what those images meant, and finally to a level of *criticizing* how media defines and represents the images of teenagers.

Yet another success was the capacity for our class to engage in civil discussions on explosive topics, such as gender identity. I have often encountered classroom struggles when showing videos such as "*Killing Us Softly 3*" (Jhally & Kilbourne, 2000), a film that explores the negative representation of women in the media, and more recently, "*Tough Guise*" (Jhally, Katz, & Earp, 1999) a video exploring the stereotypical media representations of masculinity. Thus, after the initial screening, I began the next class with a series of questions for students to answer on paper:

- What is it about talking about gender that angers people?
- If people think things are not going to change, does it do any good to talk about it? Why/why not?
- What are ways in which "other" groups are portrayed? (women, minorities, etc.)?
- How does it make you feel to realize that there are those who don't want you to know or even think about topics like those raised in the video?

In responding to these questions, we circumvented the eye of the storm. Also, because the last question fostered a measure of indignation among the students (i.e. "who wants to keep them uninformed and ignorant about a topic?") an alliance among students was created. Thus, the discussion moved away from a debate about definitions of "masculinity," to anger that people did not want them to know something. Ironically, they ended up having a fairly rigorous discussion of media representations of masculinity.

Yet in spite of such successes, this project also had several shortcomings. One setback was the too-late awareness of the need to create a safe space in which students could share their ideas. This became particularly evident as the semester drew to a conclusion. Some students did not want their videos shown in class, primarily due to the presence of one male student who seemed to intimidate others. His antagonistic presence (real or perceived) silenced those quieter students, especially those who felt personally invested in the assignment or felt that their ideas might be mocked in the class forum. One of my learning outcomes from this experience is to better ensure a "safe" environment for all students to freely participate.

Another shortcoming was our expectation that student projects would demonstrate resistance to mainstream media. Here we were both disappointed. Although Monica and I felt their projects showed an *awareness* of media literacy principles, we saw little *resistance* to media issues. Also, more than half the class seemed to view the assignment simply as a project to be done, rather than as a personal journal to explore awareness and resistance. In fact, a few groups readily admitted to stretching the truth to simply finish the project. Part of the problem, in retrospect, may have been the assignment itself. The project seemed skewed in the attempt to get the students to explain a course principle. And although they got to choose the topic and the manner of the explanation, some students were focused more on meeting the requirements of the assignment (i.e., "Is my topic 'right'?") than they were on exploring their identities.

Thus, if I had the chance to do the project again, I would have scaffolded it differently by giving the students the opportunity to hone in on something of particular interest to them. I would have asked them, "What have we studied so far that has upset or inspired you?" Then, the students could have explained a media literacy principle as part of their exploration and mastery of class material, but it would have been within the context of something personally significant to them.

Another important lesson I learned involved bringing my own agenda to the educational table, despite whatever critical pedagogical practices I espouse. As the classroom teacher in this study, I clearly had my own agenda, and the design for the class curriculum, as well as the structures of assignments all had parameters set up by me. To be sure, within that structure, students had quite a bit of freedom to explore, dialogue, and reflect, and I did my best to be a mentor, facilitator, and coach. That is why I should have been better prepared to not only tolerate, but expect and support those student viewpoints that diverged from my own. For example, one student dug his ideological heels in deeply any time we started to discuss alternate interpretations of media texts, particularly concerning gender issues. I would like to believe that I was much more tolerant of his viewpoints than he was of mine, but most likely, he sensed my resistant attitude toward his beliefs. Thus, as a teacher who practices critical pedagogy, I will still engage students to consider alternate options, but in the end, I must allow them a more open and tolerant space to disagree with both me and the course content.

Another issue that came to the fore during this study is the strong connection between reading and writing. Researchers in media literacy (Buckingham, 1998; Grahame, 1991) assert that by writing media texts, students will become better readers of media texts. Indeed, in this study, producing their video compositions facilitated their reading of the media. They became experientially familiar with manipulating production techniques, and that provided them with tools to be more critical readers of media texts. Moreover, video production allows students who have difficulty expressing themselves in writing to present their thoughts and ideas in a different modality. Providing such opportunities is important, and as non-linear editing programs become more readily available and affordable, more students will have the opportunity to express and empower themselves.

A final thought deals with researcher and participant collaboration. Ulichny and Schoener (2000) describe the reciprocity of information, rapport, and stakeholding in teacher-researcher partnerships. In the spirit of their work, we found that working as a teacher-researcher pair benefited us both. Monica and I had both read many articles about Freire's (1970) "praxis," which he defined as, "reflection and action upon the world in order to transform it" (p. 33). Through collaboration as principal teacher and principal researcher, we found that praxis occurred through dialogue and reflection of our understanding of media literacy, pedagogy, and theory in the daily life of the classroom.

LEARNING OUTCOMES
(MONICA)

To work in the field of media education (or media literacy, as it is known in the United States) is to work in isolation. After having talked to professors who teach education courses at the university level, the impression I was given was that there were only a handful of teachers who actually practice critical pedagogy. Critical pedagogy, it seemed, was mainly an academic ideal about which scholars loved to write. However, based on surveys I received from high school teachers, I found that critical pedagogy is indeed taking place. It is not a theoretical dream of progressive professors; it lives in many classrooms, and I was encouraged by this realization.

I was excited to meet David, and my field visits with him always felt much too brief. His classroom contained the living practice of media literacy/media education, and I saw his struggles as a reflection of my own struggles as a college professor teaching undergraduate communication students. For instance, one day during a class discussion grappling with the concept of "ideology," one student turned to David and said, "So, what? What if there is something called ideology?" I was happy to see that such interactions with students were not just happening in my class.

In doing this research, I also became more conscious of the complex nature of critical pedagogy in the classroom. Because I consider my form of teaching critical pedagogy, I was keen to observe it in practice in someone else's work. In doing so, I saw how the process was both fragile and powerful. The potential exists in critical pedagogy for teachers to easily lose control over the classroom. This fragile position, however, also has phenomenal power because it allows students to speak their minds about risky topics.

I also observed the truth of Buckingham's observation (1998) that when teachers allow students to speak their minds and create their own texts, students may produce texts that replicate mainstream discourse, or embrace youth pleasure such as drugs and alcohol, rather than producing oppositional texts that have the potential to be political and transformative. As David outlined above, he did not reach all his students in the way he intended.

But is it ever possible for a teacher to reach all of his/her students? And if it is not possible, should the teacher opt to reach maybe a few students and, in so doing, greatly impact those students' lives? This study revealed some student dialogue about mass media gender construction and strong statements from students that questioned and seemed to resist some media messages. Gender dynamics in the classroom, however, were oftentimes unequal. The classroom had young men—who could be at times either

charming or brutish—who regularly silenced other students by making sarcastic comments. I contemplate what line a critical pedagogy teacher must
walk between respecting students' media texts (and the pleasure they
derive from them), empowering students' voices, managing the classroom,
and listening to students' voices.

As a final thought, working with David made clear to me the need to
create more venues in the United States for scholars of media
literacy/media education and media literacy practitioners (including those
who teach video production) to meet and dialogue about our commonalities. I also believe universities need to create certification programs for high
school video production teachers, and associations need to be created to
lessen teachers' sense of isolation while teaching in this field. High schools
and universities are not as far from each other as teachers and professors
might care to think. We need to help each other make this field of research
and practice more coherent.

In my last day of fieldwork, as I was saying good-bye to David, one of
my former students from my Introduction to Video Production class at
Ohio University walked down the hall. Surprised to see him, I asked, "Jack,
what are you doing here?" Jack replied, "I came to visit Mr. Bruce." He
looked at us and said, "This is amazing. I went from Mr. Bruce's class in
high school to Monica's class at Ohio University." This story, to me illustrates the possible connections for academics and teachers to create partnerships in knowledge. The distance between David and me is not just the
physical mileage that separates Cleveland and Ohio University, but the distance that separate academia and K-12 teachers. Our work together
demonstrates that distance need not be literally and figuratively as great as
it is often perceived. A tremendous need exists to connect scholars who
work within the field of communication studies and teachers who teach
media production classes at the K-12 levels, a partnership that should be
nurtured from professors in communication schools and teachers in high
school across the United States.

NOTES

1. Critical pedagogy encourages the use of critical thinking to guide students in a
   search to deconstruct mainstream ideologies (Giroux, 1994). Teachers then dialogue with students on the constructed nature of knowledge. Through the use
   of dialogue, self-reflective essays, and presentations, students are given a forum
   to speak in the classroom.
2. The high school involved in this project is located in Cleveland, Ohio, with a
   population that approaches 19,000 (U.S. Census, 2000), composed of upper-
   middle-class professionals; and where both household parents tend to work. The

high school had nearly 1,600 students, comprised of 86% Caucasian, 6% African-American, 6% Asian, and the other 1% a mix of other ethnic backgrounds (U.S. Census, 2000). Within the student population, 94% continue toward a college education.

The communications classes at the high school were originally designed by a curricular team. Funding for a TV production studio was provided by local cable franchise fees, and a curriculum group decided that the classes should be held within the English department. The class started out as a year-long elective open for grades 9-12 with an emphasis on writing tied to production. Over the eleven years that David taught the course, the class evolved into a program that included Communications II and a Film Seminar class.

3. Legos are multicolored plastic blocks. These toys come in various sizes and are designed to connect to other pieces.

4. That feeling of sharing their identity was much different with the videos in that some students were more reserved about their identities than they were in written form, possibly because of the public nature of the videos. This became glaringly obvious on viewing day when some chose not to share their final video with the rest of the class.

5. All the names of respondents have been changed.

REFERENCES

Bazalgette, C. (Ed.). (1989). *Primary media education: A curriculum statement.* London: British Film Institute.

Buckingham, D. (1998). Media education in the UK: Moving beyond protectionism *Journal of Communication, 48,* 33–43.

Buckingham, D. (1998). Introduction: Fantasies of empowerment? Radical pedagogy and popular culture. In D. Buckingham (Ed.), *Teaching popular culture: Beyond radical pedagogy* (pp. 1–17). London: UCL Press Limited.

Ellsworth, E. (1989). Why doesn't this feel empowering? Working through the repressive myths of critical pedagogy. *Harvard Educational Review, 59,* 297–324.

Fine, M. (1993). "You can't just say that the only ones who speak are those who agree with your position": Political discourse in the classroom. *Harvard Educational Review, 63*(4), 412–433.

Freire, P. (1970/1993). *Pedagogy of the oppressed.* New York: Continuum.

Giroux, H. (1994). *Disturbing pleasures: Learning popular culture.* New York: Routledge.

Giroux, H. (1997). *Pedagogy and politics of hope: Theory, culture and schooling.* Boulder, CO: Westview Press.

Grahame, J. (1991). The production process. In D. Lusted (Ed.), *The media studies book: A guide for teachers* (pp. 146–170). London: Routledge.

Grossberg, L. (1997). Cultural studies, modern logics, and theories of globalization. In A. McRobbie (Ed.), *Back to reality: Social experience and cultural studies* (pp. 5–31). Manchester: Manchester University Press.

Hall, S. (1995). Fantasy, identity, politics. In E. Carter, J. Donald, & J. Squires (Eds.), *Cultural remix: Theories of politics and the popular* (pp. 63–69). London: Lawrence & Wishart.

Hall, S. (1980). Encoding/decoding. In S. Hall et al. (Eds.), *Culture, media, language* (pp.128–138). London: Hutchinson.

Jhally, S. (Director/Producer), & Kilbourne, J. (Writer). (2000). *Killing us softly 3: Advertising's image of women* [educational video]. Northampton, MA: Media Education Foundation.

Jhally, S. (Director/Producer), Katz, J., & Earp, J. (Writers). (1999). *Tough guise: Violence, media, and the crisis in masculinity.* [educational video]. Northampton, MA: Media Education Foundation.

McLaren, P. (1994). *Life in schools: An introduction to critical pedagogy in the foundations of education.* New York: Addison Wesley Longman.

Meyrowitz, J. (1998). Multiple media literacies. *Journal of Communication, 48,* 96–108.

Scholes, R. (1985). *Textual power: Literary theory and the teaching of English.* New Haven, CT: Yale University Press.

Ulichny, A., & Schoener, W. (2000). Teacher-researcher collaboration from two perspectives. In B. M. Brizuela, J. P. Stewart, R. G. Carrillo, & J. G. Berger (Eds.), *Acts of inquiry in qualitative research* (pp. 177–206). Cambridge, MA: Harvard Educational Review.

10

CRITICALLY READING RACE IN THE MEDIA AND IN THE CLASSROOM

A Media Literacy Project

Alicia Kemmitt[1]

Media texts are understood to make significant contributions to our sense of self and our understanding of the world around us (Gerbner et al., 2002). They also help shape our connections with the communities in which we live and those that we know only through representation (Anderson, 1992; Hall, 1997). It is therefore important to examine how media texts contribute to identity formation, especially among youth who often engage in an intensified process of shaping and reshaping their identities as they encounter new aspects of their world. In this essay, I discuss why media education is valuable for teaching students about identity formation and, in particular, the social construction of race.[2]

As a graduate student in Communication, I was introduced to media literacy through my coursework and was eager to put some of the concepts I had learned into practice. An opportunity came during the summer of 2000. While I was working as a substitute teacher in a diverse school district in San Diego County, California, a middle school teacher asked me to conduct a media literacy workshop in her class of 12- and 13-year-olds. After discussing the class curriculum in her English, Reading, and World Cultures classes, we decided to introduce media literacy as a tool to illuminate concepts of race, ethnicity, and identity formation. Through a weeklong workshop, I approached this task by encouraging students to question the dominant meanings of media texts. Beginning by exploring the symbolic meaning construction in popular media texts is a critical element of a media education that empowers students to be thoughtful participants in the symbolic and real worlds in which they live. I will discuss the learning outcomes of the media workshop in the latter half of the essay.

MULTICULTURALISM AS A POINT OF ENTRY AND CRITIQUE

Throughout my experience at the school, the students demonstrated good understanding of the concepts of multiculturalism and diversity. Many commented on how they enjoyed discussing their identity because they were able to express who they were and how they were unique. Arguably, their ability to talk openly about their ethnic and cultural identities was a result of the school's demographics and the emphasis on multiculturalism in the curriculum. San Diego is a border region in which the majority of the population is made up of people of color: Latinos, African Americans, Asian/Pacific Islanders, and Filipinos make up the largest U.S. minority groups in San Diego County public schools.[3]

The San Diego County Office of Education's web site (www.sdcoe. k12.ca.us) offers resources for teachers working in diverse classrooms. One resource, an article entitled "Diversity in the Classroom," cites the multiple ethnicities that make up San Diego County's classrooms as evidence of the importance of "value(ing) the diversity of our students and our nation within the framework of American democratic values." Diversity is cast as an American democratic value, legitimating its place in public education. The article lists a series of stereotypes it calls "myth(s)" about each ethnic group and then refutes them with an explanation of "reality," using research-based facts to debunk each stereotype. The article cautions teachers that sometimes a multicultural approach that celebrates diversity can further stereotypes if the activities are not researched for their "authenticity" in representing the culture.[4] The article encourages teachers to seek "realistic" and "authentic" portrayals of diverse cultures in order to develop "positive racial attitudes" among students. The article suggests that teachers should carefully research the cultures about which they teach to ensure that they do not exacerbate stereotyping. This approach to multiculturalism positively seeks to refute essentializing myths about ethnic groups; however, it may re-essentialize them by seeking to represent stable, "authentic" ethnic identities without taking into account multiple subject positions.[5]

In the introduction to her book on intercultural cinema, Laura Marks (2000) explores both the utility of and problems with the term *multiculturalism:*

> "Multiculturalism" has been and sometimes still is a useful term to remind us that we live in a society composed of many groups—but it implies the perspective of white or other dominant people who have been able to assume that their society continues to constitute the overarching culture. Because of its use in official policy, such as arts funding quotas, the term "multiculturalism" has come to mean the naming and slotting of difference (Bailey 1991) and often ends up homogenizing the struggles of the diverse groups it intended to empower (Marchessault 1995b). (Marks, 2000, p. 7)

San Diego County's focus on diversity may fall into this homogenizing trope. The fact that "Diversity in the Classroom" lists stereotypes of Latinos, Asian/Pacific Islanders, African American and Native Americans, but not whites, is an indication that a dominant white culture is assumed and not questioned. At the same time, however, the establishment of a multicultural perspective in public school curricula that celebrates diversity provides a point of entry for media literacy, which calls for a critical eye on the media as a site in which ethnic, racial, gender, and sexual identities are visibly played out.

INCORPORATING MEDIA LITERACY INTO THE CURRICULUM

In his discussion of diaspora in the black British context, Hall (1990) provides a complex view of multiculturalism and its relevance for media:

> Cultural identities are the points of identification, the unstable points of identification or suture, which are made within the discourses of history and culture. Not an essence but a *positioning*. Hence, there is always a politics of identity, a politics of position, which has no

absolute guarantee in an unproblematic, transcendental "law of origin."
(Hall, 1990, p. 226)

As such, media literacy concepts can be used to teach cultural positioning
by demonstrating how dominant meanings perpetuated by media representations are "points of identification" and always negotiated within the
context of embodied experiences.

The class with which I worked reflected the diversity of the school district: 80 percent were students of color, and over half spoke a language
other than English in their homes.[6] These middle school students were
familiar with defining "culture" as an aspect of everyday life as part of their
World Cultures curriculum. However, when students were presented with
the question, "What is culture?" they initially responded with answers that
did not necessarily reflect their daily experiences. Instead, they listed
examples in categories such as religion, customs, and beliefs. Yet, when
probed if *they* experienced culture, they readily disclosed the cultural
events of their everyday lives, such as waking at a certain hour each morn-
ing, eating a particular breakfast, watching specific TV shows, and going to
school. We discussed how the different assumptions we make about how
to behave in the classroom, how to watch TV or talk to friends, are part of
our cultural experiences.

I found using conceptual frameworks that students are familiar with,
such as considering the everyday experience of culture, useful to build links
between media literacy and students' lived experiences, as well as existing
curricula. Reading, English, and other subjects within Language Arts are
appropriate points of entry for media education and can be used as academic anchors to legitimize media literacy concepts in the curricula.
Responses to popular media texts and other cultural experiences are also
good to draw upon as signifying practices that students are familiar with.
Students can learn how these can be read critically and also be enjoyed,
just as students may similarly analyze and may find pleasure in reading literary texts.

The workshop I conducted focused on exploring how media representations are made meaningful through culture. We discussed how objects
and images have no inherent meaning in themselves, but we have assigned
them meanings and are able to share these meanings through our common
ideas about the world or our culture. We began with a discussion of what
it means to be critical. Students tended to assume that being critical meant
that something is inherently bad. Thus, we spent time defining "being critical" as a process of questioning why things are the way they are. I emphasized that in this way, "being critical" meant that you wanted to know how
the meaning of a particular object or image was created, and to also question why that particular image was chosen instead of another.[7]

The workshop consisted of two main activities. The first dealt with advertisements in popular magazines and the second dealt directly with racial identity. First, in order to show that meanings are constructed through culture and do not operate in a vacuum, I used a prop that is easily accessible in any U.S. public school classroom—the American flag. A national flag is a helpful tool to teach meaning construction because students can clearly see how ideological meanings are ascribed to it. When asked, students quickly assigned meanings such as "justice," "freedom," "our country," and "liberty" to the flag. I then explained how meaning can be disarticulated from an object or image such as the flag. By re-identifying the flag as rectangular fabric that showcases various colors and shapes, students also understood that it is also "a piece of cloth on a stick."

After students understood that ideas get connected to images and objects through culture and discourse, we talked about how some ideas are more prevalent and acceptable than others because some groups hold more social or economic power in society. I asked to identify dominant groups within these categories of identity: class, gender, race, religion, and sexuality. Students identified rich, male, white, Christian, and straight subject positions as holding more power in Western culture. Although naming which groups hold power in society was remarkably easy for them, they did not want to leave the dominance of these groups unquestioned. For example, shortly after the class created the list of dominant groups, a girl raised her hand and objected to the idea that men have more power. I was able to use her statement to point out that the problem with dominant culture is precisely that it does not reflect everyone, but is, in general, where most people in society assume that power lies. I also took this opportunity to discuss the possibility for alternative and counter-hegemonic meanings by returning to the example of the flag. I asked students to consider other possible meanings beside patriotism that would differ from what the majority of people would think about the flag. One student offered: "If someone in your family had died fighting for America, the flag may make you sad and mad that they had to die."

Once the students were comfortable with the basic concepts of meaning construction and cultural power, they began to work in small groups to apply these concepts to advertisements in magazines such as *YM*, *Teen*, *Seventeen*, and *Cosmopolitan*.[8] The ads were useful to show how images become connected to ideas because they often unapologetically employ images of race, gender, and social status to create a positive feeling toward the product. Small groups of students worked with an ad to create a list of dominant meanings. I asked students, "What are some of the main ideas that are connected to the images in the ad?" After they created their lists, they took the same ad and made a list of alternative meanings. Students responded to the question, "Are there ideas that you can connect to the image that you think is not the main message of the ad, and that most people probably wouldn't come up with?" Students found this harder to do, which provided an opportunity to discuss how powerful dominant culture is. Identifying alternative meanings takes more creativity and thought. With some work, students were able to come up with several alternative meanings for the ads. Often, in the alternative column, students demonstrated an understanding of the construction of meaning by writing phrases like, "they are trying to say that . . . " or "they are telling us to . . . ." In some cases, they simply listed the opposite of the dominant meaning of the ad, indicating their belief that the dominant meaning was false. In most cases, however, students' alternative meanings were more complex, grounded in their own social realities. (See Appendix 1 for a description of sample ads and student responses.)

The second group activity focused on racial stereotypes. I asked students to identify the major categories of race used by the dominant culture. They readily came up with black, white, Asian, and Latino. Some students had trouble with these limitations early on, asking "What about Indian or Arab people?" in response to which I stressed again that these are dominant categories only and leave a lot of people out. I assigned a racial category to each of the four corners of the room and asked students to choose the corner that best represented their racial identity. Despite the emphasis on diversity and multiculturalism in their curriculum, students were not familiar with dividing and categorizing themselves in this way, especially in a classroom that emphasized commonalities and working together.

When students had difficulty deciding which category to choose, I reminded them that we were not only talking about the perception of their own individual identity, but also about how the dominant culture views their race and often puts people into discrete categories. If someone got really stuck, I asked them to have their classmates tell them where they "belong." This was when the "material consequences and discursive effects" (Cottle, 2000, p. 218) of race became very clear. Although it was hard for some to decide which category they fit into, the others found it easy to tell their classmates where they should go: "Oh, you're white," one student said to another who had chosen the Latino corner. The "reassigned" student then showed her objection, confusion, and surprise as she reluctantly crossed over to the white corner, feeling the conflict between the meanings assigned to her by the dominant culture versus her own self-identity.

In order to explore representation and racial identity further, I asked the students to remain with their group and create a list of dominant and alternative ideological or symbolic meanings for their racial category, just as they had done with the ads. As they reported their findings to the class, students began to draw links between the race activity and the ad activity: Just as the images in the ads are connected culturally to certain ideas, so too are racial categories.

The difficulty students had in choosing one corner to represent their racial identity, as well as the ease with which some students placed themselves, provided a fruitful point of discussion during the debriefing session. Students were able to see just how powerful dominant categories of identity are and, simultaneously, how these oversimplified categories do not adequately reflect the ambiguous and complex realities of individual experiences and self-perceptions. Debriefing was important to allow students to discuss how each activity made them feel, especially because the racial identity activity involved mapping race onto their own bodies. I also reminded them of the power each of them holds as participants in meaning making. By understanding how dominant meanings are created and circulated, students learned they have the choice to accept, reject, or otherwise assert their own meanings in response to the dominant meanings perpetuated by the media as truth or fact. Moreover, because they had learned that meanings are culturally constructed, they could now work to deconstruct them and become aware of the power they have in responding to their media environments.

The workshop concluded with an assignment whereby the students created their own alternative ads. Using storyboards, the students created "ads" for themselves. They were encouraged to think of ideas or beliefs that represented who they are and to connect these concepts to images and corresponding text. This final activity allowed them to use what they had just learned about the social construction of racial identities to produce their own media messages.

CRITICAL LEARNING OUTCOMES
AND USING STUDENT RESISTANCE

In order to assess the learning outcomes of the weeklong workshop, the students responded to open-ended reflection questions in writing. The goals of the workshop were to help the students understand how identity markers—and in particular, race—are culturally constructed through the media. Overall, students were successful in understanding that meanings attached to cultural symbols in ads and other media, as well as those attached to racial identities, are not fixed or absolute.

The workshop promoted positive identity formation by building tools to both interpret and produce media in a way that encouraged students to use their own voices, grounded in their social realities. Students who understood how symbols are culturally constructed through their reading of ads and racial categories were empowered to apply that understanding to create alternative meanings. For example, a group of Asian American students wrote that culturally dominant meanings of Asian Americans are that they are "cheap," "Christian and Catholic," usually associated with "seafood," and "farming." After identifying images and stories in the media that help construct these dominant meanings, the students created their own, alternative meanings of being Asian American. To these particular students, being Asian American meant: "Celebrating holidays, going to their grandparents' house on Christmas Eve, eating good food, and being Filipino." The second set of meanings privileged the students' own experiences. These experiences stand in relation to, but are not the same as, the dominant construction of "Asianness" in the media.

Laura Marks (2000) explains how communities are created by common resonances in the viewing of films. In the same way, the classroom is a space of community and collaborative identity with a clear set of rules for behavior and modes of being, quite distinct from the social norms of peer groups. The classroom is set up as a place of learning, whereas the peer communities are often defined by sharing pleasures of popular culture. Thus, discussing popular culture in the classroom is likely to be qualitatively different than popular culture chit-chat among peer groups outside the classroom. The seventh grade students I worked with did express some discomfort with bringing popular culture into the classroom. For example, many students said they felt uncomfortable identifying the dominant ideas presented in some of the ads that had sexual connotations. Issues having to do with sexual attractiveness or activity are normally unspoken in the classroom and therefore caused discomfort among this class of 12- and 13-year-olds. Significantly, this very discomfort can be used productively to help students and teachers identify and break down the false divide between what is appropriate for the classroom and what is not.

In addition to students' reluctance to place themselves in single racial categories and their discomfort with discussing some aspects of popular culture in the classroom setting, some of the seventh graders showed resistance to learning about media in general because it is a topic they felt they already fully understood. In response to the question: "Do you think the media literacy workshop will change the way you experience the media?" about one fourth of the students answered "no." Some students acknowledged that they agreed with some of the dominant messages of advertisements and the media, whereas others said they disagreed with them and had their own way of looking at things. Despite students' inclination to resist the idea of changing their way of using or viewing media, I was encouraged by responses that demonstrated critical thinking and showed that they valued their own opinions. These were indeed positive learning outcome goals of the workshop. In almost every case in which a student reported that the workshop would not change anything about how he or she views the media, he or she also expressed critical ways of viewing the media. For example, a student reported: "I don't think that anything from the workshop will change my mind about the media." Nonetheless, "I learned that the media changes very simple objects into very strong ideas."

CONCLUSION: RECOMMENDATIONS FOR SUSTAINABLE MEDIA EDUCATION

Conducting a media literacy workshop for one week as a substitute teacher made for a unique situation. Although serving in this role afforded the opportunity to conduct the workshop, ideally it would have been better for their regular teacher to be present so as to incorporate the media literacy concepts into the curriculum afterward. Luckily, in my case, I worked with the long-term teacher to create the curriculum for the workshop, and she expressed interest in referring back to it throughout the year to build upon the concepts that we covered.

Introducing media literacy while serving as a substitute teacher demonstrates one of the multiple and creative ways media education can occur. However, I think the key to more effective pedagogy is to create a media literacy program that is part of a sustained effort. My experience in this seventh grade classroom points to a weakness in U.S. media literacy training: Teachers are often interested in and willing to pursue the topic, but do not always have the backing of curriculum standards or training to do so (Hobbs, 1998; Kubey, 1998). Although my presence in the classroom was temporary and serendipitous by the nature of my substitute status, it did allow me to integrate media literacy concepts into the existing course curriculum. My experience shows the potential for media education to build on existing curriculum in the Humanities and Social Sciences in order to encourage sustainability in long-term curriculum development.

NOTES

1. I would like to thank Summer Estrada and her 7th grade classes at Rancho del Rey Middle School in Chula Vista, California, for their participation in the media literacy workshop during the summer of 2000. I also extend my gratitude to colleagues, Esteban del Río and Erica Scharrer, for offering their expertise in media and pedagogical strategies during conversations at both the workshop conception and reflection stages of this project.

2. I use the term race not as having an essential biological base, but as a social construct that nevertheless has "material consequences and discursive effects" (Cottle, 2000, p. 218).
3. This demographic statistic can be found on the Sweetwater Union High School District web page. (http://www.suhsd.k12.ca.us/students_about_district.asp)
4. The article explains that a common activity for kindergarten and primary grades, such as building tepees and making headbands, may perpetuate "inaccurate stereotypes" that don't portray the "authenticity" of Native American culture.
5. See, for example, Hall's essay "New Ethnicities" (1996) in which he calls for a cultural politics of difference that does not rely on essentializing categories of identity, linked to unified notions of race or nation, but sees "ethnicities" as culturally fluid and conditional.
6. This demographic statistic can be found on the Sweetwater Union High School District web page. (http://www.suhsd.k12.ca.us/students_about_district.asp)
7. My emphasis on meaning construction as well as social inequalities involved in determinations of media content is supported by Lewis and Jhally (1998) who argue: "Media literacy, in short, is about more than the analysis of messages. It is an awareness of why those messages are there" (p. 111).
8. Most of the ads were gendered and strongly addressed the girls in the classroom. Students did use some masculine-oriented ads found in men's magazines. However, these were not geared to boys in quite the same way. Many were ads for alcohol that targeted an older male reader, whereas the ads targeting young women dealt with clothes or makeup.

APPENDIX 1

Sample Ad #1: Steve Madden

This ad displays a young white woman shot with a distorted lens to exaggerate her head, making it appear disproportionately larger than her tiny waist and long legs—which accentuate her very high-heeled black boots. She sits sideways on a motorcycle in an urban setting, lips parted, staring seductively into the camera. She is wearing large hoop earrings and has oversized eyes, outlined with thick black liner. Her tiny waist is bare, exposed by a white tank top and low-rise silver studded leather mini-skirt. A small dog sits next to her on the bike. Her thin arm is draped behind the dog, displaying a silver studded leather strap bracelet on her tiny wrist. A second dog sits on the ground next to the bike, wearing riding goggles. The Steve Madden label is in the upper right hand corner of the page, along with the store name, "Nordstrom," printed below it. The text at the bottom of the page reads: "Shoes Clothes Accessories," followed by the Steve Madden website address and phone number.

Sample Student Responses to Steve Madden Ad

Dominant Meanings:

- Buy Steve Madden shoes
- Sluttish
- Wear a lot of make-up
- To be attractive you have to buy and spend a lot of time on yourself
- You have to be skinny to be attractive
- Buy Steve Madden clothes

Alternative Meanings:

- You don't have to spend a lot of time and money on yourself
- You don't have to be skinny to be attractive

Sample Ad #2: l.e.i. jeans

This ad features Columbia Recording Artists, Blaque. Three African American young women are shot from an extreme high angle, towering up against the blue sky and puffy, white clouds behind them. They each strike a different pose, dressed in jean jackets and pants. The woman on the right stands tall with her hands to her back, pushing her right hip out. She stares into the camera through eyes like slits. The young woman in the middle stands, bending forward with hands on her knees, looking off to the left. The third young woman stands in the background, with her back to the camera, looking over her shoulder with a slight smile. The text at the top left reads: "Columbia Recording Artists Blaque." The text at the bottom right reads: "l.e.i.: life energy intelligence" and includes the l.e.i. jeans website.

Sample Student Responses to the l.e.i. jeans Ad

Dominant Meanings:

- Makes you look good in both your style and yourself
- l.e.i. is for cool people
- Cool clothes
- Tuff and sexy and a girl should be like cool or like them
- You can see that a girl should have an attitude if she doesn't have what she wants
- Cool hair styles

Alternative Meanings

- It makes them look sexy
- It makes us feel like we should act like them all the time
- They are telling us that we should have the same hairstyles as them so we can be cool
- They are trying to say we have to look like them or we will never be cool
- They say that if we wear these jeans it will give us life energy intelligence. We don't like that idea

REFERENCES

Anderson, B. (1991). *Imagined communities*. New York: Verso.

Cottle, S. (2000). Discussion of key terms and concepts. In S. Cottle (Ed.), *Ethnic minorities and the media* (pp. 215–220). Buckingham: Oxford University Press.

Diversity in the classroom. San Diego County Office of Education. Retrieved October 31, 2000, from http://www.sdcoe.k12/us/notes/9/ diverse.html

Gerbner, G. et al. (2002). Growing up with TV: The dynamics of cultivation. In D. Zillman & J. Bryant (Eds.), *Media effects: Advances in theory and research* (pp. 43–67). Hillsdale, NJ: Erlbaum.

Hall, S. (1990). Cultural identity and diaspora. In J. Rutherford (Ed.), *Identity: Community, culture, difference* (pp. 222–237). London: Lawrence & Wishart.

Hall, S. (1996). New ethnicities. In D. Morley & K. Chen (Eds.), *Critical dialogues in cultural studies* (pp. 441–449). London: Routledge.

Hall. S. (1997). The work of representation. In S. Hall (Ed.), *Representation: Cultural representations and signifying practices* (pp. 15–64). London: Sage.

Hobbs, R. (1998). The seven great debates in the media literacy movement. *Journal of Communication, 48*(1), 6–32.

Kubey, R. (1998). Obstacles to the development of media education in the U.S. *Journal of Communication, 48*(1), 58–69.

Lewis, J., & Jhally, S. (1998). The struggle over media literacy. *Journal of Communication, 48*(1), 109–120.

Marks, L. (2000). *The skin of the film*. Durham and London: Duke University Press.

11

MEDIA EDUCATION IN POST-COLONIAL HONG KONG

Cultivating Critical Young Minds

Alice Y. L. Lee

Eileen Mok

Hong Kong was a British colony for 150 years and after the handover of its sovereignty from Britain to China in 1997, numerous media education initiatives emerged. Notably, this emergence was not due to the sovereignty handover per se, but rather, was closely related to the rapidly changing social and media environments. Media education in Hong Kong is essentially a grassroots movement. Initiatives arose from different sectors of society, namely universities, secondary and primary schools, youth organizations, religious groups, social concern groups, the media industry, and the government's Education Department. The Hong Kong Association of Media Education (HKAME), a voluntary NGO, was also established in early 2000 to promote media education. One of its studies found that by the end of 2001, over 180 schools and organizations in the territory had conducted media education programs (Lee, 2002).

By assessing the performance of two major media education programs in Hong Kong, this chapter analyzes the extent to which young people have benefited from media education and what challenges media educators face in the postcolonial context. The two cases under examination are *"Media Education: An Innovative Curriculum for the Twenty-First Century"* and *"Breakthrough"*; the subjects involved were young local Chinese students. The former project was conducted in a classroom setting and the latter was carried out in both school and nonschool settings. Conclusions include that: (a) students develop critical thinking skills only with respect to the specific media topics discussed in a given media education program; (b) students are not able to immediately apply what has been learned to more broad media issues; and (c) general critical media awareness may need long-term cultivation. Piecemeal and one-off media education programs have limited effects on developing a person's general media literacy competency. However, it would appear that media education programs with a strong practical orientation that offer first-hand experience and the opportunity to learn for oneself are better at cultivating young people's critical thinking skills.

MEDIA EDUCATION IN THE POSTCOLONIAL CONTEXT

Before 1997, Hong Kong as a whole was fully engaged in the political transition process. Consequently, the community paid very little attention to social and cultural issues, and media education had no opportunity to develop under colonial rule. Furthermore, colonial education in Hong Kong was notoriously famous for its "spoon-feeding" teaching style. Critical thinking had never been articulated in the school curriculum and young people in Hong Kong were comparatively weak in creative and independent thinking (Leung & Lau, 1999; Lilley, 2001; Yu, 1992). Moreover, during the colonial period, in accordance with the government's educational guidelines, all schools adopted a "value-free" approach to education. For example, neither political nor civic education was provided for students before 1985, and even after its introduction, the educational authority did not devote many resources or much energy towards promoting such subjects. Instead, the colonial education focused on traditional mainstream academic subjects, in tandem with the hegemony of the British colonial rule (Cheung & Leung, 1998). The lack of civic education and the depoliticization of the education curriculum greatly contributed towards an apolitical attitude among the citizens of Hong Kong (Lau, 1991). Students in

Hong Kong were not cultivated as critical citizens and they were confused about their cultural identity. As they were never encouraged to critically interact with their social, cultural, and media environments, most became apathetic citizens and passive media consumers.

Immediately after the handover, the mass media in Hong Kong became apolitical, and market-driven journalism reigned supreme. In order to avoid offending the Chinese government, more and more Hong Kong media practiced self-censorship on sensitive news and played it safe by shifting their news agenda from political news to social and crime news (Lau, personal communication, March 6, 2000). Moreover, profit-making became the primary consideration of media organizations (So, 1997). As a result, sensational news stories and *infotainment* TV programs dominated the media. Violent news stories and pornographic columns flooded family newspapers and youth magazines. Ultimately, the market-driven media practices led to substantive changes in the cultural environment, which is why teachers, social workers, and community leaders began to recognize media education as an important method of cultivating critical awareness among young people. They did not regard the media as inherently bad, but nonetheless felt it was imperative to guide students towards a better understanding of the role of various media products in their lives.

Meanwhile, in 2001, the Hong Kong SAR (Special Administrative Region) government introduced a major educational reform in the territory. Under the slogan of "Learning to Learn," critical thinking and active learning became essential ingredients of the new curriculum (Curriculum Development Council, 2000). Consequently, media education grew to be a very important component of the reform (Leung, personal communication, June 16, 2001; Yiu, personal communication, December 1, 2001).

Figure 11.1 shows that "media awareness," "critical thinking," "creative expression," "action," and "project learning" are the key elements of media education. Thus, in Hong Kong, the objective of media education is to cultivate media literate youth, capable of understanding and analyzing the media, as well as using and influencing them. Media advocates believe that in addition to teaching students how to deconstruct the media, it is equally important to train them to be competent media users so that they are capable of opinion expression and media monitoring.

From Figure 11.1 we can see that the key elements of media education match the goals of the educational reform, in that great emphasis is put on the following key educational principles: empirical learning experience, holistic learning, learning how to learn, generic ability, values and attitudes. Media monitoring through social action is also part of the media education curriculum, and this encourages learning through social participation. Thus, media education is seen not only to train media consumers, but also to cultivate critical and participatory citizens. Moreover, many media edu-

FIGURE 11.1
Education Reform and Media Education

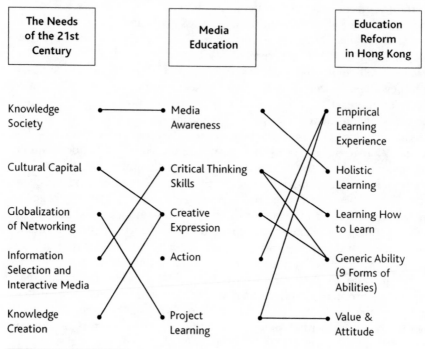

(*Source*: Research Department of Breakthrough)

cation programs facilitate project-based learning. The "social participation" element and the "project learning" element of media education underscore the importance of the empirical learning experience that is the core spirit of educational reform.

The educational reform also promotes nine generic skills: creativity, critical thinking skills, problem solving skills, communication skills, collaboration skills, information technology skills, numeracy skills, self-management skills, and study skills (Curriculum Development Council, 2000). Media education provides training for most of these generic skills and also addresses issues concerning social values and attitudes. Local educators and even government education officials therefore believe that media education can contribute greatly to the achievement of the goals of the new educational reform.

Figure 11.1 also shows that media education meets the needs and challenges of the twenty-first century. For long-term prosperity in the new millennium, Hong Kong must participate in the knowledge society and ride the wave of globalization. Thus, young people need to cultivate their creativity and learn how to master the new communication technologies. The key elements of media education, such as media awareness, critical thinking, and creative expression, fit the demands of the new century and can contribute to the training of young knowledge workers. As such, the Education Department of the SAR government willingly sponsors media education training courses for teachers (Education Department, 2001).

In addition, since 1998, the Quality Education Fund, introduced and supported by the Hong Kong SAR government, has encouraged innovative education initiatives, including media education programs. With abundant financial resources, many schools and youth organizations have started their own media education programs, and both media education projects examined here were supported by the Quality Education Fund.[1]

In sum, in response to the changing media environment, media education programs in Hong Kong focus mainly on improving young people's critical thinking skills with the aim of turning them into intelligent media consumers who also possess prosocial values. In addition, some emphasis has been put on their identity formation, self-esteem enhancement, and creative expression. Students are urged to be aware of how the media influences their personalities and characters. However, the legacy of the colonial education, the conventional top-down teaching style, students' habit of looking for model answers, heavy teaching loads, and the utilitarian approach to learning has put a lot of constraints on the media education programs conducted in Hong Kong. By examining two cases closely, this chapter describes what factors make media education programs in Hong Kong work and what constraints are present in the postcolonial context.

CASE I: "MEDIA EDUCATION: AN INNOVATIVE CURRICULUM FOR THE TWENTY-FIRST CENTURY"

The first media education case study involved a nine-school joint media education program initiated and led by the China Holiness Church Living Spirit College. This group of secondary schools developed three volumes of local media education textbooks and teachers' guides. The textbooks were developed by a team of enthusiastic teachers working in the nine schools, and they collaborated voluntarily for six months to accomplish the task. As a trial, starting from the first semester of 2000, teachers in the nine schools began using the local textbooks and curriculum materials they had developed to conduct media education as part of their formal curricula. Media education was woven into the subjects of Civic Education, Economic and

Public Affairs, Government and Public Affairs, Home Economics, Ethics, and Religious Studies. The aims of the curriculum were to develop students' critical thinking skills, cultivate students' positive social values and develop active and informed citizenry (Law et al., 1999). The subjects of the program were students in Forms 1 to 3 (equivalent to North American grades 7 to 9), and all the curriculum was conducted in a classroom setting. A teacher-training course was conducted before the teaching trial and an evaluation workshop was held during the teaching period. In order to evaluate the effectiveness of the curriculum, preteaching and postteaching surveys of the 3,295 secondary students who had received media education in class were conducted. Participating teachers also filled out the teacher questionnaires in order to share their teaching experiences.

This media education curriculum basically adopted the critical analysis model of media education. The model teaches media consumers how to deconstruct hidden media ideologies. It also urges those consumers to develop their independent critical ability so that they are not misled by the mass media. The media studied included television, advertising, comics, radio, newspaper, Internet, ICQ, film, and news. Several key concepts of media education were emphasized, namely (a) the media construct reality; (b) audiences negotiate meaning; and (c) the media contain ideological and value messages. However, according to the survey results, this media education actually did not play a significant role in affecting students' views about these concepts. However, comparatively speaking, students seemed to be more aware of the ideologies in the media messages than the way the media construct reality. This was perhaps because the curriculum design put greater emphasis on exploring the underlying values behind the media images. For example, the curriculum materials ask the students to analyze the commercial implications and gender stereotypes of TV ads.

The curriculum also aimed to cultivate informed and responsible citizens. Students were encouraged to report violent and pornographic comics to the government authority. They learned how to write complaint letters and received positive responses from the government regulating body, the Television and Entertainment Licensing Authority (TELA). This made them excited about the usefulness of their social action and, as evidenced by the survey findings, the experience gave them a sense of empowerment. Not only did they feel they could influence the content of the media, they also felt an increased sense of responsibility to monitor the performance of the mass media in the future.

The survey findings provided overall encouraging results about the effectiveness of this media education program, as students generally reported a better understanding of the mass media: 43.3 percent of the students in the eight schools and 55.6 percent of the students in the leading school said that the media education curriculum could help them develop better critical thinking skills. When asked whether the media education curriculum could help them construct their own social values, in general the students showed agreement. Many students in the nine schools said that they were interested in taking the media education courses again in the future, and after the trial teaching period, many teachers in the participating schools did indeed continue to offer media education training to their students.

With regard to classroom interaction and management, most students felt they were encouraged to express their opinion freely, with about 40 percent saying that they felt they could even present views opposing those of their teachers. However, only about 30 percent of students admitted they had actively participated in class discussions. The fact that many students were hesitant to participate in discussions, and a lot of teachers were reluctant to give up their authority by accepting students' opposing views, suggests that the conventional dynamics and practices of teaching and learning were still very much intact.

The eighteen participating teachers coming from the nine schools reported positive teaching experiences, and they generally acknowledged the usefulness of the media education curriculum in cultivating students' critical abilities (Law, 2001). Since the launch of the media education project, they tried to teach less and listen more, they were astonished to find that students were capable of expressing their independent views about various media issues. In addition, because students had an opportunity to expose themselves to different views and problem-solving alternatives during the discussion sections, the teachers found their students increasingly able to form their own social judgments. One teacher pointed out that after the media education course, one of her students told her that she had changed her newspaper reading habits. Moreover, the student persuaded her family to buy a better quality newspaper to replace the "bad-taste" popular daily newspaper they had previously purchased (Chin, personal communication, October 2, 2002). Another computer teacher was amazed by his students' favorable response to the media education class. By guiding his students to properly use ICQ, critically browse movie stars' websites, and achieve Internet literacy, he noticed that the curriculum was helpful in sharpening his students' analytical skills (Kwok, 2001). But despite these positive experiences, there were also complaints from teachers who pointed out that some students were still reluctant to think critically and express themselves. It seemed that these passive students only enjoyed watching the videotapes and joining the media literacy activities for fun.

The overall success of this nine-school media education program may be attributed to the localization of the media education textbooks. Because the textbooks were developed by the teachers themselves, they were highly motivated to make good use of them in their classrooms. Another reason may be the interactive, student-centered approach that was adopted, which is quite different from conventional classroom teaching in Hong Kong (Law, personal communication, November 10, 2002).

CASE 2: THE MEDIA AND INFORMATION LITERACY EDUCATION PROGRAM (MILE)

The second case study was conducted by Breakthrough, a well-known local youth organization. Breakthrough regards media literacy as an important skill/competency for leaders in the twenty-first century (Leung, personal communication, February 23, 2000), and the organization uses an integrated model of media education that combines the critical analysis approach and the creative production approach. Ultimately, Breakthrough believes young people acquire media literacy skills through thinking and doing.

In 2000, Breakthrough launched a large-scale, multidimensional media education project entitled "The Media and Information Literacy Education Program" (MILE). It was a two-year project (2001-2002) aimed at cultivating media awareness, critical thinking, expressive creativity, and social action among youth through a series of programs. The MILE project included several programs, each with its own set of characteristics and attributes, and had four main goals. The first goal was to set up an ongoing media education program for senior primary to junior secondary school students and teachers at school, home, and within Net environments. The second was to design a comprehensive media and information literacy curriculum. The third was to employ a contextual approach to media education that would enable participants to use the program in both intensive learning environments and personal daily living contexts. The last was to develop a network of learning circles among the users, educators, and resource people around the world for continual support and interaction. Breakthrough also developed sophisticated assessment strategies for its MILE programs, including a "Logic Model" for program design and evaluation. This model included items such as the objective, input, output, short-term outcome, and long-term outcomes (Tang, personal communication, 2001) and the "Media and Information Literacy Scales" to measure young people's critical media awareness (Breakthrough, 2000).

Although the project mainly targeted students and teachers, it also involved parents and youth workers. The project included items such as a media and Information Literacy Network, a textbook and CD-rom series, news reporting training workshops, a parenting and home series, a personal kit on media literacy games, and a media series (DJ training, magazines periodicals, a website, and a VCD portfolio). The project also operated a media resource center, established three main teacher-training programs, and designed the evaluation scales. Lastly, the project included various theoretical frameworks and models including the cultivation model, agenda-setting model, critical perspective model, information literacy and networked connectivity model, and so forth. A brief description of each program follows:

Media and Information Literacy Networks

Because the Internet is now an ubiquitous communication and interactive tool devoid of temporal or spatial constraints, an Internet platform with four media themes (popular music, advertising, television, and news) was created. "Media and Information Literacy Network" is web-based and divides into two different platforms and virtual communities for teachers and students, the "teacher zone" and "student zone," respectively. Both provided media education resources for primary and secondary teachers, as well as their students. The web site is linked to other MILE programs and each zone is further divided into four parts: the MILE resource center, MILE promotions, a discussion corner, and a game corner. This web site received an overall hit rate of 695,983 within fifteen months (Breakthrough, 2003), the success of which may be due to its strategy of using online games to attract users.

Textbook Series

Two sets of textbook and CD-ROM series were designed for primary and secondary students and both were in high demand as the requests increased from forty primary schools to sixty-seven schools. In the secondary textbook series, a "project learning" approach was adopted. The textbook series had three objectives: (a) to understand the relationship among economics, youth culture, and the media; (b) to learn how to search for useful information; and (c) to learn how to evaluate information. The Disney Empire was introduced as a case to explore the relationship among economics, youth culture, and the media. Brainstorming and information searching skills were taught with special emphasis on using "mind maps" as supplementary tools for organizing information. An information evaluation model, the START (scope, treatment, authority, relevance, and timeliness) Model was also introduced. Guided by the teachers and the textbooks, groups of students completed their own projects, and evaluation results indicated that the exercise enabled them to draw mind maps and grasp the importance of information searching skills. Some students grasped the interplay of economics, media, and youth culture; however, quite a number of students found it difficult to manage information evaluation and presentation.

The aim for the second textbook series was to help students in primary 4 to 6 understand the media, recognize its influence, and learn how to be critical of media content. The major content included analyses of advertising, the Internet, television, popular music, and news. Evaluation results showed that the textbook series was successful in teaching students to identify all the advertisements surrounding them and to differentiate the virtual media world from reality.

Camp and Workshop Series

The Camp and Workshop Series comprised of six workshops and one three-day/two-night camp that focused on news media. The course content was composed of news production reporting skills and the characteristics of news production, and the camp put great emphasis on media ethics. In addition, one of the workshops was a site reporting exercise in a youth forum, thereby exposing the participants to a practical situation.

The critical media awareness test, based on the media literacy scale measurement designed by Breakthrough, did not find any overall significant attitudinal changes in the participants after the camp and workshop series. In fact, pretest and posttest data showed that the camp did not enhance students' critical awareness and critical thinking towards media issues in general. However, program review results did reveal that student participants became more critical about the news. This positive outcome may be attributed to the news literacy focus of the Camp and Workshop Series. Participants of the camp had learned from the workshops that news selection depends on the demands of the readers, advertisers, and the editors. Many of them said that after the workshops they understood that media differ in medium characteristics and production processes. Moreover, they had mastered ways to criticize news selection and bias. They also liked the special assignment from which they learned how to research valuable angles on stories to do meaningful reporting (Breakthrough, 2002).

Since the Camp and Workshop Series was about news making, the Breakthrough workers arranged for the student participants to attend a public youth forum and make observations on news reporting. The Chief Executive of the Hong Kong Special Administrative Region, Tung Chee-hwa, and some other high-ranking government officials also joined the forum to have a dialogue with the young people. The event attracted a large group of journalists to cover the forum. After the forum, the participants reported that they had a better understanding of how news media construct reality, primarily because when they read the newspapers the following day, they discovered that the press coverage concentrated on what the Chief Executive and government officials had had to say. The youth were supposed to play a leading role in the forum, but their voices were neglected by the press, and their questions and answers were largely disregarded. This incident was useful to demonstrate how the mainstream media marginalize minority groups in society. The students also became aware of the negative externalities experienced by the public interest as a result of irresponsible and biased reporting (Breakthrough, 2001). As such, students acknowledged after the workshops that they looked at journalists and news reporting from a very different perspective. They had begun to realize that different reporters would write on the same story from different angles. They had learned how to critically read newspapers and knew the common "abuses" of the press. The concept "media construct reality" was then vivid in their minds and they acknowledged they would not trust the press as easily anymore.

Lastly, project leaders pointed out that the experiential learning approach, such as writing news headlines and attending the youth forum, seemed appealing to the participants. The interactive games introduced at the camp, such as group games and role play games, were also successful in arousing the participants' interests.

Campus Radio Community Program

In order to implement and promote campus radio community programs at school, a DJ workshop was introduced so that students could acquire radio production skills, understand the special characteristics of the radio medium, and express opinions creatively through this media format. Program evaluation results showed that by the end of the workshop, participants understood different types of radio programming and had learned how to construct the basic content of a show. Among the participants, 64.9 percent agreed that through the workshop they understood more about the dramatization skills of radio entertainment programs (e.g., the use of superstition and violence). About 41.7 percent of the respondents said they could recognize stereotypes in commercials, and 58.6 percent agreed that they understood the business relationship between music, music production companies, and radio stations.

However, when the young participants were tested using the "Media and Information Literacy Scales," there were no significant attitudinal changes after the DJ workshop. The participants were asked about issues such as crime news, biased reporting, pornographic movies, irresponsible advertising, quality of popular songs and love themes of TV dramas, and the data revealed that the overall changes were statistically insignificant.

The research results therefore indicate that the cultivation of critical media awareness is likely a long-term process.

Teacher Training Workshop and Parent Programs

The teacher workshops were called "Train the Trainer Programs," and were designed for primary and secondary school teachers interested in media education. The main aim was to help teachers introduce media education into their schools and teach students how to search, organize, and evaluate media information both on and offline. Most of the teachers who participated in the program found it helpful.

Meanwhile, the publication of a parent diary and the parental training programs also brought fruitful results. According to the findings, 64 percent of participants agreed that the overall objective of the parent training workshops was successfully achieved. Moreover, a resounding 76.8 percent said that the parent workshop had helped them understand their children better.

Overall, the MILE Project was successful at enriching young people's media knowledge about topics such as the operation and production of a campus radio station, the news-making decision processes of the press, the role of the media in youth violence, and so forth, and enhancing young people's critical thinking and analytical skills. However, results of the "Media and Information Literacy Scales" test indicated that there were no significant attitudinal changes in young people with respect to the media more generally. This disappointing finding stands at odds with the positive program review results. In fact, the results of the "Media and Information Literacy Scales" test reveal an interesting aspect of the effectiveness of media education: the scales do not directly measure the participants' response to the media topic discussed in the workshop. Instead, they assess whether the participants can apply the critical analytical skills acquired in a particular workshop on a specific media topic to media issues more broadly. In other words, the "Media and Information Literacy Scales" examined young participants' general media awareness. Take the campus radio program as an example: the pretest and posttest of the "Media and Information Literacy Scales" questionnaires did not focus their questions on radio production. Rather they asked questions on different media issues such as news reporting, advertising, and pornographic movies. Obviously, the results show that the DJ workshop did not enable the participants to immediately apply what they had learned in the workshop to other media issues. On the contrary, short-term program assessment (the program review) indicates that the DJ workshop was useful in helping the young people understand the radio industry and how to deconstruct popular songs. That means young people did actually benefit from the DJ workshop in regard to the special issue of campus radio.

CHALLENGES FOR MEDIA EDUCATORS IN HONG KONG

According to our two case studies, media education in Hong Kong has encouraged critical thinking among young people, particularly in the area of training critical media consumers. Its success, however, was limited, as not all media education participants benefited equally from the programs. In our first case study, 30 to 40 percent of the participants showed little conceptual or attitudinal changes after completing media education programs. In our second case study, the "Media and Information Literacy Scales" showed no significant change in general critical media awareness after the media education training programs. Media education can therefore not be seen as a "magic wand" that increases critical thinking skills among young people. Rather, we argue that to do so would require sophisticated teaching practices, a long-term strategy, and the ability and willingness to overcome several obstacles, which we shall now discuss.

The Legacy of the Colonial Education

Following the "spoon-feeding" tradition, students are still used to passive learning. Many students refuse to exercise their critical judgment on media issues and are reluctant to join class discussions. In a teacher evaluation workshop, one teacher complained that his students were only interested in watching the video clips he played in class, but were not interested making comments on the video afterwards, which required active thinking. Another teacher noticed that in the media education class her students found it very difficult when asked to express their opinions. In traditional classes, they were only required to pay attention to what the teacher said and take good notes. They seldom had an opportunity to express themselves and consequently were reluctant to do so.

Teaching Style

Teachers in Hong Kong are basically products of the colonial education system; that is, they were once passive learners themselves. Thus, it is hard to expect them to conduct student-centered courses such as media education with ease. The project coordinator for the "Media Education: An Innovative

Curriculum for the Twenty-First Century" project pointed out that the teacher participants were enthusiastic about the media education curriculum, but they were still inexperienced in conducting interactive classes and letting students freely express their views on media issues. Plus, they found it very difficult to accept opposing viewpoints from their students. In addition, when trying to teach students how to criticize irresponsible media practices in class, they seldom thought about contacting the authorities. The major reason for this is that these teachers grew up without any experience in civic action. Therefore, when the project coordinator made the suggestion to launch the media complaint campaign, many teachers had reservations.

Criticism for the Sake of Criticism

Students in Hong Kong always look for model answers. Colonial education has taught them how to do the "right" thing. Even in media education classes or media literacy training workshops, many students just "swallow" the media deconstruction techniques and provide standard criticisms to various media issues. In many cases, they do not practice independent judgment and provide alternative outcomes. Therefore, it can be very demanding for these young people if a teacher asks them to transfer their critical analytical skill from one media area to another. In our second case study, the Breakthrough workers found that after individual media workshops, young participants were able to make critical comments on the subject discussed but were not able to generalize their critical media awareness. Hong Kong students seemed to be over-drilled to offer the "right" answers in a defined context, and they were not able to provide creative solutions to problems arising in different contexts.

Teacher Motivation

A teacher's workload in Hong Kong is quite heavy. Therefore, some teachers were reluctant to put extra effort towards learning how to teach a new subject, especially one such as media education not yet mandated by the Education Department. Moreover, many teachers are unfamiliar with the media and show no interest in media issues. Until now, the media education teacher training programs provided for them are not comprehensive enough. According to local media education advocates, the best training for teachers is to involve them in designing and implementing their own media literacy curriculum. So far, however, only a small number of teachers have been willing to actively engage in such projects.

Banding Difference

Students in Band One schools (with higher academic standards) seem to be more capable of joining in class discussions and are more willing to exercise their critical minds. In contrast, students in Band Five schools (with lower academic standards) are less capable of performing media analyses. However, it is widely believed that Band Five students can benefit more from media education because the subject is able to stimulate their learning interests. It is therefore important for media educators to introduce media education to lower banding schools.

Utilitarian Approach

Students in Hong Kong very often adopt a utilitarian approach to learning. This attitude is also related to the philosophy of the colonial education system. In the past, the colonial government put more emphasis on teaching and evaluating mainstream academic subjects. To get good academic grades was the students' major task. Because outstanding academic achievement in school and good public examination results guaranteed a place at university and/or a better job, students were encouraged to put their time and efforts into those more "useful" subjects. Because media education is not a core academic subject, it is not surprising that some students attend media education courses without serious intent. Some of the students who joined the Breakthrough's media education programs regarded the media literacy programs simply as extracurricular activities. As a result, they were not willing to devote much effort to the learning process.

Piecemeal Program

Many media education programs, particularly those conducted in non-school settings, are one-off programs. Due to time constraints, the contents of these programs are very often too condensed and may not achieve their anticipated goals. There is therefore a need to build linkages among programs. Our case studies clearly demonstrate that participation in only one or two individual media education programs does not cultivate general critical media awareness in young people. Therefore, continued efforts should be made in terms of making more comprehensive media literacy training plans.

LEARNING OUTCOMES OF TWO HONG KONG
MEDIA EDUCATION PROJECTS
AND CONCLUSION

Although media education in Hong Kong faces great challenges in the postcolonial context, the two aforementioned media education cases offer valuable learning outcomes for the ongoing development of media educa-tion. First, if the media education programs match the requirements of the educational reform, teachers are more willing to introduce them into their schools. Moreover, if they can gain funding to conduct such programs, they will get the blessing of their school administration.

Media education must be rooted in the local culture, which is why the first thing project leaders did was develop local textbooks. Breakthrough also set up resources centers and online networks to support teachers and students who were interested in media education. The next thing they did was to provide training for teachers, the so-called "Train the Trainer Program." Armed with the training and resource backup, the motivated teachers then dared to give media education a try. Importantly, neither teachers nor youth workers had received any formal training in media edu-cation and everybody had to start from zero. As such, all the projects need-ed partnership and network support. Evidently, media education would develop better and faster with a solid partnership scheme and networking support.

To conclude, evaluation of the two case studies indicated that in gen-eral participants did benefit from the media education curriculum and workshops. Both the classroom setting and non-classroom setting media education programs were successful in enhancing young people's critical thinking skills, building up their social values, and developing their expres-sive creativity. Nonetheless, the legacy of the colonial education system has placed a number of constraints on the effectiveness of media education in Hong Kong. To overcome these constraints, media educators and young students need to gradually change their conventional passive teaching and learning approaches. In fact, because most young people in Hong Kong are still passive and uncritical learners, it is particularly compelling to intro-duce media education, which encourages a student-oriented approach to teaching.

It was found that media education initiatives that stress practical media experience, the opportunity to learn for oneself, and social partici-pation has particularly fruitful results. However, most media education programs in Hong Kong are piecemeal projects that seem to contribute more towards enhancing young people's "specific" critical analytical skills than "general" critical media awareness. Thus, continued effort is essential for the success of media literacy as a whole. It is therefore encouraging that local media education advocates plan to lobby for establishing media education as a mandatory school program.

NOTE

1. Total funding for the two projects reached US$800,000 (Quality Education Fund, 1998, 1999).

REFERENCES

Breakthrough (2000). *Development of a media and information literacy scale of Chinese youth in Hong Kong (internal report)*. Hong Kong: Author.

Breakthrough (2001). *Research and evaluation of the media & information literacy education: The interim report*. Hong Kong: Author.

Breakthrough (2002). *Research and evaluation of the media & information literacy education: The final report*. Hong Kong: Author.

Breakthrough (2003). *Research and evaluation of the media and information literacy education: The final report*. Hong Kong: Author.

Cheung, C.K., & Leung, M. (1998). From civil education to general studies: The implementation of political education into the primary curriculum. *Compare*, 28(1), 47–56.

Curriculum Development Council (2000). *Learning to learn: The way forward in curriculum development (Consultation Document)*. Hong Kong: Government Printing Department.

Education Department (2001, June). Tender for "In service teacher courses on the promotion of media education through humanities subjects/civic and moral education." Letter to education, journalism and communication departments in universities of Hong Kong.

Kwok, S.K. (2001). An interview on teacher C. K. Lau. In S. L. Law (Ed.), *Research report on "Media education: An innovative curriculum for the 21st century"* (pp. 12–13). Hong Kong: The China Holiness Church Living Spirit College.

Lau, S.K. (1991). *Society and politics in Hong Kong*. Hong Kong: Chinese University Press.

Law, S.L. et al. (1999). *Media education: An innovative curriculum for the 21st century*. Hong Kong: The China Holiness Church Living Spirit College.

Law, S.L. (2001). *Report on "Media education: An innovative curriculum for the 21st century": A final report to the Quality Education Fund*. Hong Kong: The China Holiness Church Living Spirit College.

Lee, A.Y.L. (2002). Media education movement in Hong Kong: A networking model. *Mass Communication Research, 71*, 107–132.

Leung, Y.W., & Lau, K.F. (1999). Critical thinking and political bias. In Y.W. Leung & K.F. Lau (Eds.), *Political education in Hong Kong setting: Theory and practice* (pp. 178–197). Hong Kong: Hong Kong Christian Institute.

Lilley, R. (2001). Teaching elsewhere: Anthropological pedagogy, racism and indifference in a Hong Kong classroom. *The Australian Journal of Anthropology, 12*(2), 127–154.

Quality Education Fund (1998). Media education: An innovative curriculum for the 21st century. Retrieved February 18, 2004 from http//qcrc.qef.org.hk/qef/project.phtml?proposal_id:1998/4365.

Quality Education Fund (1999). Media & information literacy education (MILE). Retrieved February 18, 2004 from http//qcrc.qef.org.hk/qef/project.phtml?proposal_id:1999/1806.

So, C.Y.K. (1997). Complete market-oriented journalism: The case of Apple Daily. In J.M. Chan, L. L. Chu, & Z. Pan (Eds.), *Mass communication and market economy* (pp. 215–233). Hong Kong: Lu Feng Society.

Yu, S.T. (1992). *Democratic education for a time of turmoil.* Hong Kong: Hong Kong Christian Institute.

INTERVIEW LIST

Chin, Kwan Ying
School Teacher
Hong Kong Truth Light College
October 2, 2002

Lau, Emily Wai Hing
Legislative Councilor
March 6, 2000

Law, Shui Lan
School Teacher
China Holiness Church Living Spirit College
November 10, 2002

Leung, Wing Tai
Associate General Secretary
Breakthrough Ltd.
February 23, 2000 and June 16, 2001

Tang, Andrew
Senior Researcher
Information & Research Unit
Breakthrough
June 25, 2002

Yiu, Ming Tak
Curriculum Development Officer
Personal, Social and Humanities Education Section
Education Department
December 1, 2001

APPENDIX 1

Media & Information Literacy Education: Reporter training course & camp (A) Focus Group Questions

Date: 28/08/2001
Interviewee: F6 students (2 Male & 7 Female)

1. Have you ever participated in a similar reporter training program before?
2. After having completed the training program, do you have different perspectives towards news reporting?
3. Are you more attentive to presentation tactics, stance point and content when reading or watching the news?
4. What are your thoughts about the Youth Forum? (e.g. straight feelings, atmosphere of the event, news reporting).
5. Of the three levels of media and information literacy (i.e., awareness, critical thinking, expression), which do you feel has been most and least enhanced? Why?
6. Do you experience righteousness, sympathy and humility in the games of the reporter camp?
7. After having participated in the course and the camp, will you consider "reporter" as your future career?

APPENDIX 2

Media & Information Literacy Education–Campus Radio Community Workshop Questionnaire

Date: 29/1/2001

Please select the appropriate option & fill up the circle (O ' ●):

1. Training Workshop/Activities:

   a. Time

	Too short	Average	Too Long
	O	O	

   b. Venue & Facilities

	Average	Good	Bad
	O	O	O

	Totally Disagree	Disagree	Average	Agree	Totally Agree
c. Program content achieved its objectives	O	O	O	O	O
d. Concrete content	O	O	O	O	O
e. Creative program format	O	O	O	O	O
f. Appropriate level	O	O	O	O	O
g. Adequate reference materials	O	O	O	O	O

2. Tutor/Lecturer:

	Totally Disagree	Disagree	Average	Agree	Totally Agree
a. Well prepared	O	O	O	O	O
b. Responsive to participants	O	O	O	O	O
c. Attentive to participants	O	O	O	O	O

3. I joined this training program because: _____

_____

_____

4. In this program I:

	Totally Disagree	Disagree	Average	Agree	Totally Agree
a. Learned a lot	○	○	○	○	○
b. Got involved	○	○	○	○	○
c. Achieved my objectives	○	○	○	○	○

5. Throughout this program, I learned how to:

	Totally Disagree	Disagree	Average	Agree	Totally Agree
a. Create sound effects	○	○	○	○	○
b. Develop a radio program using different formats	○	○	○	○	○
c. Recognize different narrative approaches and genres	○	○	○	○	○
d. Recognize gender stereotyping in advertising and to consider the implication thereof.	○	○	○	○	○
e. Use the codes and conventions available to a DJ.	○	○	○	○	○
f. Be more selective about radio stations	○	○	○	○	○

APPENDIX 2 *(Continued)*

Media & Information Literacy Education—Campus Radio Community Workshop Questionnaire

6. Opinions of the following program session:

	N/A	Very Bad	Bad	Average	Good	Very Good
a. DJ skills training & activities	○	○	○	○	○	○
b. Media education game	○	○	○	○	○	○
c. Execute workshop in radio program format	○	○	○	○	○	○

7. During this workshop, what did you most appreciate? _____

_____

_____

8. Any suggestions for improvement? _____

_____

_____

9. Have you participated in any other activities held by Breakthrough before? If so, which one(s)? _____

_____
_____
_____
_____

10. Gender: Male   Female
                  O   O

11. Age: under 12   13-15   16-18   19-21   over 22
               O   O   O   O   O

12. School Level: F.1   F.2   F.3   F.4   F.5   F.6   F.7
                      O   O   O   O   O   O   O

12

MEDIA EDUCATION TOWARD A MORE EQUITABLE WORLD

Rashmi Luthra

Critical media education at its best addresses heart, soul, and mind. If I can't get past "Why should I care?" I'm climbing uphill the entire semester. Even though I proceed at the level of intellect in the substance of each course, the class dynamic so crucial to success necessarily interweaves intellect and emotion at every juncture. Over the last decade of teaching, I have become more adept at acknowledging and working with the emotion/spirit/intellect tension. I have also discovered a lot that doesn't work, and through that back door, garnered some positive principles as well. I will discuss some of these nuggets of insight in this reflexive piece, mainly in the context of teaching Critical Media Studies and International Communication to juniors and seniors at the undergraduate level, with some observations garnered from one semester of teaching Gender and Media Studies.

Making critical media education work entails taking risks every day. I'm becoming convinced that the most successful moments are the ones that build on the totality of a particular class and semester, embracing the historical moment and the ways in which it shapes and touches the students. But, as I said, this does entail taking risks. If one wants to take advantage of the specific make-up and tenor of each class, one has to be willing to build flexibility into the syllabus, or to even go off-syllabus on occasion. In experimentation, one risks invoking student confusion, frustration, and even hostility. And worst of all, one risks failure. But it is the exciting possibilities that failure presents from which really dynamic teaching ensues.

The ultimate challenge is communicating my own passion for justice and equity in such a way as to light a spark in the students, while allowing them to explore the issues on their own, to work with their own rubrics, insights, and vocabulary to understand current problems and create alternative visions. We as educators can ask the key questions and introduce the key themes. In doing this we frame the process of exploration, which should ideally be a collective process, with no predetermined end points. The idea is not to have students mimic my analysis and conclusions, but to start them on a quest for solutions to pressing problems of global inequities and the interlocking oppressions of race, class, gender, nation, ability, and heterosexuality that result from these inequities. A further challenge in classes on media and popular culture is to communicate the centrality of these ideological institutions in both reproducing and redressing power imbalances and in constituting identities. A still greater challenge in International Communication is to convey the importance of moving towards more sustainable, humane, multicultural and cosmopolitan futures, with empathic communication across borders being a first step in this direction.

Lighting a spark isn't always easy. The first time I heard some students say in Critical Media Studies, "Why are we making such a big deal of media?" it stopped me in my tracks. Later, I heard other incarnations of the same refrain, which provided me with deeper insight. A student in a later semester noted that with so many serious events happening in the world, such as people dying and killing each other, we must realize that media entertainment is just that—entertainment. I now take every opportunity to talk about how discourse operates, and why it can be a life and death matter. On the other side of the chasm, I have students such as the African American woman last semester who said she had no idea that there were such rich ways of looking at media, and that the whole notion of the commodification of culture had opened up a new world to her.

I've also addressed the subtext of apathy and skepticism, which sometimes bursts exuberantly to the surface, by building in lots of opportunities for students to explore the material and to practice the theoretical rubrics and methodological tools first hand. By doing this, I'm communicating to the students that they don't have to take my word for any of this; they can try out the glove for themselves and see if it fits. In Critical Media Studies, students conduct an original analysis of advertising after they've grappled with the basic principles of political economy, the Frankfurt school, cultural studies, feminism, and postmodernism as applied to the context of culture and communication. Last semester, they also had the extra credit option of creating a subvertisement and explaining in what sense their practice was resistive. In addition, the semester culminates with a research paper requiring the students to apply at least one of the theoretical rubrics to a very specific communication/pop culture context, problem, or question. In this paper, they are expected to bring together scholarly work with original analysis of primary material, whether observation, interviews, or textual analysis. Some students have taken their analysis beyond the particular class to present at an undergraduate student conference. The topics have spanned from Barbara Kruger's art photography as postmodern feminist resistance, a political economic analysis of mainstream and alternative comics, to a postmodern analysis of the mainstreaming of tattooing practices. Students sometimes surprise themselves with the level of engagement with the material. When some students expressed last semester that they'd been taken into uncharted waters with the paper, or that they had ended up with conclusions that completely upset their expectations, I congratulated them in front of the class for what I considered to be a model of an organic research process. At such moments students take ownership of the ideas, and I know I've done something right.

Apathy has been a constant undertow in my International Communication class as well. Recognizing the classroom as a microcosm of the larger cultural forces at work has allowed me to move past a sense of rejection to constructive engagement with many students' lack of emotional connection with the rest of the world. The events of September 11 opened up a new window in this regard as well. We can now talk frankly in class about the possible origins and implications of our lack of engagement with other countries and peoples, and the price of this isolation. Before I can think about building student confidence or self-esteem, I am more immediately occupied with building student empathy with other places, peoples, and cultures. My teaching is premised on the belief that opening up a connection with others beyond U.S. shores will be a sturdier basis for self-confidence and self-esteem than one built on isolation and individualism. This involves a delicate process that I will call "creative destruction" for want of a better term. It is a process that tampers with ego but only to realize a larger connection with others beyond the immediate tribe or locality. I can model this process better for the students at the current juncture than ever before because of my own struggle with ego and my negotiations with it. At one time I used to take rejection of particular concepts, perspectives, and even methods quite personally. I have moved to a place where almost anything is game as long as it provides a genuine opportunity for learning.

When I say "creative destruction" I am implying a certain amount of pain on the part of students, and inevitably this extends to me as well. About a year ago, I had one white woman student in her early 20s break into tears after a session of International Communication. We had been talking earlier in the semester about the impact of September 11 on mutual understanding between different ethnic communities within Dearborn, Michigan, where I teach. Some students had been quite vocal about the lack of knowledge about the Arab American community on the part of other students. On this particular day, I had invited a former student who is doing thesis work with Arab American women to speak to the class. She spoke about the arrest of Rabih Haddad as an instance of the way in which particular groups of people were being singled out in the Dearborn/ Detroit area and neighboring locations. She also passed around the December 3, 2001 issue of *Time* magazine with the cover story "*Lifting the Veil*" about the brutalization of Afghani women under the Taliban. She spoke about the unspoken assumptions that underlie such stories and visual images of Afghani women at various stages of veiling and unveiling. When the student broke down and cried after the others had left, she explained that she had never thought about these issues deeply before. The words she spoke spelled guilt and confusion about her own relation to the processes of exclusion and bigotry exercised by white communities with which she identifies, but also a determination to pay heed to the cultural politics of the immediate region. I found her to be unusually attentive for the rest of the semester. It's almost as if she had to rise out of the ashes of her disillusionment.

I have learned to work with emotional currents that exist in the class to my advantage, such as using bonds that arise with students to create an open and even intimate classroom climate, which in turn facilitates robust discussion. One such bond I have experienced is with Arab American women students. They have generally found my class a comforting and comfortable place, a space for the articulation of their varied perspectives. The interpersonal connection they form with me is generally one of affection and mutual trust. I have sometimes suspected this has something to do with our heritage of close female relationships in what used to be gender-segregated societies; in my case an Indian heritage, in their case an Arabic one. There is just the slightest hint of our becoming "honorary sisters" for the duration of a semester and sometimes beyond. They are often anxious to talk outside of class on a more personal basis and to share little details about our families and life outside of the classroom. Sometimes, this is instigated directly by some stimulus introduced in class. After I showed a documentary on the Bhopal disaster this semester, as an example of the contradictory effects of globalization, a Lebanese woman thanked me profusely for sharing this with her, saying it had touched her deeply to know that people in India had suffered the way she suffered during the war in

Lebanon. She recounted the fear she felt as a young teen when a bomb struck their house, how the door was blasted and the walls shook. She recounted her pregnant mother's horror, and the stillborn baby that resulted because of the trauma, the sibling she never met. I thanked her from the bottom of my heart for sharing in return. In an earlier semester, an Arab American woman student told me she felt really free to participate in my class, and she spoke here more than in any other class. These little successes are significant to me even if they do not constitute formal aspects of student learning. Once a door has been opened for an empathic connection with others, or the space has been created for articulation, a positive spiral effect takes hold for the remainder of the semester.

There is another unspoken bond that emerges spontaneously in my International Communication classes. It sustains me through the many trials and challenges. The bond is built on a recognition of living an in-between life, of carrying a double or rhizomatic vision through everyday existence, of being uneasily ensconced on the borderlands (Akindes, 2001; Said, 1998). Some students are surprised to find that others experience this double life as well, and that scholars have even written about this within international communication, postcolonial studies, and diaspora studies. Last semester I began the International Communication class by asking each student to recount their experience with different cultures. The woman student with a Filipina-West Indian-African American heritage engaged to a Chinese American man and another woman student with a Nigerian and African American heritage dating an African American man warmed up to this exercise. We saw the beginnings of a relationship based on the experience of in-betweenness. We've talked about this many times in and out of class since.

The out-of-class conversations allow me to bring some interesting food for thought back to the class. For example, the woman of part–West Indian heritage spoke to me about her Indian ancestry via a Trinidadian connection. She talked about her father's hopes when they moved in next to an Indian family in a suburban neighborhood in the Detroit metropolitan area. He was excited about connecting with someone of Indian background such as his own. These hopes were dashed when her father realized that the Indian family did not consider him quite Indian. A few weeks later, we were discussing cultural imperialism in class and how it relates to the notion of cultural authenticity, how certain communities create lines to preserve the image of authenticity, and so forth. I asked her then to talk to the others about the ways in which she feels Indian and yet is not perceived as Indian, what exactly makes her feel Indian, and so forth. I did take a risk in singling her out in this way, as she could have easily felt offended. I explained after the fact the point of my questions, and her personal account became a stepping stone for further discussion.

I expected Gender and Media Studies to present no crises of motivation, because it's not required for any major. I expected self-selection to be a powerful motivating factor in itself. I was therefore surprised to find that the level of interest in the subject matter varied considerably, as did the level of identification with feminism. On the one end was a self-identified radical feminist who supplied the class with many wonderful examples of feminist music throughout the semester and who strained to be patient with the rudimentary level of some classroom discussion. On the other end was a student who took the class wondering whether she is a feminist and was skeptical of feminist standpoints throughout. A comment she and others made often was that the readings addressed mainly women and popular culture, whereas men are equally affected by media and popular culture. The point was well taken, and in response I showed *"Tough Guise,"* the film by Jackson Katz that effectively shows how masculinity is socially constructed through popular culture. In future semesters, I will foreground early on how media and popular culture affects both women and men but not in the same ways and not with the same ultimate consequences. I believe that this will address the resistance on the part of some students to identify with feminism for fear of being perceived to be a "man-hater." Inviting Susan Douglas to speak on campus this semester helped in this regard, because she explicitly addresses the broad brush strokes with which feminism has been and continues to be tarnished in the media, and does so in a humorous way that engages students. As with my other classes, I structured assignments and projects to allow students to explore gender and popular culture on their own, building on whatever degree of self-motivation already exists. Students were required to do an original gendered analysis of a current mainstream popular culture text for one project, to do a thick description of a feminist cultural intervention for another, and to create an original popular culture artifact that subverts gender expectations and/or stereotypes for yet another team project. The original creations were shared with the rest of the class, and I was gratified by the incorporation of critical feminist perspectives into these, as well as the level of innovation. The creations ranged from an alternative magazine for young men to an ethnography of girls' reception of female pop stars. Not all groups were equally explicit about the ways in which their creation subverted gender expectations, but the level of engagement was uniformly high.

The engagement with feminism in Critical Media Studies has been a troubled one on occasion. As an example, during an informal feedback session toward the end of last semester, two women students told me they didn't care for the part of the course discussing feminist approaches to the media. They felt feminists are just too touchy about the media and don't understand that women do not take this stuff seriously. They also felt that the discussion of feminism earlier in the semester had privileged voices in agreement with feminist arguments. I realized that they were referring to a particular class day when we had a robust discussion following the viewing of "*Barbie Nation: An Unauthorized Tour.*" The same women had been quite vocal about their skepticism during the class discussion. They had argued that they had played with Barbie when they were growing up and that they had come out pretty normal. They said that the feminists were not giving them credit for being able to separate fantasy from reality. Several other women then chimed in with their own Barbie stories, and tended to agree that the feminists were overdoing it. The men, who composed roughly one third of the class, mainly listened from the sidelines. A few students took a stance supportive of feminist concerns about the Barbie's influence on women's body image, but they were outnumbered by the opponents. The critique of the class dynamic as stifling voices opposed to feminism was therefore puzzling to me. It reminded me of the conservative critique of the news media as having a liberal slant. It is true that during the class discussion, when I felt the arguments attacking feminism to be misdirected or facetious, I took on the role of devil's advocate and asked several questions and provided counterarguments. I did this to deepen the thinking and provide grist for thought. But my actions were perceived as providing the frame for discussion and as constricting the space for the articulation of voices opposed to feminism. Perhaps the frame of the Barbie video was also a source of objection for these particular women students. As Lisa Cuklanz points out, the video is mild in its critique of Barbie, but the critical edge is "revealed through selection of subjects and quotations and through a juxtaposition of items that can easily be read as ironic" (Cuklanz, 2001, p. 263).

I realize in retrospect that the women in the class were providing a gut-level critique of the implicit separation between "us" enlightened feminists and the unenlightened masses of women living within false consciousness, a strain running through some of the feminist literature and also present in portions of "*Barbie Nation.*" I did try to provide, both through lectures and readings, a view of the fact that this separation has been recognized by a number of feminist scholars, and that it is part of the debate within multiple feminist approaches to media and popular culture. I did this in the hope that the discussion would be a textured one, recognizing the tensions within feminist approaches rather than using specific disagreements to reject feminist approaches altogether. The strategy did not work as well as I had expected. I think the principal problem was the short time devoted to feminism within a course that attempts to take up several different critical approaches to the study of media and popular culture. Neither professor nor students had the time to develop the complexity of particular arguments. It therefore became possible to line up for or against feminism.

It becomes clear from the examples given above, that in my mind, creating an open atmosphere for robust discussion is a must for critical media education to make a difference. Just as with original research and creative projects, sinuous discussion allows students to take ownership of the ideas and to create bridges between their lived experience and the rubrics, questions, and issues I introduce to them. When the discussion makes it possible to open new ways of seeing and thinking, it feeds into the organic process so necessary to critical media education.

Because discussion and student participation is central to my teaching, it becomes important for me to interpret instances when it is blocked or thwarted. It is also a constant challenge to keep the discussion as open and as inclusive as possible while making sure particular people do not feel marginalized, alienated, or intimidated. In the fall of 2001, this presented a particular challenge. We did meet on September 11, but spent the hour and a half in International Communication discussing news coverage of the events and students' reactions to what they had learned so far. Nearly everyone felt the need to participate on that day, to articulate their impressions and feelings at a time of great emotional stress. As the semester progressed, the two most vocal students had established a pattern. A German student spearheaded the discussion of U.S. foreign policy as a cause for the attacks, and the need for people in the U.S. to have a greater understanding of peoples elsewhere. An American student, who was more isolated but quite strident, challenged this perception and defended the actions of the United States in waging a war on terror, saying that to do otherwise and to express opinions to the contrary would be seen as suspect and unpatriotic. I was careful to accommodate both perspectives during discussion while communicating my own misgivings about the war on terror. The end result of my "equal time" policy was that the German student completely shut down after some time. It had taken some courage to express what could have been seen as an unpatriotic sentiment at the time, and the vociferous and sometimes hostile response was enough to shut her down. I attempted to draw her back by talking about the even greater importance of academic freedom at a time like this, the need to express a range of opinions without fear of retribution, even if they appeared unpatriotic. I had the class deconstruct the notion of patriotism and examine the role of the press in this regard, as a way to open up the conversation. But I had lost the German student along the way, much to the detriment of wide-ranging discussion incorporating multiple viewpoints.

One strategy to deal with the problems related to the kind of space the classroom provides for the articulation of varied views is to problematize this issue, to foreground it as a topic of discussion in itself whenever the opportunity presents itself. In the Critical Media Studies class, a natural tie-in exists with political economic approaches to the media. The discussion of the effect of concentration of media ownership on the restriction of the public sphere leads to more general discussion of the quality of public spheres today and the factors influencing the robustness of public spheres. We can then talk about the classroom as one such space. In the International Communication class, segues are provided by discussion of different models of the press, as well as discussion of the factors influencing the ability of peoples to access and disseminate various kinds of ideas and information, the imbalances between different countries and regions therein, and so forth. Last semester, I was talking about my own experience in an authoritarian press system under martial law in the Philippines in the late 1970s. I spoke about how editors, writers, and professors learned to write and speak between the lines in such a system because of the very real and painful repercussions one could face if speaking against the regime. At this point, some students pointedly asked me if I did not see parallels between this situation and shifts we're beginning to see in the United States. This led to a discussion of the changing climate in the classroom in terms of what people feel free to say and not say, and the implications of this. I cannot say for sure, but I suspect that broaching such issues sensitizes students to the need to protect the classroom space as one where free-wheeling discussion can take place without fear of repercussion.

The students' own astute observations about the changing climate for free speech in the U.S. brought home the contradiction of trying to protect the classroom as a robust public sphere while recognizing that its quality as a space for articulation is affected by a number of societal forces. We as students and professors are not immune to these forces, as I've discussed in an earlier article (Luthra, 2002). The fact of being a South Asian American professor steeped in progressive traditions has not escaped me in these trying times. The passing of the Patriot Act and its draconian implications, the detention of a number of immigrants from the Middle East and from South Asia, the virulent patriotism strutted after September 11, these transitions have seeped into conscious and subconscious crevices of my mind and informed my decisions, movements and speech in subtle ways, including the way I conduct myself in the classroom. They have coalesced to produce a subtle chilling effect. When I talk to the students about the even greater necessity today to keep the classroom climate open, I am reminding myself as much as I am imploring them. Perhaps emboldened by the larger shifts in climate, there are also efforts afoot to police professors, particularly left-leaning professors, such as the relatively new web site NoIndoctrination. org, set up by parents of college-going students for the explicit purpose of reporting by name courses and professors whose lectures, readings or class discussion exhibit "excessive bias." It would be worth our while to deconstruct the "bias" construct as a response to such efforts, discussing what it means to label particular viewpoints and ideologies as biased while others become naturalized as "unbiased" or as "just the facts." Many of us already discuss this process of naturalization in the context of media; we can usefully make analogies with what occurs in the classroom itself.

Apart from the organic aspects of classroom discussion and the unexpected paths it opens up, a willingness to introduce new topics, to go off-syllabus on particular days, and to build elasticity into assignments, all foster a flexible, responsive, organic learning process that can take advantage of the distinct historical moment as well as the unique intellectual, emotional, and even spiritual contours of each class.

For example, in the International Communication class, I assign team projects every semester. I assign a particular research-based theme to each team of three or four, and they present their findings to the class at an appointed date. The key here is to choose the theme or project in such a way as to respond to the students' imagination and interests as expressed through discussion. With rare exception, there is no repetition of team projects even across semesters. The project also often allows for team negotiation over the exact focus. For example, the goal of the first team project last semester was to demonstrate to the class the trade-offs between cultural relativism and ethnocentrism by focusing on a particular cultural practice that was alien to the students. The team was required to demonstrate what it would mean to take a culturally relativistic versus an ethnocentric approach to the practice. After negotiation, the students chose the practice of growing the boy in Papua New Guinea, which involves the transmission of semen by male elders to the boys who are being initiated. A very fruitful discussion was generated about the significance of the practice within the culture and the importance of understanding it within its own context, but on the other hand how the practice reinforces strict separation of gender roles and devaluation of women's contribution.

I tried to capitalize on the interest created during this discussion by going off-syllabus in the next session and giving an in-depth view of the practice of sex-selective abortion in the Indian context from both a culturally relativistic and feminist perspective. The fact that I have done extensive research in this area contributed to the high level of involvement that I was able to create. My own engagement in the issues communicated to the students at both an intellectual and emotional level. As a feminist myself, I had experienced the struggle between heart and mind as I raged against the practice but tried to understand the various societal supports that lead to its stubbornness in the face of laws banning it. As I communicated the various facets of the problem and the efforts being made by women's groups in India to eradicate it, students raised astute and focused questions about the practice, the relative merits and demerits of using educational versus legal methods to stop it, and so forth. I also took the opportunity that day to talk about the ways in which the practice has been reported in the U.S. media, particularly the ways in which the agency of the Indian women's movement is erased in the coverage.

As another example of the attempt to teach organically, a year ago I requested two students in International Communication to educate the class about news coverage of issues in their countries of origin and to assess the news coverage based on their own access to the history, politics, and culture of the country. A Sri Lankan student with an active interest in politics and ongoing contact with Sri Lanka enjoyed the chance to share his perspective with his classmates. On the other hand, a student with Azerbaijani heritage who had come to the United States when she was about twelve, under difficult circumstances, found the exercise to be an imposition. She was more concerned with fitting in as an American than cultivating a connection with Azerbaijan at this point in her life, and she felt somewhat singled out by my request. Similarly, last semester, one young Arab American man was disengaged from discussions throughout the semester. It was almost as if he had made a conscious decision to be disengaged. When I asked the students at the beginning of the semester to tell me about their experience with different cultures, he basically said his name, and offered no other information. He appeared to reject the whole dynamic of calling up our multiple cultural identities as a gateway to a larger understanding of some of the pressing global problems we are facing. I read his silence in a similar vein as I read the reluctance of the Azerbaijani student. These young people have been spending energy assimilating and trying to take their place in the great invisible U.S. mainstream, and I am seen as disrupting the process. Once the door is closed to learning, the particulars of which class exercises or assignments I choose are not all that relevant. The secret lies in being able to open the door and make an emotional connection.

Creating a sense of shared ownership of the class is important in an organic teaching-learning process. This allows the students to voice suggestions on course process and content, some of which can be incorporated fairly quickly. The aftermath of September 11 provides an example of this. The Arabic American students at the university were feeling vulnerable at this time, and they were making efforts to educate the larger student community about the Arabic American communities in Dearborn and about Islam. One student had invited a well-respected imam to the campus to talk about Islam as a religion advocating peace. One of the students in my class suggested inviting her brother, who holds a leadership position in the Arab American Chamber of Commerce of Dearborn, to talk about the history and current situation of Arab American communities in Dearborn. Students were quite responsive to him, asking him a number of questions about how the Arab American community is dealing with the situation, the role the media plays in community relations, and so forth. I was encouraged by this experience to incorporate student ideas into the course content and to take advantage of the cultural politics of the region as immersed in the larger global historical moment.

The Gender and Media studies class I'm teaching for the first time this semester has also afforded many opportunities to incorporate student input. I have shared examples of advertisements, music, and theatrical performances throughout the semester that students have brought to my attention. As already mentioned, I showed *"Tough Guise"* in response to student comments about the effects of media and popular culture on men. I incorporated student suggestions on class format and the order of readings. This encouraged a shared sense of ownership. The fact that the class was a new class, still being shaped, encouraged a collaborative approach between students and professor.

Another aspect to the quality of the space we create in the classroom as critical media educators is worth mentioning. As a critical media educator, I see the classroom as a potential public counter sphere (Fraser, 1990; Rai, 1995). For me this entails among other things bringing into the class voices that are seldom heard in the mainstream media. Further, as a feminist living on the borderlands, I consider it my obligation to make room for the articulation of voices of postcolonial women, third world women, women of the South, whenever possible, recognizing that these are the least accessible through mainstream media. Opportunities to bring in these voices present themselves in the International Communication class, and I have written elsewhere about the usefulness of incorporating gender perspectives into the teaching of International Communication (Luthra 1996). Last semester, for example, I took it upon myself to talk about the lost voice of Afghani women in the mainstream discourses on the war against terrorism. I showed the students the RAWA (the Revolutionary Association of the Women of Afghanistan) web site, and I discussed Saira Shah's documentary *Behind the Veil*. I shared the eloquent words of Sima Wali, President of Refugee Women in Development (RefWID) and an Afghani woman refugee herself, who had brought tears to my eyes when she spoke in Ann Arbor in November 2002. I shared her story of the courage and compassion shown by Afghani women against all odds. Some of these women, when they heard of the September 11 tragedy, wrote and sent a letter of sympathy to afflicted women in the United States, an act which could have incurred them a death sentence at the time. The class asked me why we rarely hear the words of Afghani women, why so few people know about RAWA. I asked them to enumerate the factors in light of everything we had discussed during the semester. I asked them then to imagine what it would be like if these voices were heard more often and more loudly, and I asked them what would need to change for this to happen. Once again, it was the initial emotional connection that opened up the door for this kind of exchange. It presented the possibility of creating within the classroom a "third space" from which to interrogate the limitations of mainstream media and envision alternative futures (Sreberny, 2002).

In the end, I cannot make any overarching suggestions or identify any grand principles for critical media education. From my experience, critical media education involves taking risks every day. It involves treading a delicate balance between using one's political passion in the classroom and letting the students come to their own conclusions. Perhaps the most difficult and most useful lesson is that no one principle or method works at all times with all students. Each semester and each class constitutes an organic entity, best responded to by organic teaching that responds to the particular historical moment and students' relationship to it. Such organic teaching proceeds at the level of heart, mind, and soul. Once an emotional connection is made in the classroom, many things are possible.

REFERENCES

Akindes, F. Y. (2001). Methodology as lived experience: Rhizomatic ethnography in Hawaii. *Diegesis: Journal of the Association for Research into Popular Fiction, 5,* 16–26.

Cuklanz, L. (2001). *Barbie nation: An unauthorized tour* directed by Susan Stern. Review in *Feminist Critical Media Studies, 1*(2), 261–262.

Fraser, N. (1990). Rethinking the public sphere: A contribution to the critique of actually existing democracy. *Social Text, 8-9,* 56–80.

Luthra, R. (1996). International communications instruction with a focus on women. *Journalism and Mass Communication Educator, 50*(4), 42–51.

Luthra, R. (2002). Negotiating the minefield: Practicing transformative pedagogy as a teacher of color in a classroom climate of suspicion. In L. Vargas (Ed.), *Women faculty of color in the white classroom* (pp. 109–124). New York: Peter Lang.

Rai, A.S. (1995). India on-line: Electronic bulletin boards and the construction of a diasporic Hindu identity. *Diaspora, 4*(1), 31–57.

Said, E. (1998). Edward Said: The voice of a Palestinian in exile. In E. Said (Ed.), *Third text* (pp. 39-50). London: Kala Press.

Sreberny, A. (2002). Seeing through the veil: Regimes of representation. *Feminist Media Studies, 2*(2), 270–272.

13

THE WHAT, WHY AND HOW WE KNOW OF MEDIA EDUCATION

Robyn Quin

Barrie McMahon

The reader who has reached this, the final chapter, in *Rethinking Media Education: Critical Pedagogy and Identity Politics* will likely be struck as we were, by both the diversity of the field and the commonalities within the writers' approach to their subject matter. The sense of diversity comes from the range of topics that can legitimately fall under the label of media education. The essays represent explorations in media and pedagogical theory, cultural studies, empirical research, and reflections on classroom practice. They cover a broad range of topics including violence, body image, identity, consumerism, class difference, and race.

It is not surprising that a book with the term "media education" in the title should exhibit such variance in topics, because media education embraces a broad field of study. The umbrella terms includes study of content, of transmission, of context, and of readers. In doing so it draws from other academic disciplines such as cultural and gender studies, cinema, esthetics, politics, history, civics, and economics.

Media education is not a stable category. Two decades ago a book of this title would most likely have included chapters on film, television, news media, radio, and perhaps publishing, with discussions about how their particular peculiarities could be addressed in the classroom. There is still a need for knowledge of this type but in the early years of the twenty-first century it is the overarching concerns with language, ideology, power, and representation as applied to issues of personal identity, race, ethnicity, gender, equality, and sexuality that are central concerns of media education scholars.

In order to bring the complex threads that weave through the earlier chapters together in this last chapter, we will address some fundamental questions for any educator. These are questions that still trouble those who teach in disciplines with precise boundaries and a long history of scholarly research. The questions are even more central to media education, a study that is not a neatly contained discipline and has less than fifty years of history. The key questions for the media educator are:

- What do we teach?
- How do we teach it?
- How do we know that we are being effective?

WHAT DO WE TEACH?

The authors in this collection share a belief that media education can make a difference. Although many express some concern as to whether the approaches we are currently taking are having the greatest impact, they nevertheless believe that media education can help the individual make sense of depictions of this world and, in turn, make the world a better place. In discussing the goals of media education, most of the authors have in some way given attention to:

- The disciplines or intellectual frameworks upon which we draw
- The place of values in what we teach

Goals

Rashmi Luthra in "Media Education Toward a More Equitable World" makes a bold claim for the goal of media education. It is, "to start them [students] on a quest for solutions to pressing problems of global inequities and the interlocking oppressions of race, class gender nation, ability and heterosexuality that result from these differences." Other authors express similar aims but with a different inflection. In "Cruelty, Compassion, Commonsense, and Critical Media Literacy," Bill Yousman asks by way of quoting Gerbner (1999): "If television functions as a powerful form of cultural pedagogy, to what extent can media education counter its efficacy as the primary storyteller in society?" He expands by explaining with reference to Gramsci (1971) that the popular culture industries are best understood as sites of ideological warfare, a place where the "commonsense is naturalized and determined." He illustrates his goal by challenging the student's capacity to, ". . . question and resist the commonsense notions that inform and shape our perspectives on issues of race, class, gender, sexuality, aging, power, allocation of resources, democracy, equality, freedom. . . ."

Perhaps the difference in emphasis between Luthra and Yousman is not so much in the goal itself but in the centrality of the media in its pursuit. Whereas Luthra's goal may be pursued through various forms of investigation based on the social sciences, Yousman's goal is specifically to investigate and expose the media's role in the social agenda. Alicia Kemmitt in "Critically Reading Race in the Media and in the Classroom: A Media Literacy Project" identifies a goal of questioning the dominant readings of media texts. Like Luthra and Yousman she believes that a function of media literacy is to teach cultural positioning particularly in the development of stereotypes (drawing from Stuart Hall, 1997).

Barry Duncan, a highly respected pioneer in media education, offers a simple and comprehensive purpose for media education: "helping students develop a critical understanding of how the media work, how they construct meaning, how they can be used, and how to evaluate the information presented by them." The North American context that shapes this goal is an advanced market economy that through "globalization, including free trade, transnational marketing, branding, deregulation and privatization" leads to the "corporate takeover of public space." Barry Duncan's goal to create sociopolitical critiques and oppositional readings among his students sits well with Bill Yousman's goals and with those of Alicia Kemmitt, though the context varies a little.

All the authors share a similar orientation towards improving the lot of the individual and the society through a raised social awareness, whether it be manifested by resistance to racial stereotypes (Kemmitt), commodified identities (Duncan), gendered identities (Pombo and Bruce), class inequality (Yousman), or the oppressive representations referred to in Michelle Wolf's and Kelly Briley's "Media Education and Negotiating Body Image."

Ruth Zanker's contribution, "The Media and Me: An Experiment in Reflective Writing in an Applied Broadcasting Degree," raises an interesting paradox about the goals of the students and the teacher, one that it appears, in her case, was resolved. The students had undertaken the course with the aim of pursuing a vocation. Zanker's goal in helping them to achieve this end was "to provide them with the critical tools that enabled them to analyze the forces radically reshaping the creative industries, in order to empower them to carve out (possibly as yet to be defined) niches in the reconfiguring digital mediascape." Zanker shares the goals of those above, but again with a different inflection. She too wants to produce citizens who can engage in the debates that our societies carry out in the media rather than to produce technically proficient workers (though this may be an important by-product for many students).

The degree of commonality among all authors, if not the degree of emphasis, does suggest some consensus. The absences are also significant. For example, no one has a goal of technical proficiency in media production for its own sake. Nor is there a goal to unpack the art form of a particular medium in pursuit of the high culture/low culture goals of courses many decades ago.

Values

On January 20, 2004, the Prime Minister of Australia, in decrying the public education system in that country, claimed that public school education is values neutral, whereas the private schools prosper because they embrace traditional values. In supporting his leader's attack on the public school system two days later, the Deputy Prime Minister inadvertently contradicted this values neutral assumption by stating that the public school system was "contaminated by green ideology" (Lidstone, *The Australian*, 2004). Though it may be interesting to speculate how any institution, let alone an education system, could possibly be value neutral, the question of whose values and how they are addressed is one that continues to trouble media educators as well as political leaders, albeit for different reasons.

Media educators acknowledge that education cannot be values free. Their consideration is about whether their courses should be premised on a set of values that need to be developed in students (as in an interventionist or media effects approach) or whether, instead, their courses should encourage the learners to be reflective (as in a cultural studies or critical pedagogy approach).

The apparent consensus among authors about goals implies to some extent a shared set of values that are held to be core values if we are to make any progress towards a civilized society. However, the thrust of the arguments of Kemmitt, Duncan, Lee and Mok, Zanker, Yousman, Wolf and Briley, and Luthra does not depend on student acceptance of a set of values prior to any media investigation. Their approach is different from those who advocate a media effects approach, within which the values clearly direct the curriculum. In a media effects approach values are assigned by the educator to media violence, media advertising, and so on, at the outset of the program, and the learning progresses towards this end.

In "Closer Than You Think: Bridging the Gap Between Media Effects and Cultural Studies in Media Education Theory and Practice," Erica Scharrer argues that both approaches can be integrated into a common curriculum. This is a tantalizing proposition. Her argument, based on Comstock and Scharrer (1999), is that the interventionists act because "children and teenagers are more susceptible to media influence than adults because they have a limited number of real-world experiences to use to counter media messages." Her contention of the cultural studies perspective is that it, " . . . views media education curricular that attempt to 'inoculate' against the negative effects of media exposure as misguided pursuits," because it "inauthenticates the experiences of pleasure . . . [and it] can be construed as being elitist."

Scharrer subsequently develops an argument that the difference is one of transparency. The cultural studies approach, she argues, "often carries with it an inherent moral or political stance," whereas the interventionists are more explicit in what they stand for. On this basis, therefore, there is room for accommodation because both approaches give a central role to media criticism and acknowledge that the nature of any media topic means that it carries an inherent political stance. Her point about transparency and the lack of such is well made, and Erica Scharrer is to be congratulated for pointing out that the cultural studies approach can be just as moralistic as the interventionist approach.

However, in the view of the authors of this chapter, the cultural studies and the interventionist approaches are essentially opposed positions that cannot be accommodated in the one paradigm. In our view, starting from the educators' value position on a topic is fundamentally at odds with an approach that prioritizes the issues, even though the teacher may have strong value positions on those issues. The latter approach teases out the nuance and contradictions in the various positions and in the process, empowers the students to develop their own positions on these important social issues. Indeed, Bill Yousman's research shows that the students' final positions may well be at odds with the implied values of the agenda setter. This is not to say, however, that there are not risks in opening up the space for students to formulate their own positions. As Monica Pombo and David Bruce acknowledge, without a safe space in which students can share their ideas, the classroom becomes a tool of oppression, silencing the voices of students.

Approaches

The title of this book foregrounds critical thinking, and the stated goals of many of the authors provide insights into what the critical thinking is about. The chapters consequently take as given the concept of critical media education, but it becomes apparent that the term is to some extent problematic, and the various authors' use of the term differ.

At one end of the critical media education spectrum is an implication that a critical approach is akin to a textual analysis approach. Salina Abji in "Springing Up a Revolution: Media Education Strategies for Tweens," initially equates critical media education with critical viewing skills, then takes us to a broader position that argues for "discursive spaces where tweens can instead engage in critical cultural studies." Abji sees a contrast between where we are in critical media education and where we should be, which she calls a critical cultural studies approach.

Others assign a more encompassing role to critical media education from the outset. For example, Michelle Wolf and Kelly Briley, in "Media Education and Negotiating Body Image," work from the definition of media literacy that was agreed upon at the 1992 Aspen Institute's National Leadership Council on Media Literacy Education: that media literacy is ". . . the ability of a citizen to access, analyze, evaluate and produce communication for specific outcomes."

A critical analysis approach to media education, aimed at identifying and contesting the ideologies promulgated by the media, has a rich history. It reflects the theoretical concerns of the British Cultural Studies movement, which "consistently addressed itself to the interrogation of society's structures of domination" (Turner, 1990. p. 5).

Given the range of interpretations of critical thinking in this book it is worth stating our position and, in doing so, revisiting the definitions forged in the 1980s when this was a key issue for those seeking to define the purpose of media education. Len Masterman, who was a central figure in connecting the intellectual debates of those times with classroom practice, has recently restated his position.

> . . . the whole point of media education and its interlocking conceptual structure was to investigate how the media attempt to function as consciousness industries; how they attempt to manage opinion, set agendas, construct identities, make social meanings, and how audiences make sense of and negotiate these meanings. Ideological study was the glue which provided all of the other concepts with their cohesiveness and purpose. Remove ideology and what is one left with? (Masterman, 2002, p. 32)

More important than the question of the range of definitions of what comprises critical media education is to ask what other factors need to be considered when updating a twenty-year-old concept to take into account developments in theory and in the media environment. This is not to deny a place for the theory and practice of the 1980s or to place constraints on the approaches that were not intended at the time. For example, textual analysis was seen in the 1980s as a starting point, a means to an end, although it is true that in some cases it became an end in itself. Andrew Hart's research (Hart, 2000) highlighted the fact that in England, media was studied within the discipline of English had not taken into account the broader dimensions of a critical approach to media education. His research showed that a discriminatory paradigm was the most likely frame of reference, text rather than context was studied, there was a lack of any engagement with political issues, and there was little space for young people's own media experience and knowledge. This simplistic deconstruction approach in some British English classes does not do justice to the goals of the British Cultural Studies movement and should not be seen as being any basis for discounting a cultural studies approach. The chapters in this book are rich in illustration about what needs to be added and how it can happen.

Many of the essays share a common perception of the media. They see the media not as a subject about which facts must be discovered, but as a discursive field in which the world is experienced through the media at a given time. Discourse, in this sense, refers not simply to language or social interaction but to both bodies of social knowledge and the act of producing social knowledge. It is such a concept that allows Duncan to use shopping malls as an object of study in media education. Discourse can be thought of as a set of statements around a topic, which acts to both constrain and enable what we can know about the topic. Discourse, argues Foucault, constructs the topic (Foucault, 1973, 1977). It defines and produces our objects of knowledge. It governs the way that a topic can be meaningfully talked about and reasoned about. But discourses are produced by those in a position to make authoritative statements about an object of knowledge and therefore are historically contingent and subject to change (McHoul & Grace, 1993, p. 31).

It is the fact that discourses are not immutable that makes the sorts of media education interventions described in this book worthwhile. Although Ruth Zanker knew her students to be "successful products of a consumer culture," she has demonstrated in her chapter how that discourse can be challenged and new and alternative discourses foregrounded for her students. The role of the media educator is to challenge prevailing discourses and offer students ways in to constructing new discourses, new ways of thinking about the issues.

As Salina Abji describes the shift, "the role of media studies shifts from teaching tweens critical viewing skills, towards providing discursive spaces where tweens can instead engage in critical cultural studies," and, "instead of simply teaching girls how to read critically or providing a list of consumer-based actions, today's media education strategies must go further to address the complex and contradictory experiences of tweens living in an increasingly branded world. This means recognizing tweens' agency and media savvy through peer-based approaches and venues for discussion and debate. It also involves engaging tweens in critical examination of the deeply held cultural beliefs and problematic corporate practice behind surface representations. But more than that it involves the fundamental right to unbranded discursive spaces, both virtual and real, where young women can be free to exercise their imaginative capacities, develop viable alternatives, and take control of their political, social and economic futures."

Abji in translating a Foucauldian concept into media education practice has done more than add a new dimension to approaches in media education. She is also proposing a power shift, one that empowers the learner. It is a question worthy of examination in its own right. Institutional power according to Foucault is located in strategies that operate at every level in our institutions and disseminate through our society. The pursuit of this understanding about the nature of power differs a little from the quest of the British Cultural Studies movement, but from both approaches, how the pursuit is undertaken results in a marked power shift. This is indeed a major advance on the critical media education of the 1980s.

Barry Duncan's approach in generating a power shift is to be subversive: "I examine how they can creatively cultivate points of resistance—through 'culture jamming' for example—despite the massive marketing efforts being directed at them." His chapter illustrates very effectively ways in which this can be done.

The authors of this chapter acknowledge the worth of the contributions in the previous chapters. For the purpose of developing a structure about what we teach, we paraphrase: the purpose of media education is to enable students to develop intellectual structures that will enable them to make meaning from the media texts they encounter, taking into account the media environment and its institutions.

For educators, theoretical positions have to be translated into teaching practice. How does the concept of a discursive space translate? What is the importance of media content, media genre, and media forms? Some structure is needed if we are to provide a learning path for our students. We suggest that the structure should include text, study of context, and investigation into the role of the reader. This teaching approach can apply to classes for five-year-olds through to undergraduate classes. The difference is in the content, detail, and classroom activities.

The study of the text should cover narrative, discourse, point of view, and medium. It is familiar territory for many media educators, although as Hart's research has shown, simple deconstruction separated from the political and ideological leads nowhere.

Study of context takes into account the historical, social, political, and economic contexts. Historical context includes the time, place, and people. The cultural references, justifications, and mythologies surrounding the text affect the meaning and are part of the context. The political meaning in media texts is affected by the extent to which the student connects with implied ideologies and value systems.

Understanding the role of the reader and one's own position when coming to a text must take into account the personal history and cultural experiences of the reader, the reading situation, and the intended use of the text by the reader. The cultural experiences of the reader will include many experiences with media that become deeply ingrained in the value system of the reader. The situation in which a text is read will vary. Whether one reads for pleasure or for study will affect the meaning that the reader makes of the text. The intended use or non-use the reader has in mind for the text will also affect the meaning. For example, browsing the web for the pleasure that it holds is a different use from using the web to gather evidence for developing a position on a topic.

HOW WE TEACH

Pedagogy and Student Engagement

In the past, close critical reading using textual analysis strategies has been a central pedagogical tool for the media educator. A number of the writers have addressed the limitations of the traditional pedagogical tool of critical reading. The challenge for the media educator lies in opening up the possibility of alternative discourses. This has proved to be particularly difficult. Pombo and Bruce share their disappointment in finding that students showed little resistance to media representations despite their education in media literacy principles. Similarly, Lee and Mok, in their chapter about media education in Hong Kong, report that at least 30-40 percent of the students showed little conceptual or attitudinal change after completing media literacy programs.

Sara Bragg describes her disillusionment with the use of deconstruction strategies in the classroom in "What Kevin Knows: Students' Challenges to Critical Pedagogical Thinking." She was particularly concerned that the students read her teaching practice, "as a censure of their pleasure." She also wonders "whether radical educational practices overemphasize theory at the expense of valuing what else teachers offer their students." Her strategy is to say "we should begin to consider how we work with these students' everyday poetics of association, relation, comparison, and substitution, rather than through critical pedagogy's abstract logic, revelation, rules, and application of a language the teacher supplies." Though Sara Bragg may be operating from a narrower definition of critical pedagogical thinking, and a broader definition could embrace the type of pedagogy that she is proposing, her point is well made. To ignore the function of the reader in making sense of media texts or media environments is to deny who makes the meaning. Meaning resides with the reader and emerges from the interplay of the preferred meanings in the text and those other meanings that are being brought to the text. The task of the educator is to create a learning environment where that interplay can occur.

Salina Abji in "Springing Up a Revolution: Media Education Strategies for Tweens" cites the Canadian Media Watch study and says that "the study indicated that the ability to read and critically analyze advertising images did not prevent girls . . . from experiencing negative effects, such as decreased self-esteem, as a result of media consumption." She goes on to say that contemporary media education strategies overestimate the power of critical viewing to empower students. She wants an approach that will translate into social action and believes that this can be achieved through peer-based approaches and discussion and debate.

Alice Lee and Eileen Mok also stress the need for media education to lead to social action. One of the objectives of media education in Hong Kong, they say, is to train students to use and influence the media. They describe a case study involving nine schools in a joint media education program that aimed to "cultivate student's positive social values and develop active and informed citizenry."

Wendy Barger and Kumi Silva, in "Reviving a Culture-Debating Public Through Media Education," are also concerned that media education seems to end with the critique of the media, rather than leading towards activism. They say, "[M]edia education is not only about the analysis of messages, but an awareness of why those messages are there." They voice their concern for the decline of a public sphere where in the "absence of a genuine public sphere, public opinion has become little more that a representation of the collective choices we make as consumers. . . . Without an active, engaged public sphere that truly involves its citizenry, there is no true democracy."

Barry Duncan is also keen to ensure that students move beyond the critique. He acknowledges through reference to the work of Naomi Klein (2000) that one of his prime tools in media critique (i.e., the use of the parody) can become but a harmless game if it is isolated from political or social movement and ideology. For this reason, he connects student use of parody to those such as Richard Slye and John Hartfield, who have used this approach with telling effect.

A narrow textual analysis approach without the glue that Masterman refers to and without due regard to context and reader study is clearly not achieving the outcomes that many of the authors in this book want. If textual analysis or a limited interpretation of critical analysis is not the answer to how the media educator might render the discourses of the media fragile and thus able to be thwarted, where might we look? (Foucault, 1981, p. 101). The authors in this collection offer some possibilities.

The Place of Theory

Michelle Wolf and Kelly Briley argue for the use of explicit theory as a strategy in media education. This, they say, was "the key factor that explains the more powerful and lasting impact of the classroom pedagogy." They argue for the value of theory as a means by which students are able to understand and explain the media's impact upon themselves; as a tool that the students could carry with them beyond the classroom and apply to new situations.

They would probably get some support from Ruth Zanker, who sees theory as a critical tool enabling students to "analyze the forces radically reshaping the creative industries." She argues that theory can help bridge the gap between students' own media consumption and pleasure, their learning in the craft of image production and critical analysis. She uses theory as a tool to enable students to view the media terrain through new eyes.

One would need to take into account the age of the students in developing such an approach. The chapters in this book address approaches across a wide age range. It is doubtful whether the Wolf and Briley approach would work for Kemmitt's 12- and 13-year-olds. Nevertheless, we would expect that approaches to all ages would be underpinned by a theoretical position. Whereas the learning in an undergraduate class might specifically be about the media theories, the media education in the school classroom would be unlikely to survive let alone succeed using a pure theory-based approach.

Theories cannot deliver truth, but they can provide a useful conceptual map. It is imperative, however, that the media educator acknowledges and demonstrates to students that any theory will privilege some features of the field while obscuring others. Students need to be aware that any theory acts to delimit the field; through structured presences and absences it determines what will and will not be considered pertinent to the analysis.

Context

Some authors in this collection stress the need to expand students' inquiry out from the text and into the political, economic, and social context that brought forth the particular text. Alicia Kemmitt, for example, argues for the need to understand other cultures before embarking on a study of race representations. Salina Abji stresses the need to have students explore the discourses that produce the culturally sanctioned knowledge and claims made by advertisers. Similarly, Wendy Barger and Kumi Silva believe that students need to be encouraged to go behind the image (in their case a NIKE advertisement) to look at the sociopolitical context that produced it. Erica Scharrer advocates "analyzing the system that shapes the number of choices and appeal of such choices [of media messages] that are available to audiences."

Certainly, the context will affect the way in which the reader makes sense of any media text. Contextual studies should include the examination of the contexts of both time and space, of production and consumption, including the historical, political, economic, social, and cultural dimensions. The historical takes into account the time, place, and people associated with the text and what the reader knows about these. This will influence the meaning the reader makes of the text. The social includes the cultural references, justifications, and mythologies surrounding the text, thus affecting the meaning the reader makes. The political addresses the extent to which the student connects with implied ideologies, for example, linked to gender, race, and class, generated through the point of view, suggestions of competing ideologies, and the value systems associated with portrayals of hero figures, stars, and villains. These affect the meanings in media texts. The economic context includes student perception of the economic processes behind both the medium and text and the broader processes in which they occur.

Of course, this is much easier said than done. How can media educators make students with very limited experiences of life, history, other cultures, and other places familiar with the discursive formations and contexts that produced the images they consume? How can we make visible the invisible?

The authors in this book have some proposals to do this. Rashmi Luthra advocates "bringing into the classroom the class voices that are seldom heard in the mainstream media . . . to make room for the articulation of voices of postcolonial women, third world women, women of the South, wherever possible, recognizing that these are the least accessible through mainstream media."

Another approach is to use media texts from another era that are beyond the range of the commercial media texts to which students are normally exposed. These types of texts come with very different contexts and because of their unfamiliarity and apparent mismatch with the students' familiar texts, the values will be more visible to the students. In turn the student will be better placed to see that their daily media texts are not context free.

Creating a New Public Sphere

One of the most interesting and valuable contributions this collection makes to media education is the claim for using the classroom as a new public sphere. This idea is referred to again and again throughout the essays, albeit in different terms. Rashmi Luthra speaks of the classroom as a "potential public counter sphere" in which voices absent from mainstream media may be heard. Bill Yousman offers a case study of the classroom as a public sphere in which students argue for the rightfulness of their conception of class and the American Dream. Abji recommends "providing the discursive spaces" where students can engage in critical cultural studies. Erica Scharrer calls for the classroom to be a place where, "an exchange of information or points of view can occur."

The idea is most fully explored in Wendy Barger and Kumi Silva's, "Reviving a Culture-Debating Public Through Media Education." In this paper the authors speak convincingly of using the classroom to reclaim the public sphere. The public sphere in Habermas' conception was the site in which to debate public issues of concern to the citizenry. This space has largely been replaced by the media in which persuasion and publicity for the purposes of consumption are more often seen than argument. The writers' advocacy for creating a media education classroom based on communicative action in which participants try to understand rather than persuade goes to the heart of the role of media education in a democratic society. As the media, particularly the news media, move further from their role in the democratic process, depending more on press releases and sponsored events as news and with, more recently, the invention of the embedded journalist, one effective counter is the creation of a public space where there is highly participatory, unconstrained and noncoercive dialogue.

The concept of creating an engaged student who has the capacity to undertake social action is one of the consistent searches throughout this book. Anchoring that search to Habermas provides fertile ground for further tilling. As a member of the Frankfurt School, Habermas influenced the British Cultural Studies movement of the 1960s and 1970s. The radicalism of that era is now contextualized by various authors in this book as the traditional, and the quest is to find ways to move on. Like the authors in this book, Habermas was also searching for the relationship between theory and social practice. It is fitting that his concept of the public sphere is being revisited so that the cycle of media consumers who are intellectually active but socially passive can be broken. Perhaps the lesson for us all is that understanding about media education is about conceptual growth, building on our storehouse of scholarship. It is never about starting afresh.

The Place of Practical Activity

Most of us who have taught media studies in schools have seen how effective practical media activity is in engaging the students and retaining their interest. Ruth Zanker found the same with her classes in which the students were exposed to intense craft production experiences designed to fast-track them into the mainstream media industry. Her problem was to get them to pause long enough from using the media gadgets to allow them to reflect on the "why" questions.

Our problem as media educators has not been to discover the worth of practical activity, but to theorize it so that its worth is seen as being more than the acquisition of some technical skills. We have tended to rely on the justifications of other disciplines. If it is good enough for readers of, say, English to demonstrate their progress in reading literary texts by way of writing, the same should be true of media texts.

Alicia Kemmitt's purpose in having young students create their own alternative advertisements was designed to help students understand who they are and to use this knowledge to provide insights into social construction of racial identities. Practical work in this case was used to create the attitudes and capacity to resist the media's racial stereotypes.

Erica Scharrer cites Aufderheide (1993) and Hobbs (1998) and sees media production exercises as a means of "empowering students to view themselves as creators rather than merely consumers of media, encourage rewarding and fun interactions with media and help students to understand that there are many forces, factors, and decisions made by producers that shape media content. They also allow students to use media as a means of expressing their identities by countering mainstream media portrayals that they feel do not represent them well."

There are many legitimate reasons to have students of all ages undertake media production. Past criticisms, usually by those some distance from the nature and purpose of the activity, include that it is just "playing with the toys." Indeed, if there are no learning scaffolds built around the practical activity, it can degenerate into this. But when the purpose is clear and students are equipped with some basic practical skills, media production is one of the most effective learning strategies. Selection and organization of information is at the heart of how preferred meanings are constructed in the mass media. What better way to learn about this concept than to demonstrate it? If the creation of a public sphere in the classroom is one of the democratic goals of media education, what better way to enter into the discussions than to create a perspective through a student product? In the past it has been the practicalities rather than the justifications that have been the real limitation on classroom production, such as expensive and inadequate equipment or limited capacity to allow students to move beyond the classroom. As these become less significant, the hope is that practical media education can resume or assume its place as a legitimate component of media education.

A Media Education Pedagogy

Advocates of constructivist education base their approach on engaging the student in the learning process, of assigning some of the responsibility for learning to the student, and of redefining the role of the teacher as the creator of learning scaffolds rather than one of instructor. Constructivist education is not new, not confined to a particular age group of students, nor is it discipline specific. There are many, perhaps the majority, of media educators over the past thirty years who may not be familiar with the term "constructivist education" but would identify themselves as being in this mold. Many of these teachers will have been using a cultural studies or critical thinking approach to media education. It has been a pedagogy that has served them and their students well. Pombo and Bruce make the point that using constructivist pedagogy in the classroom is not easy. David Bruce speaks for us all when he says, "The down side of the whole constructivist, negotiated classroom is that it is very messy and it makes for really difficult days."

There is a strong advocacy in this book for greater student engagement and participation in the learning process. Those thousands of media teachers around the world who have been doing this for the past thirty years may well ask, so what is new? Some may even feel affronted by the implication that what they have been doing has now been labeled ineffective, yet more of the same is proposed.

It is not the pedagogy that is under scrutiny but rather the degree to which the student has the capacity to negotiate the meanings. Is constructivist education to be applied to a simple textual analysis approach where the goal is to find the meaning that is given by the text or is it an education in pursuit of knowledge about how people make meanings and consequently the meanings that these students make?

The authors of this chapter argue for the latter, as do the authors of several other chapters. This is not to accept the oft heard cliché associated with constructivist education that the teacher becomes the guide on the side. The teacher does a lot more than create the learning scaffolds. S/he has an understanding of the theories and concepts associated with media

education and is well placed to provide the educational leadership that is
expected by both the students and the community.

HOW DO WE KNOW IF MEDIA EDUCATION IS EFFECTIVE?

As indicated in the earlier sections of this chapter, many of the contributors to this book have expressed some disappointment that the sort of
media understandings they wished to develop in their students were not
being realized by the approaches that are currently being used. To be able
to come to this conclusion, there must have been a means of monitoring
the progress of the students over a period of time. The capacity to monitor
and evaluate student progress is an essential element of the teaching and
learning cycle.

Though some means of monitoring must have been in place, as it was
not the focus in most of the chapters, the monitoring instruments themselves were not revealed. The exceptions are the chapter by Lee and Mok
and that of Scharrer, who offer categories of measures that are important
in their programs. Scharrer sees a need to measure the key concepts, the
attitudes and opinions about the media before and after participation in
media education curricula, and finally, to measure the skills of analysis or
deconstruction.

Lee and Mok describe their evaluation of two programs in Hong Kong.
They conclude that although the media education programs enhanced
students "specific" critical analysis skills, they did not raise a generalized
critical media awareness. They reason that the colonial tradition of passive
education is to blame for students' failure to transfer their critical reading
abilities from the specific instances provided in the classroom to their
media environment. We would suggest that this problem is not confined
to Hong Kong, but is a characteristic of media education outcomes more
universally.

In 1993, the authors of this chapter conducted a large-scale evaluation
of students' media literacy skills in Western Australia. The tests that were
set for 14-year-old students probed understandings about text, context,
and audience. At that time, textual analysis (depoliticized) had been the
tool of the English teacher who was teaching media education. Though the
English courses made reference to media context and audience, textual
analysis dominated media teaching in most English classes.

The study found that students were very good at using textual analysis to spot the stereotype and identify the visual symbols, but were generally unable to apply their analysis skills to the cultural framework of the

mass media. Students did not perform well in those areas that demanded more than description. We concluded that, although students leaving the compulsory years of schooling had a foundation in media analysis skills, only a small percentage had the capacity to make the link between the analysis of particular texts and the broader cultural context (Quin & McMahon, 1993).

Subsequent testing programs in Western Australia in 1996 and 2000 (Western Australian Department of Education, 2001) have tested years 3 (8-year-olds), 7 (12-year-olds) and 10 students (15-year-olds) with similar results. Students showed progress over the years in deconstructing texts, though limited improvement between years 7 and 10, but there was little evidence of understanding about media context or the role of the reader in reading media texts.

There is clearly a need to give higher priority to the cultural context and the role of the reader as we teach students about media's sense-making processes. We also need to develop the instruments that will allow teachers and students to monitor progress in the dimensions of text, context, and reader in the process of making meaning. The proposal here is to start at the end point, with the monitoring instrument, so that we know where we want the students to be. If this progression is clearly articulated, curricula, support materials, and even teacher professional development can be built towards achieving this end.

In broad terms the task is to progress the students from familiar texts in familiar situations through to unfamiliar texts in complex and challenging situations. This is where they will need to be in their understanding of media through their lives. The problem is not the starting point, textual analysis; though devoid of the political and ideological dimensions, it is difficult to understand its purpose. Students do need a language and a structure if they are to engage with the media. We have all experienced those horrible classroom moments when a viewing finishes, discussion is supposed to commence and is thwarted by the student who sums up his experience with "It sucks." The problem is not in textual analysis per se but in the assumption that media education ends with textual analysis.

An instrument is needed that takes into account the dimensions of critical media analysis that are in addition to textual analysis, those dimensions that contributors to this book outlined. The authors of this chapter are working with a small group of media educators across four countries to develop and apply such an instrument in various countries, all with their own priorities and courses (McMahon & Quin, 2002).

The Media Literacy Learning Continuum, the working title of the instrument, is a way to monitor and assess the progress that students are making at any stage of their education, from primary school through to undergraduate classes. One media activity in one year may give an indication about where the student is on the media education journey, but unlike the one-off mark we sometimes give in the classroom, it plots merely a point in time. It enables teacher and students to know what is learned and what needs to be tackled next. We also need to recognize that student progress will be uneven and influenced by many variables, some of which are beyond classroom control. The Media Literacy Learning Continuum will also help us to chart those glitches in student progress, but not the reasons for them.

A Learning, Monitoring and Assessment Model

The Media Literacy Learning Continuum can be used as a planning instrument, as a means for monitoring student progress, and as a basis for student assessment. It is outcomes based in that it places the emphasis on the result rather than the teaching intention. The instrument can be used for assessment of all types, both formative and summative. The types of assessment will include teacher, peer and, most importantly, self-assessment. The latter is so important if the student is to make the conceptual transition from a school media activity to the development of a critical framework for lifetime use.

The continuum uses text, context, and reader position as the organizers for the development of a critical framework. These three organizers have subcategories to pinpoint the types of outcomes that are expected.

	Identification	Interpretation	Transposition and reflection
TEXT			
Narrative			
Discourse			
Point of view			
Medium			
CONTEXT			
Historical			
Political			
Economic			
Social, cultural			
READER			
Cultural experiences			
Reading situation			
Intended use			

There are eight levels of outcomes that spread across the identification, interpretation, and transposition phases. Progress through these levels will take students from the familiar texts in familiar situations through to unfamiliar texts in complex and challenging situations.

The approach being used, as the international project develops, unashamedly foregrounds monitoring and assessment (the forgotten element of teaching and learning) in its broader sense.

There are many reasons why we assess, the most obvious being to recognize student achievement and for diagnostic purposes. The Media Literacy Learning Continuum is intended to take into account all the dimensions of assessment—formative, summative, teacher, self, and peer assessment. There are also political reasons for assessing to do with status and credibility, aspects that are particularly important for media education.

A less obvious reason is to keep the program on track. Reference was made earlier to the different approaches that are used in media education. The richness of media study opens up the possibility of many tangents, some exciting, most worthwhile, and all part of the learning process. As previously mentioned, some of the contributors to this book have expressed disappointment that the outcomes of their approaches have fallen short of their expectations. This highlights the need for checkpoints both during and after the learning journey, some indicators of what our focus is and how we are progressing. Good assessment instruments, known by all in advance, will provide that direction.

Assessment must be seen as a component of the learning rather than an interruption to the learning. Unless assessment is built into the teaching and learning cycle, stopping to take a test is an interruption of learning and often a denial of the validity of good teaching and learning practices. Embedding a rich performance task into the curriculum or as an end of course project and using it as an assessment instrument is a validation of good teaching and learning and an example of authenticity in assessment.

The various forms of assessment need to be rigorous and true to the concepts that are inherent in the outcomes rather than focused on the specific lesson content. Assessment models that emphasize content above conceptual outcomes run the risk of taking students on tangents that may or may not achieve the required outcomes. For example, in a video production activity, if the production skills are the exclusive basis of assessment rather than the means to the conceptual ends, there is little likelihood that the students will develop the sort of transferable skills that are necessary to address the big questions posed in and by the media. Little progress will have been made on ways of making sense of the media.

The teaching and learning cycle is about what we teach, how we teach it, and how we know where we have been and how we are going. As it is a cycle, we suggest that the starting point is what has often been seen as the end point, the critical monitoring and assessment component. If we educators do this we will be forced to clarify what it is we intend to teach and students to learn and how we go about it. The ensuring transparency in content and pedagogy we anticipate will lead to effective student critical thinking and action in regard to the media.

This anthology brings together the most up-to-date, cutting-edge thinking about the nature and purpose of media education. Its strengths are in the clarity of thinking exhibited in each of the chapters, the diversity of views and perspectives presented, and its thoroughly international outlook. Our congratulations to the editors and contributors on producing a much needed and long overdue look at media education from a global perspective.

REFERENCES

Aufderheide, P. (1993). *National leadership conference on media literacy. Conference report.* Washington, DC: Aspen Institute

Comstock, G., & Scharrer, E. (1999). *Television: What's on, who's watching, and what it means.* San Diego: Academic Press.

Foucault, M. (1973). *The order of things: Archaeology of the human sciences.* New York: Vintage Books.

Foucault, M. (1977). Nietzsche, genealogy, history. In D. Bouchard (Ed.), *Language, counter-memory, practice: Selected interviews and essays by Michel Foucault* (pp. 139–164). Ithaca, NY: Cornell University Press.

Gerbner, G. (1999). Foreword: What do we know? In J. Shanahan & M. Morgan, *Television and its viewers: Cultivation theory and research.* Cambridge: Cambridge University Press.

Gramsci, A. (1971). *Selections from the prison notebooks.* New York: International.

Hall, S. (1997). The work of representation. In S. Hall (Ed.), *Representation: Cultural representations and signifying practices* (pp. 15–64). London: Sage.

Hart, A. (2000). Innovation and inertia: Media teaching in English. *Communications, 25.*

Hobbs, R. (1998). The seven great debates in the media literacy movement. *Journal of Communication, 48*(1), 16–32.

Klein, N. (2000). *No logo: Taking aim at the brand bullies.* Toronto: Random House.

Lidstone, J. (2004, January 14-15). Bring teachers into play. *The Australian,* p. 20.

Masterman L (2002). Down cemetery road: Why the BFI's proposals for moving image education are no good. Wirral, England: Alpha Media.

McHoul, A., & Grace, W. (1993). *A Foucault primer: Discourse, power and the subject.* Melbourne: Melbourne University Press

McMahon, B. & Quin, R. (2002). The media literacy learning continuum. (Unpublished).

Quin, R., & McMahon, B. (1993). Monitoring standards in media studies: Problems
    and strategies. *Australian Journal of Education, 37*(2), 182–197.
Turner, G. (1990). *British cultural studies: An introduction.* Boston: Allen and Unwin.
Western Australian Department of Education. (1996, 2000). *Monitoring standards
    in education, viewing.*

AUTHOR INDEX

SUBJECT INDEX

Printed in the United States
78367LV00002B/79-120